PASSING THE SOUTH CAROLINA US HISTORY AND CONSTITUTION END-OF-COURSE TEST

Kindred Howard

American Book Company
PO Box 2638
Woodstock, GA 30188-1383
Toll Free: 1 (888) 264-5877 Phone: (770) 928-2834
Fax: (770) 928-7483 Toll Free Fax: 1 (866) 827-3240
www.americanbookcompany.com

ACKNOWLEDGEMENTS

The authors would like to gratefully acknowledge the formatting and technical contributions of Becky Wright and Marsha Torrens as well as the editing and proofreading contributions of Susan Barrows.

We also want to thank Carrie Owen and Eric Field for developing the graphics for this book.

Printed in the United States of America

12/11 01/12

Table of Contents

Chapter 3: Territorial Expansion during the Antebellum Period 61

Chapter 4: Secession, Civil War, and Reconstruction 79

South Carolina U.S. History Preface

Passing the South Carolina U.S. History and the Constitution will help students who are learning or reviewing standards for the history and Constitution sections of the **South Carolina End of Course** test. The materials in this book are based on the high school core area assessment standards as published by the South Carolina Department of Education.

This book contains several sections:

1) General information about the book itself
2) A diagnostic test
3) An evaluation chart
4) Eleven chapters that teach the concepts and skills needed for test readiness
5) Two practice tests

Standards are posted at the beginning of each chapter and in the diagnostic and practice tests as well as in a chart included in the answer manual.

We welcome comments and suggestions about this book. Please contact the author at

American Book Company
PO Box 2638
Woodstock, GA 30188-1383

Call Toll Free: (888) 264-5877
Phone: (770) 928-2834
Toll Free Fax: 1 (866) 827-3240

Visit us online at
www.americanbookcompany.com

Preface

About the Author:

Kindred Howard is a 1991 alumnus of the University of North Carolina at Chapel Hill, where he graduated with a B.S in Criminal Justice and national honors in Political Science. In addition to two years as a probation and parole officer in North Carolina, he has served for over seventeen years as a teacher and writer in the fields of religion and social studies. His experience includes teaching students at both the college and high school level, as well as speaking at numerous seminars. He is currently completing a M.A. in Biblical Studies at Asbury Theological Seminary, as well as a M.A. in History from Georgia State University. Mr. Howard lives in Kennesaw, Georgia, with his wife and five children.

Diagnostic Test

1. William strongly disagrees with the US government's economic policies. He organizes a rally at which he declares the US financial system corrupt and calls on average citizens to boycott major US banks and businesses. William's right to do this is protected by which of the following? 1.5

   A. the Declaration of Independence

   B. the Thirteenth Amendment

   C. the Nineteenth Amendment

   D. the First Amendment

2. What economic impact did railroads have during the 1800s? 4.1

   A. They decreased exports.

   B. They ended support for Manifest Destiny.

   C. They expanded national markets.

   D. They limited demand for land and resources.

3. Eli is a western frontiersman living in rural Missouri in 1822. Which of the following would Eli **most** likely support? 2.1

   A. populism

   B. democracy

   C. tariffs

   D. conservatism

4. The European Union directly impacts the United States in which of the following ways? 8.6

A. militarily

B. economically

C. socially

D. domestically

5. Which of the following causes would a government leader in the region depicted above have **most** likely supported? 2.3

A. protective tariffs

B. expansion of slavery

C. Jacksonian democracy

D. doctrine of nullification

6. In 1820, Congress passed a law regulating how slave states and free states would be admitted to the Union. It was meant to maintain the balance of power in Washington, DC. By what name was the law known? 3.1

   A. Civil Rights Act

   B. Fugitive Slave Law

   C. Monroe Doctrine

   D. Missouri Compromise

7. What effect did overproduction have on farmers in the 1920s? 6.3

   A. Farm prices rose because there was more to buy, thereby making farmers rich for a time.

   B. Farm production increased even more, and farmers prospered.

   C. Farm prices fell, causing farmers to struggle even prior to the Great Depression.

   D. Farmers had to rely on President Coolidge's price controls to survive.

8. The cartoon above appeared during which period? 3.3, 3.4

   A. Reconstruction

   B. the Great Depression

   C. the Harlem Renaissance

   D. colonial America

9. Which of the following individuals might be referred to as a "robber baron?" 4.3

A. a train robber in the 1800s

B. a striking worker

C. a capitalist businessman in the late 1800s

D. a politician at the beginning of the 20th century

10. Which of the following African Americans founded the Tuskegee Institute, believed that segregation was acceptable, and felt that African Americans would win the respect of whites if they learned a trade and gained economic independence? 3.5

A. Frederick Douglass

B. Booker T. Washington

C. W.E.B. DuBois

D. Martin Luther King Jr.

> "The United States must expand its borders. White civilization has naturally progressed. White Americans and Europeans have an obligation to share the benefits of democracy, Christianity, and capitalism with the less developed and under civilized peoples of the world. We need not apologize for our ability to control regions of the world. We must, however, recognize the weight of our responsibility in how we do it."

11. The above quote makes an argument for US imperialism based on which of the following? 5.1

A. industrialism

B. isolationism

C. Social Darwinism

D. New Federalism

- Seward's Folly
- Banana Republics
- Dollar Diplomacy

12. Which of the following would be the **best** heading for the list above? 4.2

    A. Policies and Decisions Affecting International Markets

    B. Military Decisions that Have Impacted Foreign Relations

    C. Domestic Economic Trends of the Late 1900s

    D. Foreign Policies Supporting Isolationism

13. Which of the following encouraged the United States to go to war in 1917? 5.4

    A. the bombing of Pearl Harbor

    B. isolationism

    C. U-boat attacks on US ships

    D. a US alliance with Germany

14. An economist during the 1930s who believed in deficit spending and direct intervention by government to deal with an economic depression would have been supportive of which of the following? 6.3, 6.4

    A. the New Deal

    B. trickle-down theory

    C. New Federalism

    D. *laissez-faire* economics

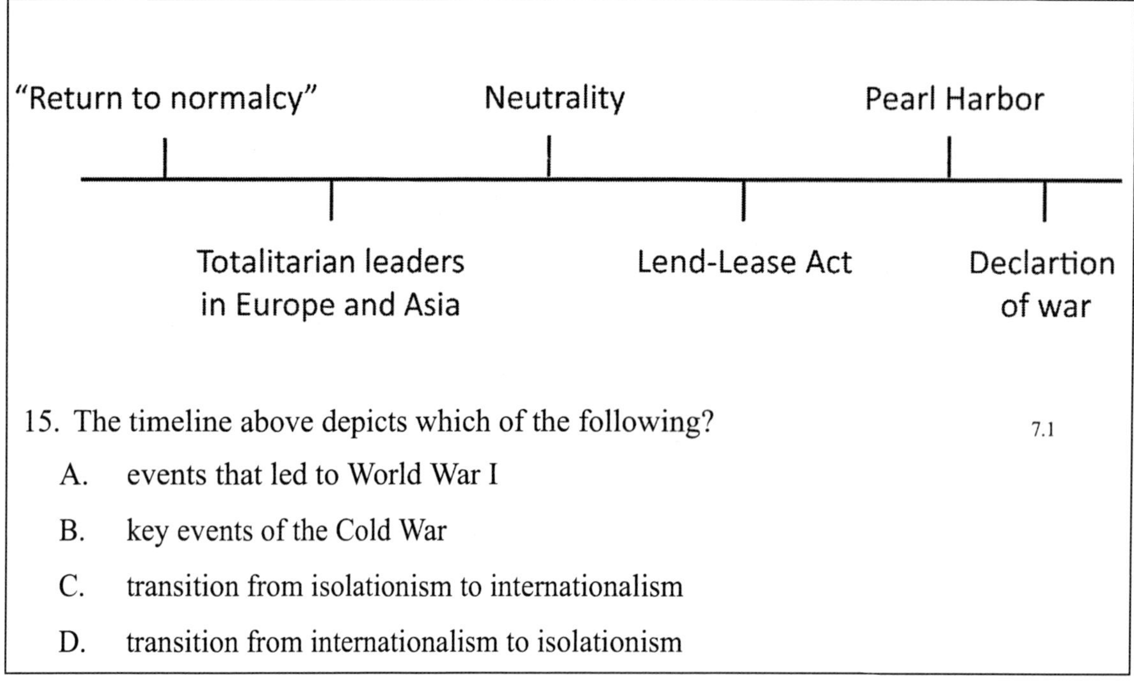

15. The timeline above depicts which of the following? 7.1

A. events that led to World War I

B. key events of the Cold War

C. transition from isolationism to internationalism

D. transition from internationalism to isolationism

16. Andrew is very suspicious of a strong national government. He tends to favor the interest of southern landowners and favors few government regulations on businesses. He also opposes tariffs and believes that each state should pay its own debts after the American Revolution. Andrew is **most** likely a member of which party? 1.6

A. Federalist

B. Democratic-Republican

C. Conservative

D. New Democratic

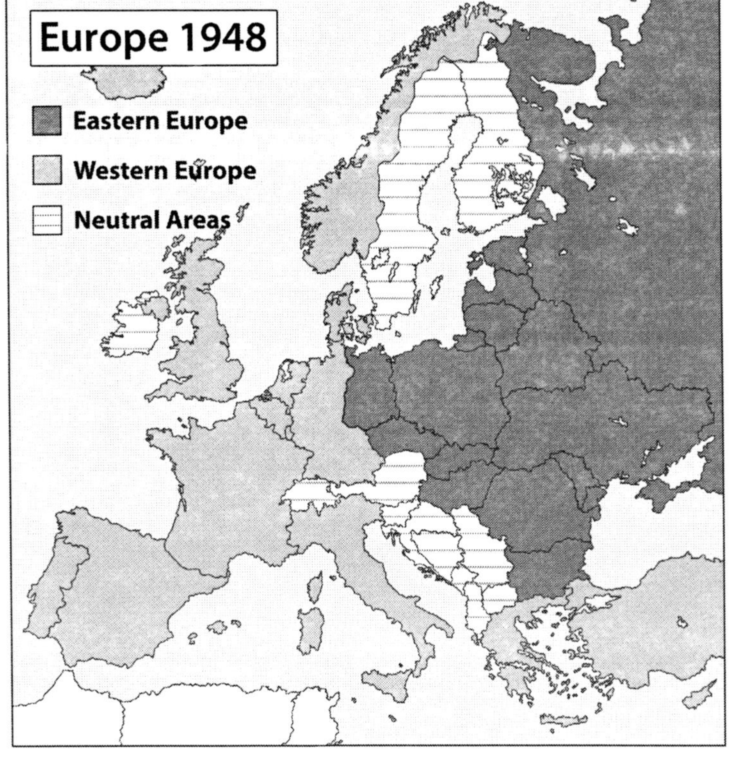

17. The map above depicts which of the following? 7.3

A. Iron Curtain

B. Berlin Wall

C. 38th Parallel

D. European Union

18. In the mid-1800s, William Lloyd Garrison wrote: 2.4

> "Be faithful, be vigilant, be untiring in your efforts to break every yoke, and let the oppressed go free…
> No compromise with slavery! No union with slaveholders!"

What cause did Garrison make this statement in support of?

A. the plantation system

B. Social Darwinism

C. abolition

D. temperance

19. Which of the following was an executive order that outlawed slavery in the South while still allowing slavery in states loyal to the Union? 3.2

    A. Three-fifths compromise

    B. Emancipation Proclamation

    C. Thirteenth Amendment

    D. The Lincoln Draft

20. The Marshall Plan was part of a Cold War strategy meant to stop the spread of communism. The Marshall Plan's main objective was to provide which of the following? 7.4, 7.5

    A. economic relief to help rebuild European nations

    B. military support to NATO allies

    C. nuclear weapons for use as defense

    D. political advisors to plot against communist countries

21. With which of the following statements would both President Lyndon Johnson and President Richard Nixon agreed? 8.2

    A. "States are limited in their capabilities. We must allow the federal government to regulate more in when it comes to social issues and education."

    B. "Civil rights must take precedence over any claim to property rights."

    C. "Communism is a threat to freedom, and the US must do all in its power to stop its spread."

    D. "It is in the United States' interest for its president to recognize Mao's government in China."

22. What role did children often play in the US urban labor force at the beginning of the 20th century? 4.4

    A. They worked long hours for low pay.

    B. They rarely worked because they were in school.

    C. They worked limited hours because of strict child labor laws.

    D. They were rarely hired because employers had to pay them a minimum wage.

23. What effect did new technology, increased mechanization, and mass production have on the US? 6.1

    A. People started saving more money than they had before the 1920s.

    B. Businesses produced more at more affordable prices, helping the US to become a "consumer society."

    C. The economy suffered because consumers did not yet trust innovative modes of production.

    D. Businesses produced less, and inflation increased.

Supreme Court Rules New Immigration Law Unconstitutional

24. The above headline reflects a judicial power stemming from which precedent court case? 1.7

    A. *Brown v. Board of Education*

    B. *Plessy v. Ferguson*

    C. *Marbury v. Madison*

    D. *Bush v. Gore*

25. Which of the following was a cause supported by the conservative movement of the 1960s? 8.4

    A. civil rights

    B. feminism

    C. property rights

    D. direct relief

26. Which one of the following statements would a fundamentalist opponent of John Scopes **most agree** with? 6.2

A. "Science is not to be feared or thought ill of."

B. "God must not exist. How could he with so much suffering in the world."

C. "Evolution is an evil lie! The Bible tells us where humans come from."

D. "*Laissez-faire* economics is immoral because it is oppressive."

27. The fact that US citizens elect representatives to make laws and implement public policies on their behalf is evidence that the United States government is what? 1.2

A. confederation

B. a federalist system

C. based on separation of powers

D. a republic

28. In 1945-46, a number of Nazi leaders faced trial in Nuremburg, Germany, and were sentenced to death. They were convicted largely because of their role in supporting the 7.4

A. bombing of Pearl Harbor

B. attacks on neutral ships by U-boats

C. Holocaust.

D. executions of anti-communists

1.4

> *"Gentlemen, I believe that this compromise presents the best possible solution to this dilemma. Since those in the North feel strongly that slaves are not citizens and therefore should not be counted in the population, while our Southern representatives feel just as adamantly that they should be, I see no other solution."*

29. The above quote is referring to which of the following?

    A. the Three-fifths Compromise

    B. the Connecticut Plan

    C. the Slave Trade Compromise

    D. the Virginia Plan

30. A practice which contributed to the stock market crash of 1929 in which investors would buy stocks by paying less cash than they were worth and then borrowing the difference was called what? 6.3

    A. buying on margin

    B. buying on speculation

    C. black market dealing

    D. *laissez-faire* economics

31. Trevor has a relative who was a WAC during WWII. Trevor's relative is **most likely** who? 7.2

    A. his great grandmother

    B. his great grandfather

    C. his grandfather

    D. his European uncle

32. Who of the following opposed monopolies? 4.6

A. John Rockefeller

B. robber barons

C. advocates of social Darwinism

D. progressive reformers

33. Which of the following policies would **most likely** be favored by a conservative? 8.5

A. more government social programs

B. wealth redistribution

C. fewer welfare programs

D. higher taxes

34. What land purchase roughly doubled the size of the United States at the time and meant that the US could focus on westward expansion rather than strictly depending on trade with foreign nations? 2.1

A. the Gadsden Purchase

B. Land Ordinance of 1785

C. the Louisiana Purchase

D. Oregon territory

35. Why did the United States become involved in Vietnam? 8.3

A. The US feared that the Vietnamese would cut off needed shipments of oil.

B. The US feared that if Vietnam fell to communism, then all of Southeast Asia might fall.

C. The US was allies with North Vietnam and had promised to protect it from China.

D. The US was allies with France and sent troops to help France.

36. Which of the following statements **most accurately** describes African Americans in the English colonies? 1.1

   A. The first Africans who arrived in the colonies were landowners.

   B. Black slaves actually outnumbered whites in certain colonies for a time.

   C. Only in the southern colonies did African Americans live as slaves.

   D. Due to discrimination, only whites could purchase a slave's freedom or own slaves.

37. Which of the following would have been a role of the Freedmen's Bureau? 3.4

   A. to help southern soldiers readjust to life after the war

   B. providing education to Union soldiers after the war

   C. providing money to help rebuild the South's postwar economy

   D. providing assistance and relief to emancipated slaves

38. Which of the following individuals would have been **most likely** to visit Ellis Island during the first few years of the 20th century? 4.5

   A. an Italian immigrant

   B. a farmer moving to New York

   C. a Chinese immigrant

   D. an emancipated slave

39. Which of the following resulted from Jim Crow Laws? 3.4

   A. Japanese Americans experienced unfair treatment during World War II.

   B. African Americans could finally attend white schools.

   C. Women gained the right to vote.

   D. African Americans could not eat at the same restaurants as whites.

> *"We must make women unhappy with what they have... we must make them so unhappy that their husbands can find no happiness or peace in their excessive savings."*

40. The above quote is **most likely** from whom? 7.6
    - A. a feminist supporting the Equal Rights Amendment
    - B. a member of the HUAC during the Red Scare
    - C. a politician advocating that women work during WWII
    - D. advertisement trying to appeal to housewives

41. The impact of western expansion on Native Americans can **best** be described as what? 2.1
    - A. Negative, because many suffered and died as they were stripped of their land and way of life.
    - B. Important, because exposure to white settlers meant the Native American escaped poverty.
    - C. Limited, because white settlers and Native Americans rarely interacted.
    - D. Beneficial, because Native Americans grew wealthy selling goods to white consumers.

42. How did Manifest Destiny impact US relations with Mexico? 2.2
    - A. The two nations became allies to fight European imperialism.
    - B. The two nations fought a war over territory in the Southwest.
    - C. The two nations avoided war after Mexico invaded Texas.
    - D. The two nations worked together to build a transcontinental railroad.

43. In which of the following ways did the Spanish-American War help transform the United States in terms of international affairs? 5.2

A. It weakened the US in the eyes of other nations.

B. It caused the US to sink further into isolationism

C. It established the US as a world power.

D. It hurt the US economically by limiting markets.

44. What African American leader preached nonviolent, civil disobedience as the most effective method for blacks obtaining civil rights? 8.1

A. Dr. Martin Luther King Jr.

B. Malcolm X

C. Frederick Douglass

D. John F. Kennedy

> *"We, as civilized white men, are called by God to move west. It is our sacred duty to settle the western territory, teaching and civilizing the savage as we go. If we do not, I believe we not only fail to take advantage of the abundance before us, but we also sin in that we have failed to fulfill our God-ordained purpose."*

45. The above statement was made by a government official advocating which of the following? 2.2

A. sectionalism

B. the Monroe Doctrine

C. imperialism

D. Manifest Destiny

> *"The war will be an uphill struggle. The other side has more factories for production, more railways, and far more people for supplying an army and labor. But our cause is noble! Never underestimate those who fight for their homeland and their liberty!"*

46. The above quote is **most likely** from whom? 3.2

    A. a southerner during the Civil War

    B. a northerner during the Civil War

    C. a slave during the Civil War

    D. President Abraham Lincoln during the Civil War

47. Which of the following **best** describes the impact of the Declaration of Independence? 1.3

    A. It established the US government by dividing power between an executive, a legislative, and a judicial branch.

    B. It made the colonies' split with England official by formally proclaiming the United States to be a free nation.

    C. It has been used by many totalitarian governments to put down rebellions world-wide.

    D. It revolutionized political thought by rejecting the ideas of the Enlightenment as it established a body of laws for the new United States.

48. The idea that certain races are entitled to conquer and rule over other races because they are genetically superior, and it is only natural to do so is consistent with what? 4.3

    A. Social Darwinism

    B. fundamentalism

    C. conservatism

    D. progressive reform

49. Which of the following statements **most** accurately describes the mood of US citizens immediately following WWI? 6.1

    A. Most were eager to expand and conquer new territories.

    B. Isolationism became popular as most just wanted a "return to normalcy."

    C. The desire for a permanent military force increase.

    D. Most people in the US wanted to forget about the war and focus on economic problems because of the Great Depression.

50. The principle that no imperialist nation would be allowed to use debt collection as an excuse for occupying territory in the Western Hemisphere was the basis for which of the following? 5.3

    A. big stick diplomacy

    B. dollar diplomacy

    C. missionary diplomacy

    D. moral diplomacy

51. The term "Cold War" referred to which of the following? 7.5

    A. the war between Germany and the USSR

    B. the war between the US and Germany

    C. the tension that existed between the US and USSR after World War II

    D. the dividing line between Western Europe and Eastern Europe

52. Which of the following greatly expanded the president's powers and ultimately led to the increased presence of US military forces in Vietnam? 8.3

    A. the War Powers Act

    B. detente

    C. the Gulf of Tonkin Resolution

    D. the Pentagon Papers

53. Martin Luther King Jr. advocated a strategy for winning Civil Rights that was 8.1

    A. non-violent.

    B. ineffective.

    C. militant.

    D. timid.

54. Why did the US Senate refuse to ratify the Treaty of Versailles? 5.5

    A. Most senators felt that it did not punish Germany enough.

    B. Most senators felt that it did not give enough land to the US.

    C. Most senators felt that it treated the US unfairly.

    D. Most senators feared it would pull the US back into war.

55. To which of the following is the cartoon above referring? 5.3

    A. Roosevelt's economic policies

    B. Roosevelt's progressive battle to end monopolies

    C. Roosevelt's isolationist views

    D. Roosevelt's readiness to intervene in international affairs

EVALUATION CHART FOR SOUTH CAROLINA US HISTORY AND THE CONSTITUTION END OF COURSE TEST

Directions: On the following chart, circle the question numbers that you answered incorrectly and evaluate the results. These questions are based on the South Carolina Competency Standards. Then turn to the appropriate topics (listed by chapters), read the explanations, and complete the exercises. Review other chapters as needed. Finally, complete the practice test(s) to assess your progress and further prepare you for the ***South Carolina US History and the Constitution End of Course Test.***

***Note:** Some question numbers may appear under multiple chapters because those questions require demonstration of multiple skills.

Chapter	Diagnostic Test Question
Chapter 1: British North America	27, 36
Chapter 2: The Birth of a Nation	1, 16, 24, 29, 42, 47
Chapter 3: Territorial Expansion during the Antebellum Period	3, 5, 18, 34, 41, 45, 48
Chapter 4: Secession, Civil War, and Reconstruction	6, 8, 10, 19, 37, 39, 46
Chapter 5: Expansion, Industrialization, and Reform	2, 9, 12, 22, 32, 38, 48
Chapter 6: International Expansion and Conflict	11, 13, 43, 50, 54, 55
Chapter 7: Roaring 20s and the Great Depression	7, 14, 23, 26, 30, 49
Chapter 8: World War II	15, 17, 28, 31
Chapter 9: Birth of the Cold War Era	20, 40, 51, 53
Chapter 10: Transformational Years	21, 35, 44, 52
Chapter 11: End of Cold War and Modern America	4, 25, 33

Chapter 1
British North America

This chapter addresses the following standard(s):

New Indicators	1.1, 1.2
Old Indicators	1.1, 2.1, 2.5

1.1 THE ENGLISH COLONIES

Beginning in the fifteenth century, European nations began establishing colonies in the Americas. Eventually, Spain, France, and Great Britain (England) claimed colonies in North America. Spain occupied much of the southern portion of the continent. The French used rivers and inland waterways to occupy much of the North American interior. The British established colonies along the eastern coast between the Atlantic Ocean and the Appalachian Mountains.

13 Original Colonies

Unlike many French and Spanish colonies, most English settlers came to North America with the intention of staying long term, rather than simply making money and then returning to Europe. During the sixteenth century, many people left England and journeyed to North America for a variety of reasons. These settlers established colonies along the Atlantic coast from Georgia to Maine. Their different motivations, as well as the geographic diversity of the land, contributed to a great deal of economic, political, and social diversity within the English colonies.

The English colonies were divided into three geographic regions. The **New England Colonies** included Massachusetts, New Hampshire, Rhode Island, and Connecticut. The **Middle Colonies** consisted of New York, New Jersey, Pennsylvania, and Delaware. The **Southern Colonies** were made up of Maryland, Virginia, North Carolina, South Carolina, and Georgia.

Chapter 1

SOUTHERN COLONIES

John Rolfe Visits Powhatan

The first successful English settlement was **Jamestown,** Virginia founded in 1607. It was established by a joint-stock company (a company owned by a group of investors) called the Virginia Company. The Virginia Company hoped to make money off of the products and raw materials the colony would provide.

The first few years were hard. Bitter cold winters, disease, and starvation killed many of the settlers. Fortunately, the local Native Americans helped, allowing Jamestown to survive and grow. Many new settlers came to the colony hoping to get rich and obtain land. Ultimately, the colony was saved when a man named John Rolfe discovered a new crop — tobacco! To attract laborers to help cultivate more tobacco, Virginia instituted the **headright system**. This system promised fifty acres of land to those who would settle in the colony.

ECONOMY

Tobacco Indigo

North American tobacco became incredibly popular in Europe and ended up being an important cash crop for Virginia, Maryland, and North Carolina. Meanwhile, the hot and wet climates of South Carolina and Georgia made rice and indigo important crops further South. Southern colonies also produced tar, pitch, and turpentine from the abundant forests that existed in the region.

The South's reliance on **staple crops** (crops that are in large demand and provide the bulk of a region's income) like tobacco and rice led to the rise of the **plantation system.** Plantations were huge farms owned by wealthy landowners who raised cash crops. Because these plantations required lots of manual labor, indentured servants and slavery became important parts of the southern economy.

Plantation System

Indentured servants were people who could not afford to come to North America on their own. They agreed to work for a landowner for up to seven years in exchange for the landowner paying for their trip. This system eventually gave way to **slavery** (a system in which people are "owned" like property).

By the mid 1600s, slavery was firmly rooted throughout the colonies, especially in the South. In South Carolina, black slaves actually outnumbered free Europeans throughout the 1700s. Because these large plantations tended to lie along rivers and inland water ways, plantation owners often had direct access to shipping without having to first transport their products over land to major ports. As a result, the South did not develop the major centers of commerce and large cities that arose in the North (cities like New York, Boston, Philadelphia, and Baltimore).

Southern Society

Southern society tended to be divided between rich plantation owners, poor farmers, and slaves. Overall, southern society tended to accept class distinctions and the idea that the wealthy, upper class (known as the **gentry**) is superior to the lower, poorer class. People believed that male members of the upper class should be the ones in positions of power and authority.

Wealthy Southern Landowner and Servants

Public education did not exist for some time in the Southern Colonies. Any education that occurred among poorer Southerners took place in the home. Meanwhile, wealthy Southerners either schooled their children at home, hired private tutors, or sent them to Europe to receive a formal education.

Unlike colonies further north, the Southern Colonies were established predominantly for economic reasons rather than religious (Maryland, which was started as a colony for Catholics, was the one exception). For this reason, rich landowners tended to remain part of the Church of England (Anglican Church) because it was in their political and economic interest. Over time, Methodist and Baptist congregations became common among poorer southerners and settlers along the frontier because they were willing to adopt new methods for reaching rural areas.

New England Colonies

Puritans

In addition to wealth, there were other reasons people came to America. Religious dissent (disagreement with the Anglican Church) was one of the most common. Since Europeans strongly identified religion with nationality, any protest or refusal to follow Anglican teachings was seen as a betrayal. As a result, those with different religious views saw North America as a place to escape persecution. One such group was the **Puritans**. They wanted to establish a community built solely on "pure biblical teaching" rather than Anglican traditions. In 1620, a group of Puritans established a colony at Plymouth, Massachusetts. These Puritans became known as the "Pilgrims" and celebrated the first Thanksgiving in 1621.

Later, another group of Puritans settled further north and established the Massachusetts Bay Colony. Eventually, Roger Williams and Anne Hutchinson helped form Rhode Island after they left Massachusetts over disagreements with Puritan leaders. Other Puritan settlers founded Connecticut and New Hampshire, as well. New England was a region founded on religion and strongly influenced by the Puritan faith.

Economy

Rather than raising cash crops, the New England Colonies relied heavily on the Atlantic Ocean. Shipbuilding, trade, and fishing became leading industries in the region. New Englanders transported goods from England to other regions, like the West Indies. From these regions, they acquired products like sugarcane, molasses, and rum that they could then trade for African slaves. Although New Englanders farmed as well, their farms tended to be smaller and for the primary purpose of allowing families to be self-sufficient. Meanwhile, Boston, Massachusetts became a booming urban center for shipping and New England commerce.

Shipping

New England Society

The Puritan church was a central part of life in New England. In Massachusetts, for instance, every settler had to attend and support the Puritan church. Dissenters were often banished from the colony. In 1692, this commitment to protect the Puritan faith resulted in one of the darkest episodes in American history—the **Salem Witch Trials**. Claiming that they had been possessed by the devil, several young girls in Salem, Massachusetts accused various townspeople of being witches. Before it was over, colonial authorities actually brought the accused to trial and condemned a number of them to death.

Colonial Education

Other aspects of Puritan Society were more positive. The Puritans had a strong sense of faith, family, and community. They were the first to promote **public education**. Puritans believed that everyone should be able to read the Bible. Therefore, they put a high priority on literacy. This emphasis on education eventually spread to other fields as well. In 1647, Massachusetts passed laws requiring public schools for towns of fifty families or more. In addition, towns of one hundred or more families were required to establish grammar schools for the purpose of preparing young boys for college. Generally, only boys attended these schools, while girls were trained for "womanly duties" at home (although there were some exceptions). Colonists in New England also founded two of the nation's earliest colleges: Harvard and Yale. Initially, the primary purpose of these colleges was to train ministers.

Middle Colonies

Sandwiched between the New England and Southern colonies were the Middle colonies. Because of their geographic location, the degree of religious tolerance, and the fact that settlers from other countries, such as the Swedes and the Dutch, had successfully colonized parts of the region prior to England, the Middle colonies were the most culturally diverse.

Economy

The Middle Colonies depended on both farming and commerce. Farmers raised staple crops like wheat, barley, and rye. Unlike the Southern Colonies, however, the Middle Colonies also boasted large cities like New York, Philadelphia and Baltimore. These urban centers were home to diverse groups of people and a variety of businesses. In addition, they were important ports for shipping products overseas.

Because of the nature of the economy, slaves in the Middle Colonies were not as numerous as in the South. Slaves that did live in the Middle Colonies often worked in shops and cities, as well as on farms. Due to waterways that granted colonists access to the heavily wooded interior, the Middle Colonies also benefited from a thriving fur trade and forged an economic relationship with Native Americans like the Iroquois.

Society in the Middle Colonies

The Middle Colonies featured a more diverse population than either of the other two colonial regions. Under the leadership of William Penn, Pennsylvania became a homeland for **Quakers**. This religious group did not recognize class differences, promoted equality of the sexes, practiced pacifism (non-violence), and sought to deal fairly with Native Americans. They also made Pennsylvania a place of religious tolerance, thereby attracting not only the English Quakers, but German Lutherans, Scotch-Irish Presbyterians, and Swiss Mennonites as well.

William Penn

Because New York was originally a Dutch colony, it exhibited linguistic and cultural diversity, as well as religious differences. Jews, as well as Christians, made New York their home, making the city site of the colonies' first synagogue (place of Jewish worship).

Due largely to the diversity and tolerance that the Middle Colonies tended to offer, the region featured a frontier that was continually pushing west as more and more settlers made their way from New England and southern colonies, as well as from overseas. Meanwhile, as urban areas continued to grow and develop (Philadelphia eventually became the colonies' largest city), a social order also emerged. Merchants who dealt in foreign trade formed the upper class "aristocracy" of the region, while sailors, unskilled workers, and some artisans comprised the lower classes. The middle class consisted of craftsmen, retailers, and businessmen.

Chapter 1

Colonial Government

House of Burgesses

Due to the colonies' great distance from England, the British adopted a policy known as **salutary neglect**. Except for limited efforts by the crown to assert its control in the mid 1600s, the English government basically let the colonists govern themselves.

Greatly influenced by England's model of representative government and new political philosophies which taught that people should have a say in their government, the colonies established **representative governments** (governments in which the people elect their own officials and have a voice). While colonial governors appointed by the crown were technically in charge, colonial legislatures consisting of local residents came to possess most of the power. These legislatures typically consisted of two houses (much like the British Parliament). One was an advisory council appointed by the governor. The other was a body elected by eligible voters.

Signing of Mayflower Compact

In New England, the first efforts at self-government were defined in the Mayflower Compact. The Puritan settlers at Plymouth drafted this document while still onboard the Mayflower (the ship that transported them to North America). It established an elected legislature and asserted that the government derived its power from the people of the colony. It also implied the colonists' desire to be ruled by a local government, rather than England.

This belief in representative government often took the form of town meetings, in which local citizens met together to discuss and vote on issues. Once again, it gave citizens a say in their government and helped to firmly establish a belief in democratic ideals.

However, despite advocating representative government in principle, the Puritans still believed firmly that government should seek to enforce the will of God rather than satisfy the will of the people. For this reason, power tended to rest in the hands of church leaders and could often be very authoritative (dictating to colonists what the rules of society would be). Tensions sometimes arose between church/government leaders and the people. In 1636, colonists under the leadership of Thomas Hooker left Massachusetts because they felt that the government there was too much like a dictatorship and did not serve the people. They established a new colony at Hartford, Connecticut and wrote a body of laws for their colony called the Fundamental Orders of Connecticut. It stated that the government's power came only from the "free consent of the people" and set limits on what the government could do. Such principles eventually provided a foundation for the government of the United States following the American Revolution.

Colonial Women

Colonial Woman and Child

In most cases, **colonial women** were considered to be second class citizens. Although they tended to enjoy greater freedom and more expanded roles than women in England, they still could not vote, nor could they usually attend school. By law, they were normally considered to be under their husband's or father's control. Their main responsibilities were bearing and raising children, as well as taking care of the home. In some cases, when a husband or father was unavailable or had died, women owned property or took on roles traditionally held by men. It was not unusual, in the case of some southern women, to hear of a wife or daughter running a plantation in the absence of her husband or father. At times, the lack of available labor also resulted in women taking on roles traditionally held by men. Some colonial women worked as shopkeepers, hostesses in taverns, printers, and even doctors.

African Americans and Slavery in the Colonies

Colonial Slavery

The first **African Americans** in the English colonies arrived in 1619 at Jamestown. Many arrived as indentured servants. They attained their freedom after a set number of years, owned land, and some even became masters of indentured servants and slaves.

In time, however, economic concerns, racism, and rationalizations on the part of white European settlers led to the institution of African American slavery in North America. In South Carolina and Georgia, where rice was the predominant crop, African American slaves tended to be used mostly in the fields and remained somewhat segregated from white society. Since cultivating tobacco took less time than rice, slaves in Virginia, North Carolina, and Maryland served in more expanded capacities and had more direct contact with whites. As a result, they tended to adopt more European customs and behavior. In the Middle Colonies and New England, owners often trained slaves in a craft and then put them to work in shops and cities. Some masters even permitted their slaves to make money provided they paid a share of their earnings to their master. In this way, some blacks were able to buy their own freedom.

Practice 1.1: English Colonies

1. Historians traditionally divide the original thirteen English colonies into which of the following categories?

   A. North, West, East, and South
   B. North, Middle, South
   C. New England, Middle, Southern
   D. New England, Middle, Plantation

2. Which colonial region was **most** known for plantations, large numbers of slaves, and the production of rice and tobacco?

   A. New England
   B. Southern
   C. Middle
   D. Atlantic

3. In what ways were the motivations for founding the Southern Colonies different from those for founding the New England Colonies? How did these differences affect the practice of religion in each region?

4. What factors led to the Middle Colonies being more diverse than the New England and Southern Colonies?

5. What does the term "salutary neglect" refer to?

1.2 Foundations of Representative Government

Magna Carta and Parliament

Signing of Magna Carta

Colonial government was based on principles established in England. Even before the end of the Middle Ages, England's monarchy (government ruled by a king or queen) felt the first rumblings of limited government. **Limited government** is government based on the **rule of law**. Governments based on the rule of law must obey a body of rules. Both government and citizens are subject to the law. These laws are usually in the form of a written document, such as a constitution or charter.

Documents

In 1215, a group of English nobles forced King John I to sign such a document. Known as the **Magna Carta** or "Great Charter," this document granted the nobles various legal rights and prevented the king from imposing taxes without the consent of a council. This idea of a council eventually gave birth to the British **Parliament**.

Originally formed in the thirteenth century, Parliament came to be comprised of two houses. The upper house, known as the House of Lords, consisted of appointed noblemen. The lower house, known as the House of Commons, was made up of elected officials.

Through Parliament, English citizens gained a voice in their national government. In 1689, Parliament gained additional power as a result of the **English Bill of Rights**. Under the English Bill of Rights, the monarch could not interfere with Parliamentary elections, nor could he or she impose taxes without Parliament's consent. It also granted citizens the right to a speedy trial, forbade cruel and unusual punishment, and granted citizens the right to petition the government. Both Parliament and the English Bill of Rights became models for the US Constitution and the government it established.

English government also submitted to **common law**. First established during the Middle Ages, common law is based on tradition or past court decisions, rather than on a written statute. Today, the idea of relying on past legal decisions where no formal statute (written law) exists is an important aspect of the US legal system.

Chapter 1

Impact of the Enlightenment

John Locke

Beginning in the late 1600s, Europe experienced the Enlightenment. The Enlightenment was a time that featured revolutionary ideas in philosophy and political thought. During this time, a number of philosophers introduced concepts that later helped form American ideas about government. One influential figure was John Locke. Locke's thoughts on government challenged the old view that monarchs possess a God-given right to rule with citizens obligated to obey. Locke believed that people were born with certain **"natural rights"** that no government could morally take away. These rights include life, liberty, and property. He also advocated what is often referred to as **social contract theory**. According to this philosophy, there is an implied contract between government and citizens. Citizens are born with freedom and rights. However, for the good of society, people agree to give up certain freedoms and empower governments to maintain order. Locke believed that if a government failed to fulfill its role to serve citizens, then that government should be replaced. His views were eventually used by many to justify the American Revolution.

Self-Government in the American Colonies

Most colonists believed in the idea of representative government long held in England and reinforced by the Enlightenment. Town governments in New England, colonial legislatures like the House of Burgesses, and the urban governments that eventually developed in places like Boston and New York, were all based on the principle that the people should have a voice in their government.

Due to England's policy of *salutary neglect* (letting the colonies govern themselves), settlers in America became accustomed to sovereignty. They made their own decisions and established their own policies without England imposing too many restrictions. England allowed this freedom because of the great distance between Europe and America, the strong tradition of local government that existed in England, and the fact that most colonists were proud to be British citizens and did not need to be forced to comply with British laws.

Colonial Legislatures and Governors

The first example of limited self-government in the British colonies was Virginia's **House of Burgesses**. This body consisted of two houses: one elected by the people, and the other appointed by the royal governor. In theory, **colonial governors** appointed by the king possessed most of the power. However, because the **colonial legislatures** created and passed the laws, determined how taxes would be levied, set the salaries of royal officials, and consisted of rich landowners within the colony, they — rather than the governors — actually came to possess more influence. This often caused **tension** between governors who had been appointed to serve the king and legislatures concerned with colonial interests. As the time of the American Revolution grew closer, legislatures often featured powerful

Colonial Legislature

personalities who favored independence, while colonial governors continued to be men appointed by the king and whose position and livelihood depended on the colonies remaining united to England.

Practice 1.2: Foundations of Representative Government

1. Which of the following describes the idea that a government cannot do whatever it wants, but rather is constrained by a set of laws?

   A. limited government
   B. representative government
   C. colonialism
   D. salutary neglect

2. Which of the following **best** describes John Locke's philosophy of government?

   A. Because each citizen has certain "natural rights" it is the duty of government to impose its will regardless of what citizens think.
   B. Social contract theory is an outdated philosophy and should be replaced with the idea of classical republicanism.
   C. It is the privilege of citizens to replace any government that fails to protect "natural rights" and uphold the common good.
   D. Subjects of the Crown are there to serve their king without question.

3. How did the history of British government and the ideas of the Enlightenment affect colonial government?

4. Why did conflict often arise between royal governors and colonial legislatures?

Chapter 1 Review

A. Key terms, People, and Concepts

New England Colonies
Middle Colonies
Southern Colonies
Jamestown
headright system
staple crops
plantation system
indentured servants
slavery
gentry
Puritans
Salem Witch Trials
public education
Quakers
salutary neglect
representative governments
colonial women
African Americans
limited government
Magna Carta
Parliament
English Bill of Rights
common law
natural rights
social contract theory
House of Burgesses
colonial governors
colonial legislatures

B. Multiple Choice

1. Tobacco and rice can **best** be described as which of the following?
   A. staple crops of the Southern Colonies
   B. cash crops of New England
   C. staple crops of the Middle Colonies
   D. crops raised in urban centers of commerce

2. Which of the following **best** describes the economic differences between the Southern and New England Colonies?
   A. The Southern Colonies found it profitable to trade with other countries, whereas New England Colonies did not.
   B. Southern landowners sought to make large profits, whereas New Englanders sought only to make enough to survive.
   C. Southern landowners did not have to depend on urban centers of commerce to trade their goods overseas as much as New Englanders did.
   D. The Southern colonies relied on the Atlantic Ocean to a greater extent than did the New England Colonies.

3. Who of the following would have **most** likely come to North America seeking religious freedom?

   A. a Catholic missionary from Spain

   B. an Anglican minister from England

   C. a southern plantation owner

   D. a Puritan

4. Which of the following did colonial Boston, New York, and Philadelphia, all have in common?

   A. they were each located in the Middle Colonies

   B. they were each important centers of commerce and ports for shipping

   C. they were each originally settled by nations other than England

   D. they were each cities founded and built by the Puritans

5. Which colonial region was the **most** diverse?

   A. the Middle Colonies
   C. New England

   B. the Southern Colonies
   D. the Carolinas

> *"Their place in history is interesting. On one hand, they came to the New World to escape religious persecution, only to persecute those who disagreed with them. They even executed people for being 'witches'. Yet, at the same time, they gave us the Mayflower Compact as a model of government and introduced public education to the colonies."*

6. The above quote is referring to which of the following?

   A. the Anglican Church
   C. the Puritans

   B. members of a joint-stock company
   D. the Quakers

7. Which of the following **best** describes the role of colonial women?

   A. They enjoyed more freedom and expanded roles than women in Europe, but were still denied many of the rights and respect given to men.

   B. They were not permitted to own or administer property, nor were they ever allowed to hold jobs.

   C. They did not enjoy as many rights as women in England

   D. They were allowed to attend school and vote, but they were never allowed to run for public office.

8. Which of the following statements is **true** regarding African Americans in the English colonies?

   A. The first African Americans came to Jamestown as slaves in the 1700s.

   B. All African Americans in the colonies were slaves.

   C. African American slaves in South Carolina outnumbered free whites through much of the 1700s.

   D. Although African Americans could sometimes earn money, they were never allowed to buy their own freedom.

9. A government that must obey a written constitution is a government that is what?

   A. free of authority

   B. dependent on salutary neglect

   C. representative in nature

   D. based on the rule of law

10. Who of the following would have **most** likely opposed one of the king's policies?

    A. a royal governor

    B. an official appointed by the governor

    C. a member of Parliament

    D. a colonial legislator

Chapter 2
The Birth of a Nation

This chapter addresses the following standard(s):

New Indicators	1.3, 1.4, 1.5, 1.6, 1.7
Old Indicators	2.2, 2.3, 2.4, 2.5, 2.6, 2.7

2.1 The American Revolution

Causes of the Revolution

The roots of the American Revolution went all the way back to the late 1600s. During that period, many nations in Europe began to accept the idea of *mercantilism*. Under this theory, countries grow wealthier and maintain their national security by consistently **exporting** (selling goods to other nations) more than they import (buy goods from other nations). As a result, countries tried to maintain a favorable balance of trade (export more than they import). To maintain such a balance, nations needed colonies for additional resources and markets.

In 1660, England began passing a series of laws known as the Navigation Acts. These laws required the British colonies to sell certain goods only to England. The few products the colonies could sell to other countries were charged a British duty (tax). Strict enforcement of the Navigation Acts ultimately contributed to the call for revolution.

The French and Indian War

French and Indian War

The desire for territory produced by mercantilism also meant that nations ended up fighting over land and resources. As British colonists moved west, they found themselves fighting French settlers and Native Americans. In 1754, this tension between French and British colonials resulted in the **French and Indian War**. It was so named because Britain fought the war against France and its Native American allies. After nine years of fighting, France finally surrendered and gave up its claims in Canada and all lands east of the Mississippi River. France's defeat meant that Great Britain stood alone as the one, true colonial power in North America.

Chapter 2

TENSIONS RISE BETWEEN GREAT BRITAIN AND THE COLONIES

Soon after the French and Indian War, relations between England and its colonies deteriorated. The colonists had lost respect for Britain's military, viewing it as ill-prepared and unsuited for fighting on the American terrain. Meanwhile, Great Britain was heavily in debt after fighting to defend its colonies and felt that the Americans should help pay for the expense. As a result, it took a number of steps the colonists found offensive. In 1760, England began issuing ***writs of assistance***. These were general search warrants that allowed British authorities to search whatever they wanted and for whatever reason. The British used these writs to board and search colonial ships as a way of enforcing the Navigation Acts.

Three years later, in response to Native American attacks in territories won from the French, King George III issued the **Proclamation of 1763.** It forbade colonists from settling west of the Appalachian Mountains and put the territory under British military control. Colonists resented the King's restrictions and many ignored the proclamation.

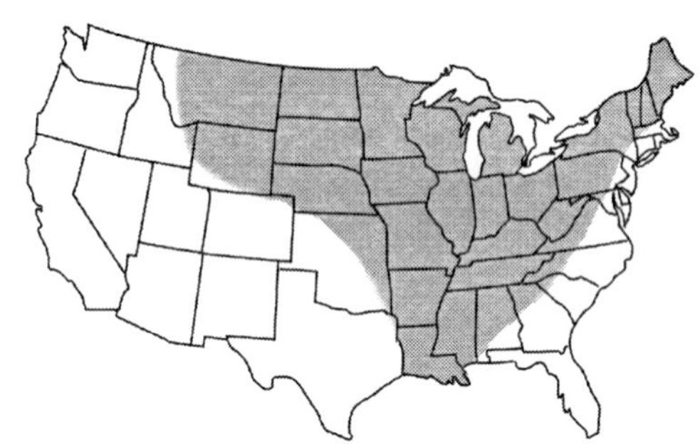

French Territory

Beginning in the mid 1760s, Parliament passed a series of laws and taxes that infuriated the Americans. The Quartering Act required colonists to house and supply British soldiers stationed in North America. The **Stamp Act** taxed nearly all printed material by requiring that it bear a government stamp. Many printers protested the new law. In response, a delegation of colonists met in what came to be known as the Stamp Act Congress. One of its leaders, James Otis, protested the tax proclaiming, **"No taxation without representation!"** Remember, under British law, no tax could be imposed except one approved by Parliament. Since the colonies had no representation in Parliament, Otis and others believed that they should not be subject to new taxes. In protest, the colonies imposed a **boycott** of British goods. A boycott simply means that they refused to buy them, thereby withholding money that would otherwise go to English businesses. A group called the Sons of Liberty took it upon themselves to enforce the boycotts and used violence and intimidation to prevent the implementation of British laws. The boycotts, along with violent responses to the Stamp Act, eventually led England to repeal (cancel) the law.

Tarring and Feathering of British Loyalists by the Sons of Liberty

However, on the same day that it repealed the Stamp Act, Parliament passed the **Declaratory Act**. This act stated that Parliament had the authority to impose laws on the colonies. In effect, England was telling the colonies that it expected them to comply with British laws whether they felt represented or not.

In 1767, Parliament passed the Townshend Acts which taxed imported goods like glass and tea. So violent was colonial reaction to these laws that England sent troops to Boston. On March 5, 1770, British soldiers who felt threatened by a mob of angry protesters fired shots that left several colonists dead or dying. The event became known as the **Boston Massacre**. A famous engraving by Paul Revere depicted the incident as a brutal slaying of innocent civilians. As a result, colonial resentment increased.

Boston Massacre

THE REVOLUTIONARY CAUSE

Boston Tea Party

Shortly after the "massacre," Townshend Acts (except for the duty on tea) and tensions subsided. They did not, however, go away. Years of salutary neglect would not allow Americans to accept England's firm control over them. One group took bold action in December 1773 when it dressed as Mohawk Indians and marched to Boston Harbor. There, in what became known as the **Boston Tea Party**, its members raided ships hauling British tea and threw the crates overboard. In response, Parliament passed the Coercive Acts (because of their harshness, the colonists labeled them the **Intolerable Acts**). These acts closed Boston Harbor and placed a military governor over Massachusetts. In addition, England expanded the Canadian border, taking land away from certain colonies.

To deal with the crisis, representatives from nearly every colony (only Georgia did not attend) gathered for the **First Continental Congress** in September 1774. In a statement to the King, the Congress wrote that the colonists had a right to be represented in their government. Since the colonies were not represented in Parliament, they were entitled to govern themselves.

Then, in April 1775, all hope of a peaceful resolution was lost when fighting broke out at **Lexington and Concord**. As British troops were on their way to seize arms and ammunition stored by colonists at Concord, Massachusetts, they were met at Lexington by colonial militia (voluntary, local military units consisting of private citizens rather than full-time soldiers). It was there that someone (to this day no one is sure who) fired the "shot heard 'round the world" that started the American Revolution.

Thomas Paine

Signing of the Declaration of Independence

Less than a month later, colonial delegates met for the **Second Continental Congress** to discuss how to deal with the situation. The following January, in 1776, Thomas Paine published his famous pamphlet, *Common Sense*. In it, he made a compelling case for independence that won many to the cause. Due to the influence of Paine and others, the Second Continental Congress eventually stopped seeking resolution with England and chose, instead, to draft the **Declaration of Independence**.

THE DECLARATION OF INDEPENDENCE

Declaration of Independence

Thomas Jefferson

In June 1776, the delegates to the Second Continental Congress decided to declare independence from Great Britain and appointed a committee to prepare a statement outlining the reasons for this separation. A young delegate named **Thomas Jefferson** drafted the statement. Strongly influenced by men like Locke and the Enlightenment, Jefferson asserted the principle of **egalitarianism** (the idea that all men are created equal) and proclaimed that men are born with certain **"inalienable rights"** (natural rights that government cannot take away). Among these rights are "life, liberty, and the pursuit of happiness." Claiming that Great Britain had failed to fulfill its duty to respect and uphold these rights, the **Declaration of Independence** concludes with a list of complaints against the king and asserts the colonies' right to declare independence.

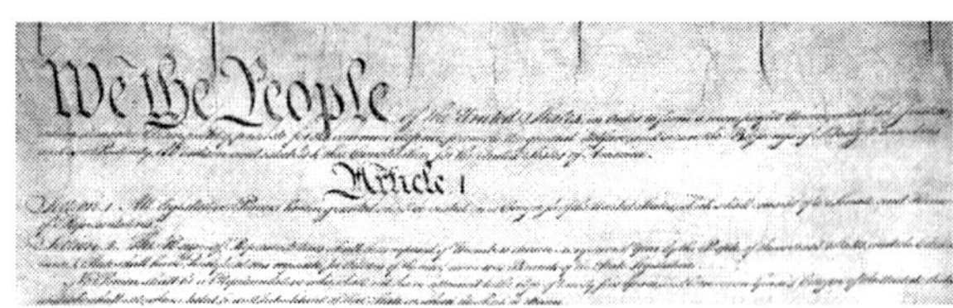

US Constitution

Both the Declaration of Independence and the American Revolution had a profound impact on the new country and the ideals of a republican form of government. Once it was signed, the 13 colonies became states and began drafting their own state constitutions (body of laws by which a state/country is governed). These constitutions usually included a bill of rights (something that would impact ratification of the US Constitution) and were to a large extent based on the principles and ideas set forth in the Declaration. Eventually, the Declaration's ideas also formed the groundwork for the **United States Constitution**.

In addition, the Declaration of Independence also caused US citizens to wrestle with their consciences. The document claimed the nation's right to independence based on the fact that Britain had imposed laws without allowing the colonies representation. It also expressed outrage that Britain had failed to uphold the natural rights of its citizens. Yet, the United States continued to sanction the institution of slavery, failed to recognize the rights of Native Americans, and did not grant women or minorities the right to vote. By forcing citizens to face such sad contradictions, the Declaration of Independence helped to ignite debate over these and other issues regarding the rights and freedoms of citizens. Over the centuries, the Declaration of Independence has served as the foundation on which countless crusades for social justice and reform have been based.

The success of the Revolution also meant that these ideas gained credibility abroad. The idea that government must be responsible to the people and respect certain rights helped ignite other movements, such as the French Revolution. In 1789, the French Revolution even produced a document directly modeled after the Declaration of Independence called the Declaration of the Rights of Man and of the Citizen. Over time, the Declaration of Independence has served as a model for numerous documents and national declarations of independence. Even today, the principles it proclaims continue to shape the world we live in.

The War for Independence

The American Revolution actually began long before the Declaration of Independence was ever written. By the time delegates to the Continental Congress signed the document in July 1776, colonists and British forces had been fighting for over a year. King George III of England did not expect a long war. After all, the British possessed the world's most formidable army and its mightiest navy. How could a disorganized band of untrained colonists possibly defeat them? The colonists, however, enjoyed one advantage that the British did not. They were fighting for their homeland and the right to govern themselves! This made them more determined, if not more prepared, to win the war. In addition, many colonists had fought alongside the British in the French and Indian War and were familiar with their tactics. Colonial leaders also knew that, if they failed, they would all hang for treason. In short, the American colonists had no option but victory!

King George III

Loyalists and Patriots

Not all colonists supported independence. Loyalists wanted to remain loyal to the king. Landowners in the South who depended on the British for protections and certain businessmen who relied on economic relations with England did not want war. Many Anglican church leaders and others whose livelihood were tied to the king also supported Great Britain.

Patriots supported the revolution. They wanted independence from Great Britain. No war in history (not even the Civil War) divided neighbors and members of the same communities as much as the American Revolution.

George Washington

Following Lexington and Concord, nearly 20,000 Patriots surrounded Boston where British soldiers were stationed. In June 1775, British troops launched a series of attacks against two hills occupied by American forces. The British eventually won the battle but suffered far greater casualties than the Americans. Although most of the bloodiest fighting took place on Breed's Hill, the battle was actually named for the second hill and became known as the Battle of Bunker Hill.

A month later, General **George Washington** arrived, having been newly appointed by the Continental Congress as commander of the Continental Army. In March, 1776, the British left Boston and eventually made their way to New York. There, despite his best efforts, Washington was forced to abandon the city and start a long and humiliating retreat.

General George Washington

Plagued by a lack of supplies, undisciplined soldiers, and the desertion of many of his troops (either illegally or because their enlistments had expired), Washington and his army seemed on the brink of defeat in December 1776. Then, in a daring move, Washington surprised his enemy by crossing the Delaware River on Christmas night and attacking the Hessians (Germans hired to fight for the British) encamped at Trenton, New Jersey. Having finally tasted victory, Washington's troops did not let up. Leaving their camp fires burning so as to make the enemy think they were still there, Washington's army then slipped away in the middle of the night to launch another surprise attack at Princeton.

The Northern War

British Surrender at Saratoga

In September 1777, General Horatio Gates won another key US victory at **Saratoga**, New York. This victory was especially important because it convinced the French that the US could possibly win the war. As a result, France and the United States forged an alliance that proved crucial in defeating Great Britain.

Following the victory at Saratoga, the Continental Army (official name given the US forces) endured a harsh winter at Valley Forge, Pennsylvania. Poorly supplied and lacking warm clothes, many of Washington's men proved too sick to serve. A number of them even died. Fortunately, once the warm weather returned, Washington's army returned to battle more determined and better trained than they had been before.

The Southern War

Fighting broke out in the South as early as 1775. On June 28, 1776, South Carolina militia resisted an attack on Charleston when their palmetto log fort was able to absorb the blows of the British artillery and forced the British naval fleet to turn away. To commemorate the victory, South Carolina put the palmetto on its state flag.

Thomas Sumter

Francis Marion

In the final weeks of 1778, the British began focusing more of their efforts on the South. By the summer of 1780, the British had seized both Savannah and Charleston and were ready to try and bring all of the Carolinas under their control. British forces under the command of General Lord Cornwallis sought to invade North Carolina following their victory at Camden, only to be defeated and turned back by Patriot victories at Kings Mountain and Cowpens. Inspired by the victory at Kings Mountain, guerilla forces (small bands of mobile combat troops who strike quickly then disappear; they are often more concerned with inflicting damage than with winning battles) under the command of men like Francis Marion (nicknamed "the Swamp Fox") and Thomas Sumter (nicknamed "the Gamecock") grew in numbers and caused headaches for the British.

Eventually, Cornwallis did invade North Carolina, pursuing the southern US forces under the command of Nathanael Greene. After leading the British on a long chase that extended into Virginia and forced Cornwallis to exhaust many of his supplies, Greene eventually engaged the British forces at the Battle of Guilford Courthouse at what is today Greensboro, NC. Cornwallis won, but at a heavy cost. To win the battle, he found it necessary to fire his cannon into the midst of the battle, killing many of his own men. In need of supplies, Cornwallis then marched his forces north to the coastal town of Yorktown, Virginia, where he hoped to receive what he needed from British ships.

YORKTOWN

Realizing that Cornwallis was trapped on the Virginia peninsula, Washington marched south to pin him between the Continental Army and the Atlantic Ocean. Meanwhile, the French navy provided a blockade that prevented British ships from coming to Cornwallis' rescue. On October 19, 1781, Cornwallis surrendered to Washington at **Yorktown**. Although negotiations would go on for two more years, Yorktown effectively ended the Revolutionary War. The war officially ended in 1783 when the two sides signed the Treaty of Paris and Great Britain formally recognized US independence.

Battle of Yorktown

Surrenders at Yorktown

Practice 2.1: The American Revolution

1. Which of the following was **not** a contributing factor to the start of the American Revolution?

   A. British writs of assistance

   B. Stamp Act

   C. taxation without representation

   D. France's decision to side with the United States

2. Thomas Paine's contribution to the Revolutionary cause can **best** be described as what?

   A. important, because he drafted the document that proclaimed US independence

   B. memorable, because he introduced the phrase, "no taxation without representation!"

   C. inspiring, because his writings won many to the cause of independence

   D. radical, because he led a group of colonists who dressed as Mohawk Indians and dumped tea in Boston harbor.

3. Which one of the following would Thomas Jefferson have **most** likely considered an "inalienable right?"
   A. the right to guaranteed happiness
   B. the right to take whatever you want
   C. the right to pursue success
   D. the right to a public education

4. What effect has the Declaration of Independence had on the US and the world?

2.2 Establishing a Government

Articles of Confederation

Initially, the newly independent states were cautious about giving too much authority to a central government. They preferred a confederation, in which each state would maintain its sovereignty while being loosely unified as a nation. For this reason, Congress drafted the **Articles of Confederation** to serve as the nation's first set of laws.

Finally ratified in 1781, the Articles of Confederation failed because it did not give enough power to the federal (national) government to lead effectively. In order for any law passed by Congress to be final, at least nine of the thirteen states had to agree. Since the states often had different interests, such agreement was rare. Also, the Articles did not grant Congress the power to impose taxes. The federal government had to *ask* the states for money. This was not very effective and made it practically impossible to administer the government or provide for a national defense. Foreign countries quickly realized the glaring weaknesses in the Articles of Confederation as well. As a result, Britain refused to withdraw troops from the Ohio Valley and Spain closed its port at New Orleans, cutting off the Mississippi River. Unable to raise a formidable army, the United States was in no position to oppose such actions.

After the revolution, the United States experienced an economic crisis. The nation was experiencing a depression in which the value of US currency was very low, paper money was scarce, and falling farm prices left many farmers unable to repay outstanding loans. At the same time, in order to pay war debts, the state of Massachusetts raised taxes (the national government could not impose taxes, but state governments could). Outraged, a Massachusetts farmer and Revolutionary War veteran named Daniel Shays led a number of farmers in rebellion. Without an adequate national government,

Shays's Rebellion

Massachusetts was forced to deal with the revolt on its own. The event made it evident that a stronger central government was needed, and leaders called a convention to revise the Articles of Confederation.

The Constitutional Convention and Ratification

In 1787, a delegation met in Philadelphia to revise the Articles of Confederation. Soon after the convention began, however, the delegates decided to do away with the document altogether and write a new set of laws. The result was the **United States Constitution**.

Constitutional Convention

All the delegates in attendance (only Rhode Island did not send representatives) agreed that change was necessary. However, how the national government should be reorganized was a matter of much debate. As a result, a number of compromises (decisions reached as a result of disagreeing parties being willing to give up a little of what they want) emerged.

The Great Compromise

Edmund Randolph and James Madison of Virginia introduced the Virginia Plan. They proposed a federal government made up of three branches: a legislative branch to make the laws, an executive branch to enforce the laws, and a judicial branch to make sure that the laws were administered fairly. For the legislative branch, the Virginia Plan called for two houses with representatives from each state. In each house, the number of representatives per state would be determined by population. The greater a state's population, the more representatives it would have.

Larger states loved the idea; but smaller states hated it because they would be left with less representation. As a result, one of New Jersey's delegates proposed the New Jersey Plan. Like the Virginia Plan, it also called for three branches of government, but it wanted the legislative branch to consist of only one house with each state getting a single vote. In the end, the delegates decided on a compromise. It became known as the **Great Compromise**. It established a legislative branch with two houses. One house, called the *House of Representatives*, would be elected directly by the people and each state granted a certain number of seats based on population. The other house, called the *Senate*, would be elected by state legislatures with each state having two senators, regardless of population. Together, the two houses would comprise Congress.

The Three-Fifths Compromise

Slavery also proved to be a point of contention. Northern states had fewer slaves and argued that, since slaves were not voting citizens, they should not be counted as part of the population. Southern states, however, had far more slaves and wanted to count them. The answer to this question was important because it affected how many representatives each state would have in Congress. Again, a compromise was reached. It was known as the **Three-fifths Compromise** because it stated that each slave would count as "three-fifths of a person."

James Madison

The Slave Trade Compromise

Slave Trade

Meanwhile, debate about the slave trade resulted in a **Slave Trade Compromise**. Under this agreement, Northerners who opposed the slave trade agreed to allow it to continue for twenty years, after which time Congress could impose regulations. This was important to Southerners who insisted that their economy could not survive without the slave trade.

The Bill of Rights

Although the new document was an amazing improvement from the Articles of Confederation, it was not without controversy. A number of states refused to ratify it, claiming it did not do enough to guarantee the rights of citizens. Finally, in late 1788, the last of the nine states needed approved the Constitution once Congress agreed to consider a number of amendments protecting civil liberties. Only North Carolina and Rhode Island held off until after these amendments had actually been submitted to Congress. When Congress met in 1789, one of its first orders of business was to pass the **Bill of Rights**. It consists of the first ten amendments (additions) to the Constitution and stems from many of the principles expressed in the Declaration of Independence.

Federalists vs. Anti-Federalists

There was also controversy surrounding the new Constitution concerning what role and powers the national government should have. Many favored the Constitution because they believed that the United States needed a strong federal government with a powerful president at its head. Others opposed the Constitution because they feared that a powerful federal government would trample on their rights. Because of the debate, political leaders split into opposing factions. The faction that favored a strong central government and supported the Constitution was called the **Federalists**. Among their leaders were Alexander Hamilton, James Madison, and John Jay (first chief justice of the Supreme Court). The faction that opposed them and wanted to see stronger state governments was called the **Anti-federalists** (author of the Declaration of Independence, Thomas Jefferson, was an Anti-federalist).

Federalists had a **loose interpretation of the Constitution**. They believed that the Constitution allowed the federal government to take certain actions not specifically stated so long as such actions were deemed necessary for carrying out the government's constitutional responsibilities. By contrast, Anti-federalists held to a **strict interpretation of the Constitution**. They believed the federal government could only do what the Constitution specifically said. This was because the Anti-federalists feared that the central government would become too powerful and infringe on the rights of citizens.

To make their case for the Constitution, Hamilton, Madison, and Jay wrote a series of essays known as the ***Federalist Papers***. The essays were written to persuade New York's legislature to ratify the Constitution by easing fears that the document left the government susceptible to any one faction seizing too much power. Eventually, with the support of men like George Washington, Alexander Hamilton, and John Adams, the Federalist view won. Anti-federalists did succeed, however, in securing the Bill of Rights.

Alexander Hamilton

Practice 2.2: Establishing a US Government

1. The Articles of Confederation proved ineffective as a national body of laws for which of the following reasons?

   A. It gave too much power to the Congress without providing for a commander of the nation's armed forces.

   B. It did not give the federal government enough power to effectively lead.

   C. It imposed taxes that led to a rebellion of farmers in New England.

   D. It prevented individual states from having their own constitutions.

2. Why did smaller states oppose the Virginia Plan and how did the Great Compromise set their fears at ease?

   A. They opposed the Virginia Plan because it wanted to include slaves in the population count, thereby giving southern states even more power in Congress. The Great Compromise eased their fears by stating that after twenty years, Congress could decide not to include slaves in such a count.

   B. They opposed the Virginia Plan because it wanted to leave slaves out of the population count and smaller states needed their slaves counted if they were going to compete with the larger states. The Great Compromise eased their fears because it stated that slaves would be counted as three-fifths of a person in the population.

   C. They opposed the Virginia Plan because it advocated only one house in Congress that would be based on population. The Great Compromise eased their fears because it said that each state would be represented equally.

   D. They opposed the Virginia Plan because it advocated a legislative branch in which both houses of Congress would be based on population. The Great Compromise eased their fears because it called for one house to be based on population but the second to provide equal representation for each state.

3. What is the Bill of Rights and what purpose does it serve?

4. Political faction which favored a strong national government, loose interpretation of the Constitution, and wanted to see the Constitution ratified was known as what?

   A. Federalists

   B. Anti-federalists

   C. supporters of the New Jersey Plan

   D. delegates to the Constitutional Convention

2.3 Hamilton, Jefferson, and the Emergence of Political Parties

Hamilton's Economic Plan

Alexander Hamilton

Thomas Jefferson

When the new US government took power in 1789, the nation was deep in debt and the value of the new currency was low. **Alexander Hamilton**, a trusted officer during the Revolutionary War and President Washington's secretary of the treasury, developed a plan to help. Hamilton proposed that the federal government take on state debts that were largely due to the war. To raise revenue and strengthen the economy, Hamilton wanted to establish an excise tax (a tax per unit produced) on whiskey, impose tariffs (taxes on imports) which would strengthen and protect US businesses, and start a national bank. Hamilton's economic plan gained the support of President Washington, but it was not without controversy.

Many opposed Hamilton's views. One opponent was Washington's secretary of state and author of the Declaration of Independence, **Thomas Jefferson**. Jefferson had a strict interpretation of the Constitution and argued that the federal government must restrict itself to those powers specifically stated in the document. Since the Constitution did not give the federal government the authority to open a national bank, Jefferson argued that it could not. Hamilton, on the other hand, had a loose interpretation. He believed that the *necessary and proper clause* of the Constitution gave the government the right to charter a bank if it was necessary to exercise its constitutional duties (in this case, coining money).

Southerners opposed Hamilton's plan because they were against tariffs. Tariffs would lessen competition from foreign countries and raise prices on finished goods. They would also encourage other countries to respond with tariffs of their own, thereby raising prices on southern exports and hurting the South's economy. Southerners also did not want to help pay the debts of other states.

The whiskey tax was very unpopular among farmers in the western regions of Pennsylvania, Maryland, Virginia, and North Carolina. Many of these farmers made their living converting grain into whiskey. Their protest eventually resulted in the Whiskey Rebellion of 1794, when Pennsylvania farmers refused to pay the tax and resorted to violence. The uprising ended when President Washington organized a military force that halted the resistance. While the event showed that the new government had the power to enforce its laws, it also led many farmers and frontiersmen to see Hamilton's form of government as tyrannical. More of them flocked to Thomas Jefferson as a defender of states' rights and a champion of their cause.

The Rise of Political Parties

Washington's Farewell Address

Shortly before leaving office, President George Washington gave a farewell address in which he emphasized three key points. First, Washington expressed his view that the United States should stay neutral and avoid permanent alliances with other nations. Second, he believed that good government is based on religion and morality. Third, he spoke about the dangers of forming political parties (organized political factions established to support and elect candidates which support the party's ideals/agenda). He warned that political parties would cause people to work for their special interests rather than for the public good.

Despite Washington's warnings, opposing political parties did indeed form. The **Federalist Party** believed in a strong national government, felt that political power should be entrusted to the educated upper classes, and supported business over agriculture. Hamilton was a key figure in the Federalist party.

The **Democratic-Republicans** arose in opposition to the Federalists. Their leader was Thomas Jefferson. Democratic-Republicans favored stronger state governments and a weaker national government. For this reason, many of them originally opposed the Constitution because they feared it made the national government too strong. The Democratic-Republicans tended to favor the interests of small farmers and debtors, rather than those of business.

Federalists

- favored a strong central government
- wanted power in the hands of the wealthy and well-educated rather than in the hands of the people
- thought the nation's economy should be based on manufacturing, shipping, and commerce rather than agriculture
- interpreted the Constitution loosely as giving powers not specifically stated

Democratic-Republicans

- favored states retaining authority
- wanted power in the hands of the people because they felt the people were the safest store of power
- thought the nation's economy should be based on agriculture
- interpreted the Constitution strictly as giving powers only as stated

Conflicts Between the Federalists and the Democratic-Republicans

Debt was not the only problem facing the new nation. Global politics was another major source of concern for Washington's administration. France and Britain were at war, and while the US wanted nothing more than to remain neutral and establish good diplomatic relations with both nations, this proved impossible. The Federalists and Democratic-Republicans again had different views. While neither party wanted war, the Democratic-Republicans favored the French — believing that the French Revolution would produce a government close to America's political leanings. The Federalists, on the other hand, favored neutrality. The

Federalists, unlike Jefferson and the Democratic-Republicans, believed that the French Revolution was a negative influence. Because the Federalists believed in a strong central government with power in the hands of a few, they feared the spread of ideas that the success of such a rebellion might bring. As a result, Congress passed several laws during John Adams' administration. The **Naturalization Act** required fourteen years of residency before US citizenship could be obtained. The **Alien Act** allowed the government to arrest, detain or remove foreigners deemed untrustworthy. Finally, the **Sedition Act** severely limited free speech and expression. Federalists often used the Alien and Sedition Acts to silence critics (usually Democratic-Republicans). Jefferson and others saw these acts as abuses of power. Such laws also helped the Federalists because immigrants who had been in the country for only a short time tended to be poorer and drawn to the Democratic-Republicans. Under these laws, such people could not vote in elections.

Thomas Jefferson and James Madison produced a response to the Alien and Sedition Acts in the form of the **Virginia and Kentucky Resolutions** (named after the states that adopted them). These resolutions stated that if a state believed a federal law to be unconstitutional, then it did not have to obey or enforce it. The idea that individual states have such a right came to be known as the **Doctrine of Nullification**, because it claims that states can nullify (not be bound by/ignore) a national law that they believe violates the Constitution.

Eventually, with the end of the War of 1812, the Federalist party faded. The existence of political parties and the role that they play in US politics, however, continues to this day in the form of the Republican and Democratic parties.

Practice 2.3: Hamilton, Jefferson, and the Emergence of Political Parties

1. How did Alexander Hamilton and Thomas Jefferson interpret the Constitution differently?

   A. Hamilton saw the Constitution as the law of the land, whereas Jefferson thought it had little authority.

   B. Hamilton had a strict interpretation of the Constitution and believed the federal government could only do what the Constitution specifically gave it the authority to do. Jefferson, on the other hand, had a loose interpretation and thought that the federal government could take just about any action that the Constitution did not specifically forbid.

   C. Hamilton wanted to revise the Constitution to let the states have more power, whereas Jefferson wanted to do away with it altogether in favor of a document that better protected the rights of businessmen.

   D. Hamilton had a loose interpretation and believed that the Constitution allowed the federal government to take actions like establishing a national bank. Jefferson had a strict interpretation and worried that if the federal government was not limited to powers specifically mentioned, it would infringe on the rights of states.

2. What two political parties formed in the early days of the nation, and how did they view government and economics differently?

3. How did the Virginia and Kentucky Resolutions come into being, what doctrine did they establish, and what did this doctrine state?

2.4 Principles of the Constitution

The Founding Fathers of the United States based the US Constitution on the ideals of limited government and the rule of law. In the United States, the government must abide by the Constitution.

Republicanism and Democracy

The US Constitution founded a republican government. A republican government is one in which members of an elite, leadership class, represents members of society overall. Under the Constitution, only males who owned property could originally vote to determine what members of the ruling upper class would represent them in Congress and state legislatures. State legislatures then elected members of the Senate and delegates to the Electoral College who would elect the president.

Over time, the US government changed to become more of a democracy. In a democracy, the people elect leaders directly. Leaders need not come solely from an elite ruling class. The Seventeenth Amendment allowed private citizens to elect US senators instead of relying on state legislators to do so. Eventually, presidents were elected directly. Delegates' votes in the Electoral College came to be determined by popular vote rather than by state representatives.

Separation of Powers and Checks and Balances

In order to prevent any one leader or body from becoming too powerful, the framers made sure that the new government featured a **separation of powers**, in which each branch shares governmental authority.

The US government consists of three different branches (legislative, executive, and judicial). Each possesses certain powers that the others do not. For instance, the president is the commander of the nation's military, but only Congress may declare war. In the same way, Congress has the power to pass laws, but the federal courts have the power to rule on whether or not they have been properly applied (or even if they may be applied at all).

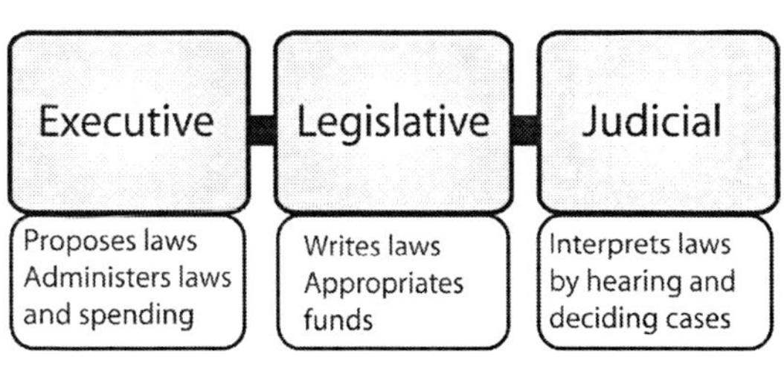

To make sure that no one branch tries to use its authority to overpower the others, the framers of the Constitution also included a system of **checks and balances**. Although one branch might enjoy a certain power, another branch can still "check" or "balance" its power if need be. For example: Congress has the power to propose and pass bills that become laws. The president, however, has the authority to "check" this power by vetoing (rejecting) the bill Congress passes, thereby preventing it from becoming a law. In turn, if Congress has enough votes to "override" the president's veto (ignore the president's rejection), then the bill becomes law anyway. This is just one example of how checks and balances work.

FEDERALISM

Another feature of the US Constitution is **federalism**. Two levels of government share power. In the United States, power is shared between the national (federal) and state governments. Certain powers belong to the federal government (negotiating treaties, declaring war) and some belong to the states (regulating public schools and local governments, deciding how elections will be run). The federal and state governments share a few powers as well (the authority to build roads or impose taxes). Powers that are delegated to the federal government by the Constitution are called delegated powers; powers that are reserved for the states are called reserved powers; and powers that are shared between the two are called concurrent powers.

SECTIONS OF THE US CONSTITUTION

THE PREAMBLE AND ARTICLE I (THE LEGISLATIVE BRANCH)

The first sentence of the US Constitution is known as the **Preamble**. It serves to explain the purpose and intent of the document. The preamble is followed by seven articles that establish the US government.

We the People of the United States, in Order to form a more perfect Union, establish Justice, insure domestic Tranquility, provide for the common defence, promote the general Welfare, and secure the Blessings of Liberty to ourselves and our Posterity, do ordain and establish this Constitution for the United States of America.

Preamble

The articles are followed by twenty-seven amendments. These are additions to the Constitution added at different times in US history after the document was originally drafted. Article I establishes the **legislative branch**, known as Congress. It is the role of the legislative branch to make the laws. Congress consists of two houses. Population determines how many representatives each state has in the **House of Representatives**. The greater a state's population, the more representatives that state has. The second house is the **Senate**, which is comprised of two senators from each state. Originally, state legislatures rather than the people elected senators. However, in 1913, the Seventeenth Amendment changed this. Now, citizens directly elect their US senators.

Congress

The Constitution grants each house of Congress certain powers and responsibilities. Some powers are shared by both. For instance, both houses must approve a bill (a proposed law) before it can become a law (a rule which society is legally bound to uphold and abide by). Other powers are possessed by one house, but not the other. Only the House of Representatives may introduce tax bills or impeach public officials. Only the Senate has the power to block or confirm presidential appointments (people the president nominates to fill cabinet positions, seats on the federal courts, or other public offices).

Article II (The Executive Branch)

Article II establishes the **executive branch** of government to enforce the laws. The **president of the United States** serves as the chief executive of this branch and the nation's head of state (leader).

Al Gore

The president is elected to office by the Electoral College. This is a body of delegates that meets every four years solely to elect the president and, under the Twelfth Amendment, the vice president as well.

The Constitution lists the qualifications for president and defines his or her powers and responsibilities. The Constitution also takes steps to make sure that the president is bound by the rule of law. Article II / Section 4 states that the president may be impeached (charged with wrongdoing) by the House of Representatives if he or she is suspected of treason, bribery, or "other high crimes and misdemeanors." If this occurs, the president then stands trial in the Senate. If two-thirds of the Senate finds him or her guilty, then he or she is removed from office.

George W. Bush

Article III (The Judicial Branch)

Article III creates the **judicial branch**. This branch consists of the federal court system with the Supreme Court acting as the highest court in the land. The role of the judicial branch is to make sure that laws are applied appropriately.

One of the most important powers of the judicial branch is not specifically granted by the Constitution, but rather was established by precedence in 1803. **Precedence** means a court uses past legal decisions to make rulings because the law is open to interpretation, or there is no written statute.

John Marshall

The case involved a conflict between the Federalists and the Democratic-Republicans. In 1801, Thomas Jefferson (a Democratic-Republican) became president. However, just before leaving office, his predecessor, John Adams (a Federalist), appointed a number of federal judges. Because he did this at the last minute, these appointments came to be called the "midnight judges." Although the Senate had confirmed these judges and Adams had signed their appointments, the documents making their appointments official had not yet been delivered when Jefferson took office. Fearing that Federalist judges might interfere with his plans, Jefferson refused to deliver the documents (commissions), preventing some of the judges from ever taking office. When several of the appointees challenged this move, the Supreme Court intervened to hear the case.

In ***Marbury v. Madison (1803)***, Chief Justice **John Marshall** stated that the appointees were entitled to their commissions *but* that the US Supreme Court did not have authority under the Constitution to force the president to issue them. In so doing, Marshall led the court in striking down part of a national law passed by Congress and establishing the Court's authority of **judicial review**. Judicial review is the Courts' power to declare acts of Congress and/or state legislatures "unconstitutional". This means that even if Congress passes a law and the president signs it, the federal courts can still nullify the law by ruling that it violates the Constitution.

The Bill of Rights

Of the twelve amendments that Congress passed in 1789 for the purpose of protecting civil liberties, the states chose to ratify ten of them. Greatly influenced by the English Bill of Rights and the Declaration of Independence, these ten amendments are known as the US Bill of Rights.

The First Amendment guarantees citizens' freedom of speech, freedom of the press, freedom to petition the government, and freedom to assemble. It also protects freedom of religion and establishes the principle of separation of church and state through the Free Exercise Clause, which forbids Congress from making any law prohibiting the free exercise of one's religious beliefs; and the Establishment Clause, which forbids Congress from establishing a religion.

Freedom of Religion

The Second Amendment guarantees the right to bear arms. Although there is much debate today about the extent to which firearms should be available to private citizens, in the early days of the nation this right was considered crucial for maintaining local militias. The first shots of the revolution were fired because the British attempted to take arms stored by private citizens at Concord.

The Third Amendment restricts quartering (housing) of federal troops in the homes of US citizens. Prior to the revolution, the British angered colonists by forcing them to house British soldiers.

The Fourth Amendment protects citizens against unreasonable searches and seizures. The memory of Great Britain's writs of assistance inspired this amendment.

The Fifth Amendment clearly defines criminal proceedings by which a person may be arrested and charged with a crime. It ensures that no person shall be imprisoned or deprived of their property without due process. In addition, this amendment protects citizens from the possibility of "double jeopardy." A person cannot be tried for the same crime more than once. Neither can defendants be forced to testify against themselves in court. This is called protection from self-incrimination. Finally, this amendment also places limits on eminent domain. Eminent domain is the government's power to take private property for public use.

The Sixth Amendment protects the rights of the accused. This includes the right to a public and speedy trial by jury. This amendment also guarantees the right to legal representation (a lawyer) and the right to call and confront witnesses.

The Seventh Amendment extends this right to a trial by jury to civil cases as well (i.e., when one person sues another for money).

Jury Trial

The Eighth Amendment protects those arrested or found guilty of a crime. It prohibits the government from imposing excessive bail/fines. Bail is money an arrested person must pay to get out of jail until the date of his or her trial, while fines are amounts of money imposed as punishment for a crime one has been found guilty of. This amendment also forbids cruel and unusual punishment of those convicted of a crime.

The Ninth Amendment simply says that the rights specifically mentioned in the Bill of Rights are not necessarily the only ones enjoyed by the people.

The Tenth Amendment says that those powers not restricted by the Constitution, nor delegated to the US government, are reserved for the states. The Constitution grants the states the authority to decide certain matters of law.

Practice 2.4: Principles of the Constitution

1. The fact that even Congress, the president, and the courts are bound by the Constitution is evidence of which of the following principles?

   A. implied powers

   B. limited government

   C. federalism

   D. democracy

2. The president appoints a promising young judge to the United States Supreme Court. However, to ensure that the appointee is qualified, the US Senate must first confirm (approve) the nomination. This is an example of what?

   A. checks and balances

   B. judicial review

   C. legislative process

   D. impeachment

3. Congress passes a new federal law making it illegal to call public officials "boneheads." The president gladly signs it. However, the Supreme Court nullifies the law by ruling that it violates the Constitution. What power has the Court exercised?
   A. the power to impeach
   B. judicial appointment
   C. judicial review
   D. constitutional amendment

4. The fact that the Constitution delegates some powers to the federal government while reserving other powers for the states is evidence that the US government is modeled after what?
   A. republicanism
   B. democracy
   C. separation of powers
   D. federalism

5. The Second Amendment is designed to protect which of the following rights?
   A. the right to free speech
   B. the right to peaceful assembly
   C. the right to religious freedom
   D. the right to bear arms

6. How are some of the rights and principles expressed in the Declaration of Independence also evident in the US Bill of Rights?

Chapter 2 Review

A. Key Terms, People, and Concepts

French and Indian War
writs of assistance
Proclamation of 1763
Stamp Act
"No taxation without representation"
Declaratory Act
Boston Massacre
Boston Tea Party
Intolerable Acts
First Continental Congress
Lexington and Concord
Second Continental Congress
Thomas Jefferson
egalitarianism
inalienable rights
Declaration of Independence
George Washington
Saratoga
Yorktown
Articles of Confederation
United States Constitution
Great Compromise
Three-fifths Compromise
Slave Trade Compromise
Bill of Rights
Federalists
Anti-federalists
loose interpretation of the Constitution
strict interpretation of the Constitution
Federalist Papers
Alexander Hamilton
Federalists Party
Democratic-Republicans
Naturalization Act
Alien Act
Sedition Act
Virginia and Kentucky Resolutions
Doctrine of Nullification
republic
democracy
separation of powers
checks and balances
federalism
legislative branch
House of Representatives
Senate
executive branch
president of the United States
judicial branch
precedence
Marbury v. Madison
John Marshall
judicial review

B. Multiple Choice

1. Which of the following contributed to the start of the American Revolution?
   A. British debt following the French and Indian War
   B. The *Federalist Papers* rebellion
   C. Shays's rebellion
   D. ratification of the Constitution

2. The following quote is **most** likely from whom?

   > "While I agree that power must be divided among several branches of government, I cannot agree to this plan. It proposes that both houses of the legislative branch be comprised of representatives from each state. That is fine and good. But it also proposes that, in each house, the number of representatives per state is to be based on population. Should we, the smaller states, have less of a voice in our own government because we are fewer in number? Did not our citizens spill blood to make this nation free as well. No! To approve this plan would be to impose a form of tyranny on us again. What good is representation if it is destined to mean nothing."

   A. a delegate to the First Continental Congress from a large state

   B. a delegate to the Constitutional Convention who is protesting the New Jersey Plan

   C. a delegate to the Second Continental Congress who is opposing the Constitution

   D. a delegate to the Constitutional Convention who is opposing the Virginia Plan

3. Which of the following statements is **untrue** regarding the Declaration of Independence?

   A. It echoed many of the principles of the Enlightenment.

   B. It was written after delegates witnessed the success of the French Revolution.

   C. Congress chose Thomas Jefferson to write it.

   D. It has inspired other political movements and documents around the world.

4. The US victory at Saratoga was especially important for which of the following reasons?

   A. It was the first US victory of the American Revolution.

   B. It was the result of a daring move by General Washington on Christmas night 1776.

   C. It convinced France that the US could win the war, thereby giving the US a crucial ally.

   D. It resulted in Britain's immediate surrender and served as the final decisive battle of the war.

5. Someone who supported ratification of the Constitution, believed that the president should have a lot of power, and held a loose interpretation of the Constitution, was **most** likely a member of which faction?
   A. Federalists
   B. Anti-federalists
   C. Democratic-Republican
   D. First Continental Congress

6. A poor Pennsylvania grain farmer in the early 1790s who feared having his rights trampled on by a powerful national government would have **most** likely supported who of the following leaders?
   A. John Adams
   B. Thomas Jefferson
   C. Alexander Hamilton
   D. John Jay

7. Which of the following statements reflects the views of a Federalist?
   A. "We must not put the interest of business above that of agriculture. After all, it is on the backs of farmers that this nation of ours was built."
   B. "If left unchecked, greedy businessmen will exploit and devour the lower classes."
   C. "We must interpret the Constitution strictly. If the Constitution does not specifically grant certain powers to the government, then the government has no right to assume such powers; even if it claims it is doing so in the interest of carrying out its constitutional responsibilities."
   D. "The national government must have ultimate authority above that of the states. Likewise, we must not hinder the national government's ability to function, but rather we must grant it the freedom to undertake any action it sees as necessary and proper for carrying out its obligations and duties."

8. Which of the following was added to the Constitution after its ratification for the purpose of protecting civil rights?
   A. the Articles of Confederation
   B. the Bill of Rights
   C. writs of assistance
   D. the Great Compromise

9. Which of the following was established by the case of *Marbury v. Madison*?
   A. republican
   B. judicial review
   C. doctrine of nullification
   D. federalism

10. Which of the following resulted from the court's ruling in *Marbury v. Madison*?
   A. The power of government became more limited.
   B. The power of the president increased.
   C. The power of the judicial branch expanded.
   D. The Bill of Rights became part of the Constitution.

Chapter 3 Territorial Expansion during the Antebellum Period

This chapter addresses the following standard(s):

New Indicators	2.1, 2.2, 2.3, 2.4
Old Indicators	3.1, 3.2, 3.3, 4.1

3.1 Territorial Expansion

With victory over the French in the French and Indian War, Britain took possession of the Northwest Territory (the area lying north of the Ohio and east of the Mississippi rivers). Following the American Revolution, Congress passed the Northwest Ordinance which divided the area into even smaller territories and provided guidelines under which new states could be admitted to the union. It eventually resulted in the formation of five states: Ohio, Indiana, Illinois, Michigan, and Wisconsin. Under the ordinance, slavery was not permitted in the new territories.

Northwest Territory

The Louisiana Purchase

Once in office, President Thomas Jefferson wanted to secure United States trading on the Mississippi River. He sent representatives to France to negotiate the purchase of New Orleans. Initially, Napoleon was not interested in selling New Orleans because he hoped to revitalize the French colonial empire in the western hemisphere. However, when the colony of Haiti revolted and Britain resumed its war with France, the French emperor surprised Jefferson by offering to sell not only New Orleans but the entire Louisiana region.

Thomas Jefferson

The **Louisiana Purchase** of 1803 was the United States' largest land purchase, roughly doubling the country's size. It marked a turning point for the new nation economically as it began to pursue prosperity from within its own borders rather than from foreign nations.

The Lewis and Clark Expedition

Lewis and Clark Expedition

Even before the Louisiana Purchase in 1803, President Jefferson had chosen his personal secretary, Meriwether Lewis, to find a water route to the Pacific Ocean. Lewis chose William Clark to help him lead the expedition that departed from St. Louis in May of 1804. Finally, in November of 1805, the Lewis and Clark Expedition reached the Pacific Northwest coast. Many people thought the explorers had died along the way, but the group returned to St. Louis in September of 1806 with valuable information about the Oregon and Louisiana territories. This exploration led to the rapid migration of settlers to the Pacific Northwest.

The War of 1812

As US settlers attempted to move west, they often confronted Native Americans who resisted them. Many settlers blamed the British for encouraging such resistance in order to protect their own interests. They also felt threatened by the British presence in Canada. This, combined with the British navy's policy of impressing US seaman (taking them captive and forcing them to serve on British ships), meant that many in the United States wanted war. Finally, on June 18, 1812, Congress declared war on Great Britain.

The **War of 1812** began with many in the US hoping to win land from the British in Canada and the Spanish in Florida (Spain had ties to the British). At times, it appeared that the US was in trouble, especially when the British invaded and burned Washington, DC in August 1814. The US won an inspiring victory shortly after losing the capital, however, at the battle of Fort McHenry. The bravery of the US soldiers who held the fort despite intense British fire inspired Francis Scott Key to write the initial draft of the *Star Spangled Banner* (today's US national anthem).

War of 1812

US Commander **Andrew Jackson** won victories over the Creek Indians (British allies) at the Battle of Horseshoe Bend and against British forces that had him outnumbered at the Battle of New Orleans. The US also secured the signing and ratification of a treaty ending the war (the battle of New Orleans actually occurred after the treaty, but the US victory ensured that the British would honor its terms). The Treaty of Ghent did not grant any official land gains to the United States, but it did keep the Mississippi River and the frontier open, thereby encouraging further western migration. It also served as evidence to the United States' ability to defend itself and assert its interests in North America against foreign powers. Meanwhile, due to its opposition to the war and an ill-timed protest that reached the capital at the same time as news of the treaty and Jackson's victory, the Federalist party lost its credibility and faded from importance in national politics.

Andrew Jackson

NATIONALISM

The War of 1812 led to a rise in US **nationalism** (pride citizens feel in their country). The young nation's ability to stand tall against the mighty British a second time filled many citizens with confidence in their government and military. Also, the fact that US manufacturers proved capable of supplying the country with goods during a time when foreign trade was limited did much to boost morale and the economy. US citizens began to view their country as one of the greatest on earth.

Chapter 3

The Monroe Doctrine

James Monroe

With the end of the War of 1812 and the Federalist party, the United States entered a period of national pride and political unity known as the *Era of Good Feelings*. It was during this period that President James Monroe issued the **Monroe Doctrine** in 1823. Monroe stated that the United States would not tolerate European intervention in the affairs of any independent nation in the Americas. He also made it clear that the American continents were no longer open to European colonization and that the US would view any future attempts to colonize as acts of aggression. Monroe was especially concerned because several Latin American nations had recently established themselves as independent of Spanish rule. He did not want another European power taking control of these territories and possibly threatening the United States.

In reality, Monroe did not have the power to enforce his proclamation. The United States was still a young nation and lacked a strong military. But Monroe was fortunate. He benefitted from the fact that Great Britain wanted to trade with these new nations and also wanted them to remain independent. Thanks to the power of the British Navy, no European country challenged the Monroe Doctrine.

Manifest Destiny

As the United States approached the middle of the nineteenth century, a great sense of nationalism inspired many to want to add to the US territory. Many leaders and citizens believed it was the country's destiny to expand and possess territory all the way to the Pacific Ocean. Those who shared this conviction referred to it as **"Manifest Destiny,"** and it inspired many to see western settlement as a sacred duty.

The Missouri Compromise

No political issue caused more division in the United States as it expanded west than the institution of slavery. Free northern states opposed the addition of new slave states. Conversely, southern states feared that the addition of free states would leave them at a political disadvantage.

In 1819, a debate raged in Congress over Missouri's application for statehood. Slave states and free states were equally represented in the Senate. Missouri's admission would disrupt the balance of power. Senator Jesse B. Thomas of Illinois proposed a bill calling for the admission of Missouri as a slave state and Maine as a free state. In addition, the southern boundary of Missouri, 36°30' N, would become a dividing line for any new states admitted to the Union. All new states north of that line would be free states, while those to the south would be slave states. Thanks largely to the efforts of Kentucky Senator Henry Clay, Congress passed the bill and President Monroe signed it into law in 1820. It became known as the **Missouri Compromise**, and it was designed to maintain the balance of power in Washington, DC.

TEXAS: INDEPENDENCE AND ANNEXATION

Santa Anna

Sam Houston

In 1821, Mexico gained independence from Spain. Along with its independence, Mexico also gained control of **Texas**, a region which included a large number of US settlers. In 1834, General Antonio Santa Anna assumed power over the Mexican government and tightened his control over Texas. In response, Texans under the leadership of Sam Houston launched a rebellion.

The Alamo

On March 2, 1836, a convention of Texas delegates declared the territory to be an independent republic. Santa Anna answered with military force. On March 6, a small group of Texans took their stand against the Mexican leader at an old mission called The Alamo**.** Despite the Texans' brave resistance, Santa Anna's forces were too strong. Every Texan who fought at the Alamo perished in the battle or was executed after his capture.

After a series of battles, the Texans eventually defeated Santa Anna and took him hostage. In exchange for his freedom, the Mexican leader promised to recognize the Republic of Texas and withdraw his forces back below the Rio Grande River. Wanting to become part of the United States, Texas asked to be annexed (made part of the US). President Andrew Jackson was in favor of annexing Texas, but he could not overcome northern opposition. Northerners knew that Texas would be admitted as a slave state. They also feared that, because of its large size, the area might be divided into *several* slave states. Texas remained an independent nation until 1845.

The **annexation of Texas** was a critical issue in the election of 1844. As a result, the Democratic party split and James K. Polk became the first "dark horse" (unexpected winner) presidential nominee in US history. Polk took a strong stand as the Democratic candidate, calling for the annexation of both Texas and Oregon. Polk won the election. Inspired by Polk's victory, his predecessor, President John Tyler, called for a joint resolution of Congress prior to leaving office. At his urging, Congress passed a resolution admitting Texas to the Union as a slave state in 1845.

OREGON

In 1827, the US and Great Britain had reaffirmed their agreement to occupy the **Oregon territory** jointly. Beginning in 1843, thousands of US settlers moved to Oregon seeking a better life. President Polk approached Britain, arguing that the US had rightful claim to the territory up to 54°40'N. Thus arose the slogan, "54-40, or fight!" Polk's aggressive tone irritated the British, but they were ready to give up Oregon because the territory was no

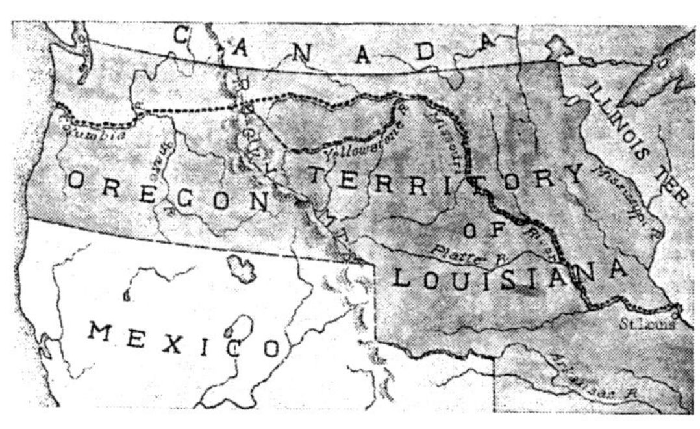

Oregon Territory

longer profitable. Furthermore, the United States had become an important consumer of British goods, leading Britain to desire friendly terms with the US. The United States accepted a treaty declaring the 49th parallel as the official boundary and, in 1846, Oregon became a US territory.

War With Mexico and the Gadsden Purchase

Mexico considered the United States' annexation of Texas to be an act of aggression. This did not deter President Polk who, along with many members of Congress, believed in Manifest Destiny. In June 1845, Polk ordered General Zachary Taylor to lead his troops to the Texas border. He also sent John Slidell to Mexico to settle disputes over the US-Mexico border and negotiate for the purchase of California and New Mexico (the area between Texas and California). After the Mexican president refused to meet with Slidell, Polk ordered Taylor to move into the disputed territory between the Nueces and Río Grande rivers. In response, Mexican troops crossed the Río Grande and attacked Taylor's forces. Immediately, Polk demanded that Congress declare war on Mexico, proclaiming that the Mexicans had "shed American blood on American soil." Though some representatives disagreed, Congress passed a declaration of war on May 13, 1846.

Gen. Zachary Taylor

The war was a series of US victories leading up to September 14, 1847, when General Winfield Scott finally marched his troops into Mexico City and forced Mexico to surrender. After months of negotiations, the US and Mexico finally ended the war with the **Treaty of Guadalupe-Hidalgo** on February 2, 1848. The treaty required Mexico to surrender the New Mexico and California territories to the United States in exchange for financial compensation.

In 1853, boundary disputes with Mexico still remained. President Franklin Pierce sent James Gadsden to settle the problem and to purchase land for a southern transcontinental railroad. The **Gadsden Purchase** gave the United States parts of present-day New Mexico and Arizona in exchange for $10 million. The acquisition of these territories all but completed the continental expansion envisioned by those who believed in Manifest Destiny.

THE CHEROKEE AND THE TRAIL OF TEARS

Territorial expansion greatly affected Native Americans. One tribe that was prominent in western North Carolina and northern Georgia was the **Cherokee**. The Cherokee had assisted Andrew Jackson in his victory at Horseshoe Bend during the War of 1812. They had also adapted their way of life to accommodate white settlement more than any other Native American people. They farmed, owned private land, and some even owned black slaves.When gold was discovered on Cherokee land in Georgia, however, the US government took action to move the tribe and claim their territory for white settlement.

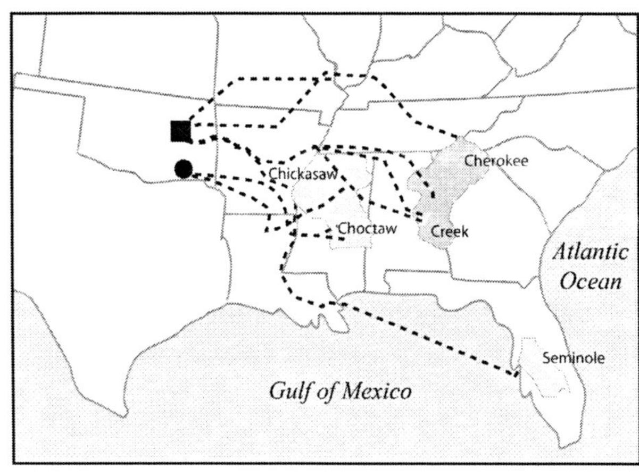

Map of Trail of Tears

In 1830, Congress passed the Indian Removal Act. This law authorized the removal of the Cherokee and several other tribes from the southeast United States. The Supreme Court ruled that the Cherokee had a right to remain on their land and could not be forcibly removed. President Andrew Jackson disregarded the Court's decision, however, and would not enforce the court's decision. In 1838, after Jackson left office, the US government forcibly removed the Cherokee. The very people who had saved Jackson at Horseshoe Bend were now forced to march eight hundred miles to reservations in Oklahoma. Over one quarter of the Cherokee people died from disease, starvation, and exposure to the bitter cold during the journey. Their march became known among the Cherokee people as the **"Trail of Tears."**

CALIFORNIA BECOMES A STATE

In 1848, gold was discovered just north of Sacramento, California. The following year, gold seekers came from all over the world as part of the California Gold Rush of 1849. These new arrivals came to be known as "49ers," and they served to rapidly increase California's population. This growth produced a need for stable government almost overnight. For this reason, when the debate over slavery prevented Congress from organizing the territory, Californians took matters into their own hands by drafting and approving a state constitution. Finally, thanks to the **Compromise of 1850**, Congress admitted California as a free state on September 9, 1850.

Practice 3.1: Territorial Expansion

1. What land acquisition doubled the size of the United States in 1803?
   A. Oregon territorial acquisition
   B. Louisiana Purchase
   C. Northwest Territory
   D. Indian Territorial Purchase

2. Which of the following describes an effect of the War of 1812?
   A. Great Britain reclaimed large portions of land in North America.
   B. The United States won control of much of Canada.
   C. US nationalism and manufacturing increased.
   D. The United States developed one of the world's strongest militaries.

3. What was the Trail of Tears? What impact did it have on Native Americans?

3.2 Sectional Differences

The West

Joseph Smith

Settlers had different motivations for venturing west. For some, it was their religious faith. Many Christian missionaries ventured into the new territories in hopes of spreading the message of Jesus to the Native Americans. One group, the Mormons, moved west to escape religious persecution after their founder, Joseph Smith, was murdered in Illinois. Under the leadership of Brigham Young, the Mormons journeyed west and settled in present-day Utah.

Brigham Young

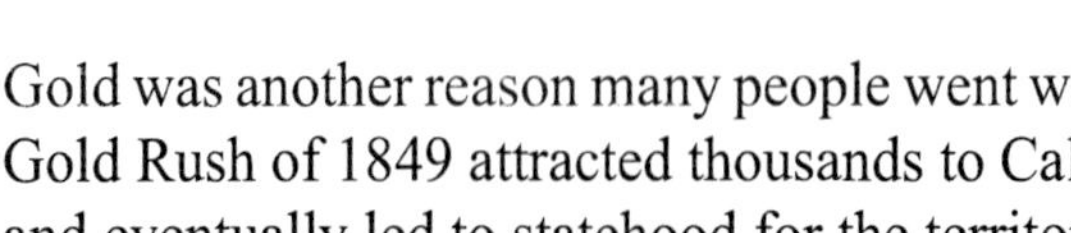

Gold was another reason many people went west. The Gold Rush of 1849 attracted thousands to California and eventually led to statehood for the territory. Ten years later, in 1859, large numbers of people rushed to the region of western Nevada after discovery of the Comstock Lode. Named for a miner involved in its discovery, the Comstock Lode was the richest discovery of precious ores in history. Gold ultimately became one of the major reasons for conflict between white settlers and Native Americans.

Panning for gold

Land also drew people west. Many settlers saw available land as a chance to claim their own property and make their fortune. As cotton became more and more profitable, many southerners pushed west to grow cotton, spreading the institution of slavery and increasing debate about slavery in new territories.

The frontier fostered a strong sense of independence among those who moved west. Western settlers grew to value their independence. They wanted to govern themselves locally and did not want intrusion from a strong national government.

Economic Differences Between the North and South

By the 1800s, slavery was a major part of the nation's economy. In 1793, Eli Whitney invented the **cotton gin**, a machine that separated seeds from cotton. The gin made cotton the most profitable crop in the South and resulted in the region becoming known as a "cotton kingdom." As plantations produced more cotton, plantation owners needed more slaves.

Cotton Gin

In the North, however, it was another of Whitney's innovations that helped shape the economy. After starting a business manufacturing muskets, Whitney implemented the concept of **interchangeable parts**. Instead of simply making entire muskets one at a time, Whitney mass produced individual parts that could be used on any musket. His ideas soon spread to other industries and resulted in the increased use of factories for production.

Sectionalism and tensions over slavery continued to grow as the South increasingly relied on its **plantation system** for agriculture, while the North relied more and more on its **factory system** for manufacturing. In the North, where slavery was abolished (done away with) in the first half of the 1800s, businessmen resented the fact that they were paying for workers while plantation owners in the South had the benefit of slave labor. Meanwhile, more and more people in the North were beginning to see slavery as a moral issue and calling for its abolition. Southerners answered that the conditions under which many poor immigrants and factory workers lived in the North were just as bad, if not worse, than those of slaves on the plantations.

Political Differences Sparked by Sectionalism

Major differences arose between the different regions politically. Southerners and western settlers tended to believe that the federal government should restrict itself to powers specifically stated in the Constitution, and that all else should be left to the states. Southerners did not trust northern politicians whom they believed were out to end slavery. Many westerners resented eastern politicians and business leaders who they felt favored big business over small, independent landowners. Northerners were more prone to support a strong central government that could enact policies that favored national commerce.

Southerners opposed **tariffs** (taxes on imports from other countries) because they raised the price on manufactured imports and invited other countries to impose tariffs of their own. Such actions hurt the South's ability to sell cotton and other agricultural products overseas. Northerners, however, supported tariffs because they made imports more expensive and their own products more attractive to consumers.

Henry Clay

Because the South's economy depended heavily on agriculture and large plantations, southern politicians fought to uphold slavery and to see that it was expanded into new territories. Conversely, northern politicians wanted to see the expansion of slavery halted, if not the entire institution brought to an end. Some leaders took this stand on moral grounds, seeing slavery as an abomination. For others, their opposition was economical and/or political in nature.

HENRY CLAY'S AMERICAN SYSTEM

Erie Canal in 1800s

During the first half of the 1800s, there were a number of political confrontations which made the differences between different regions evident. One was the nation's reaction to Kentucky senator Henry Clay's **"American System."** It was a plan designed to unite the nation and make it more economically independent following the War of 1812. It called for a *tariff* to protect the nation's young manufacturing industry; *internal improvements*, such as better canals and roadways funded by the federal government's tariff revenue; and a *strong national bank* because the charter for the first national bank had expired. Clay, however, underestimated the nation's growing sectionalism. While many Northerners supported the plan, Southerners tended to oppose it because they saw the tariffs as benefitting northern businesses at the expense of southern farmers. They also believed that it gave far too much power to the federal government. Meanwhile, those in the West also felt that the plan was designed to help eastern business interests at the expense of other regions of the country.

Practice 3.2: Sectional Differences

1. Which of the following describes how **most** western settlers felt about a strong national government?

   A. They wanted the government to regulate farming and commerce in the west.

   B. They trusted the government and believed the government should own most of the land.

   C. They valued their independence and did not want intrusion from the government.

   D. They opposed slavery and relied more on factories than on farming.

2. What impact did cotton have on western settlement?

   A. Cotton was a southern cash crop that had no impact on the West.

   B. Most western settlers opposed slavery and moved west to get away from cotton plantations.

   C. Cotton's profitability discouraged many from moving west for economic reasons.

   D. Cotton's profitability encouraged many people to move west to acquire land.

3. Who would have **most** likely supported Henry Clay's "American System"?

   A. a New York City banker

   B. a small southern farmer

   C. a western settler

   D. a Native American

3.3 Democracy

As more and more people moved west to settle the frontier, the cry for democracy increased. In a democracy, eligible citizens have an equal say in their government. The US Constitution established the national government as a republic. Only members of an elite ruling class tended to win election to high offices. Only white men who owned property could vote. They elected members to Congress and to state legislatures. These elected officials then chose members from their own ruling class to serve as US senators or as delegates to the Electoral College (the Electoral College elected the president).

Most westerners were small landowners and pioneers. Some did not own enough property to qualify to vote. These people did not trust eastern elites to protect their interests. They wanted more democracy and a greater voice in who served in public office.

ANDREW JACKSON

Westerners and poorer Americans eventually found their leader in **Andrew Jackson**. Jackson was viewed as a "common man." He was not born into the rich upper class, but, instead, achieved his success despite growing up relatively poor and uneducated. As a result, he was very popular with western frontier settlers and "common folk." In 1824, he decided to take advantage of his popularity and ran for president.

Andrew Jackson

A "CORRUPT BARGAIN"

John Quincy Adams

More than any previous election, the presidential election of 1824 was evidence of the sectional differences in the United States. New England backed the current secretary of state, John Quincy Adams, while the southern candidate was William Crawford of Georgia. Henry Clay and Andrew Jackson were formidable western candidates. The election came down to Adams and Jackson and was so close that the House of Representatives had to decide the winner. When Clay threw his support to Adams, it was enough to give the son of former President John Adams the victory. Jackson and his followers soon protested, however, when it was learned that Clay would be named secretary of state. Jackson and his supporters denounced it as a "corrupt bargain" made to give Adams the presidency. Four years later, Jackson defeated Adams to become the nation's president.

UNIVERSAL (WHITE MALE) SUFFRAGE

Jackson's brand of politics and the changes he inspired came to be called **Jacksonian Democracy**. Jackson believed strongly in western expansion and the rights of white frontier settlers. He, like many westerners, resented "eastern elites" and political leaders who seemed to favor the upper class and passed laws Jackson believed helped the wealthy over small landowners.

Jackson favored **universal suffrage**. He believed that all white men should be free to vote, not just those who owned property. With the support of men like Jackson, all but a few states dropped property requirements for voting. Expanding suffrage made the nation more democratic and enabled "simpler men" like Jackson to win public office, rather than

Western Farmer

simply those from the upper class. (It is important to remember, however, that even Jacksonian Democracy did not attempt to extend the right to vote to women, blacks, or Native Americans.)

The "Spoils System," Strict Interpretation, and *Laissez-Faire* Economics

Andrew Jackson

Once in office, Jackson instituted a policy of rewarding his political supporters with government positions. This policy became known as the spoils system, and set a precedent for rewarding faithful supporters with government jobs. Jackson believed it was a great way to encourage common people to become politically involved and ensure that wealthy politicians would not continually dominate the government. However, it ultimately led to corruption and a call for reform in later administrations.

Jackson and his followers also favored *laissez-faire* economics. In other words, they did not think that the government should regulate business or pass policies to help U.S. businessmen (although Jackson did occasionally support tariffs so long as he did not think they were so high as to hurt small farmers). They believed that such measures tended to favor wealthy easterners while hurting southern farmers and landowners along the western frontier. Jackson did not want to hurt large U.S. businesses and landowners, but he did want to make sure that smaller merchants and small landowners had every bit as much chance to succeed as rich manufacturers.

National Bank Controversy 1832

Jackson also had a strict interpretation of the Constitution. Although he often pushed the bounds of presidential power (Jackson believed the president should have more power and say than Congress) and was even accused by his enemies of acting more like a king than a president, Andrew Jackson believed that the federal government should be restricted to only those powers the Constitution specifically gave it. He opposed policies he viewed as giving big businessmen and members of the upper class an unfair advantage of small landowners and farmers. This conviction led to a huge battle between Jackson and the **Second National Bank** in 1832. Jackson opposed the bank. He saw it as a violation of the constitution. His opponents favored the bank. Although the bank was not due to be re-chartered for several years, Jackson's political enemies convinced the bank to apply for its charter early so that it would become an issue in the 1832 presidential election. Jackson's opponents thought that the president's opposition to the bank would damage his credibility and cause him to lose the election. They were wrong. Jackson succeeded in convincing people the bank was an example of national government favoring big business over poorer Americans. Jackson won the election, and the bank lost its charter. The banks closure meant that federal monies were placed in state banks. The new system worked poorly, and the nation soon faced a national economic crisis.

Chapter 3

RETURN OF THE TWO-PARTY SYSTEM

Martin Van Buren

Eventually, sharp differences between Jackson and men like Henry Clay, Daniel Wester, and John C. Calhoun led to a break in the Democratic-Republican Party. Jackson's wing took the name "Democrats," while his opponents adopted the name "National Republicans."

Eventually, many of the National Republicans formed a new party, the "Whigs." They chose this name because it was the name of the British party that opposed King George III during the Revolutionary War. Since they accused Jackson of acting like "King Andrew," they adopted the name "Whig" to show their dislike for the president. After an "era of good feelings," the **two-party system** returned to national politics with a vengeance. Jackson left office after his second term, allowing his vice president and fellow Democrat Martin Van Buren to win the presidential election of 1836.

Practice 3.3 Democracy

1. Who would have **most** likely supported Andrew Jackson?

   A. a wealthy eastern businessman
   B. Henry Clay
   C. a western farmer
   D. John Quincy Adams

2. What was Andrew Jackson's view concerning suffrage?

   A. He believed everyone living in the United States should be allowed to vote.
   B. He believed any white man should be allowed to vote.
   C. He favored restricting suffrage to landowners.
   D. He thought that whites and Native Americans should be allowed to vote, but not blacks.

3. Describe Jackson's views regarding the government's role in economic matters and interpretations of the Constitution.

3.4 Social Reforms

Revival of the Second Great Awakening

A number of **social reform movements** began during the 1800s. These movements aimed to transform society in beneficial ways. Many of those who participated in such movements were inspired by religious movements like the **Second Great Awakening**. As part of the "Awakening," many zealous Christian preachers traveled from revival to revival preaching the Gospel and calling on believers to become socially active and impact society through good works. As a result, religion motivated many to become social reformers. Others without strong religious beliefs became active, simply to try to improve the world they lived in.

Temperance

During the early nineteenth century, the **temperance movement** began gaining popularity. Members of this movement wanted to moderate the use of alcohol. Later, they advocated total abstinence from alcohol and succeeded in convincing several states to pass laws prohibiting its sale. The temperance movement owed much of its success to the efforts of women and church leaders in the United States.

The Abolitionist Movement

William Lloyd Garrison

In the 1830s, the **abolitionist movement** gained momentum, despite being seen by most as a movement of fanatics. As always, slavery remained a hot topic in the nation. The South found itself dependent on the practice for economic support. Meanwhile, in the North, a movement to abolish slavery was growing. White members of this movement were mostly middle class, educated, church people from New England (many of whom were Quakers). Black abolitionists were mostly former slaves. Eventually, the movement gained enough support and respectability that it helped give birth to a new political party and changed the course of the nation. (We will discuss abolition more in chapter 4.)

Chapter 3

WOMEN'S RIGHTS MOVEMENTS

Elizabeth Cady Stanton
and
Susan B. Anthony

Women had participated in the abolitionist and temperance movements, only to face discrimination from the men with whom they'd served. The offense these women suffered led to the birth of the **women's rights movement**. The movement eventually made women's suffrage (the right to vote) its main cause.

Practice 3.4: Social Reform

1. An abolitionist supported which of the following causes?

   A. outlawing alcohol

   B. ending slavery

   C. limiting slavery to southern states

   D. ending women's suffrage

2. What was the Second Great Awakening? What impact did it have in terms of social reform?

CHAPTER 3 REVIEW

Key Terms

Northwest Ordinance
Louisiana Purchase
War of 1812
Andrew Jackson
Battle of New Orleans
Monroe Doctrine
Manifest Destiny
Missouri Compromise
Annexation of Texas
Oregon Territory
Treaty of Guadalupe-Hidalgo
Gadsden Purchase
Compromise of 1850
Cherokee
Trail of Tears
cotton gin
sectionalism
plantation system
factory system
tariffs
American System
democracy
Andrew Jackson
Jacksonian Democracy
universal suffrage
Second National Bank
temperance movement
abolitionist movement
women's rights movement

1. Which of the following is **untrue** regarding the Louisiana Purchase?
   A. It was the result of a congressional resolution urged by President Tyler.
   B. It roughly doubled the size of the United States at the time.
   C. It gave the US access to the Mississippi River and New Orleans.
   D. It was authorized by President Thomas Jefferson in 1803.

> *"The president has firmly established that any further attempts to colonize this hemisphere shall be viewed by the United States as an act of aggression. I commend his resolve and hope that this nation is willing to take all steps necessary to uphold this position."*

2. The above quote is **most** likely expressing support for which of the following?
   A. the Jacksonian Democracy
   B. Manifest Destiny
   C. the Treaty of Guadalupe-Hidalgo
   D. the Monroe Doctrine

3. A US congressman in the 1840s who favored western expansion on the grounds that it was the nation's role to control and "civilize" the territory from the Mississippi river to the Pacific coast was undoubtedly a believer in what?
   A. universal suffrage
   B. Manifest Destiny
   C. the Monroe Doctrine
   D. abolition

4. Although President Jackson and others wanted to annex Texas after it won its independence from Mexico, political leaders in the North opposed annexation. The reason for this opposition was primarily for what reason?
   A. Northern politicians were afraid that it would be seen as an act of aggression by Mexico and cause future wars.
   B. Northern politicians hated Jackson and wanted to wait until another president was in office.
   C. Northern politicians feared that the South would gain too much of an economic advantage because of the new industry and laborers Texas would bring.
   D. Northern politicians feared that the South would gain a political advantage because Texas would be admitted as a slave state.

5. A southern plantation owner would have been **most** excited about
   A. interchangeable parts.
   B. the cotton gin.
   C. abolition.
   D. the Seneca Falls Conference.

6. Negotiations with the British, war with Mexico, and annexation of Texas were all part of

   A. sectionalism between the North and South.

   B. westward expansion.

   C. Jacksonian Democracy.

   D. social reform.

7. Andrew Jackson would have been **most** supportive of

   A. a slave's right to freedom.

   B. woman's suffrage.

   C. the Whig Party.

   D. white frontiersmen having a voice in politics.

8. A U.S. senator from Connecticut introduces a bill using government regulations to help New England manufacturers. President Andrew Jackson will **most** likely

   A. oppose the bill.

   B. support the bill.

   C. have no opinion on the bill.

   D. sign the bill.

9. Jacksonian Democracy favored

   A. wealthy business leaders.

   B. New Englanders.

   C. the "common man."

   D. Native Americans and blacks.

10. Someone who believed women should have the right to vote in the 1800s would have **most** likely supported

    A. Jacksonian Democracy.

    B. women's suffrage.

    C. disfranchising women.

    D. temperance.

11. What effect did Manifest Destiny have?

    A. It improved relations between the United States and Mexico.

    B. It made Texas a free republic.

    C. It extended US territory all the way to the Pacific.

    D. It resulted in the end of universal suffrage.

Chapter 4
Secession, Civil War, and Reconstruction

This chapter addresses the following standard(s):

New Indicators	3.1, 3.2, 3.3, 3.4, 3.5
Old Indicators	4.2, 4.3, 4.4, 4.5, 5.7

4.1 States Rights and Slavery

In 1861, the Civil War divided the nation. It was a war fought between northern states that remained loyal to the Union and southern states that decided in favor of secession (they elected to leave the Union) with the intention of ruling themselves. Several issues led to the break. Two of the most notable were states's rights and slavery.

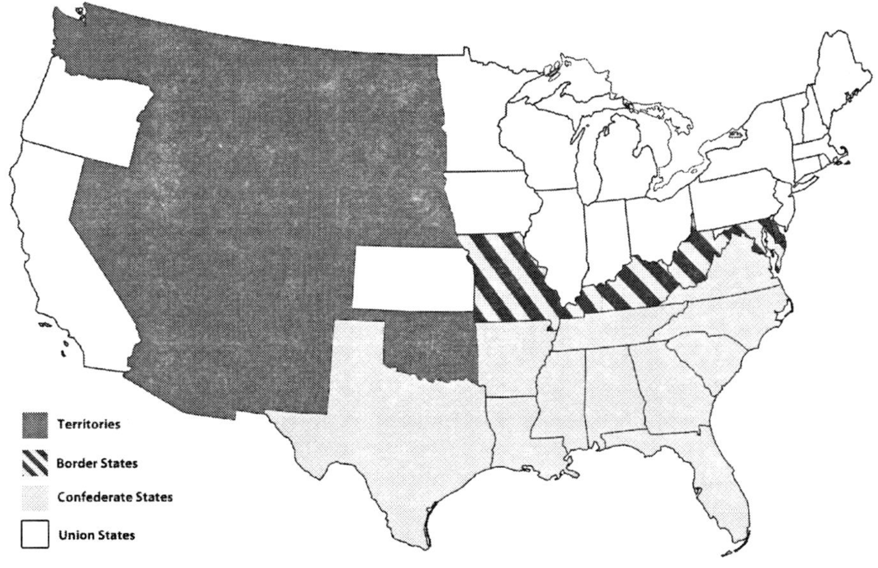

Map of Union and Confederate States

States' Rights

As the nation grew, so did the debate over the role of the federal government. Some favored a stronger federal government that could unify the nation economically and provide infrastructure. They wanted the federal government to be able to pass legislation that state governments would have to follow.

Many leaders in the South opposed such ideas. With anti-slavery forces growing in the North, southern politicians and landowners feared a federal government with the power to impose legislation on the states. They argued that any power not specifically delegated to the federal government by the Constitution was a power that only state governments could claim. In an attempt to protect southern economic interests and the institution of slavery, southern leaders advocated states' rights: the right of state government to establish their own laws where the Constitution does not specifically empower the national government.

South Carolina Nullification Crisis

Andrew Jackson

One episode that exemplified the tension between states rights and federal power was the South Carolina Nullification Crisis in 1832. South Carolina began protesting high tariffs on British goods. One of South Carolina's senators, **John C. Calhoun**, took center stage for his pamphlet entitled, *Exposition and Protest*. In it, Calhoun argued for **states' rights** and asserted that any state could refuse to enforce a law it saw as unconstitutional. In 1832, South Carolina threatened to invoke this right and secede if the offensive tariffs were not repealed. Enraged, President Andrew Jackson prepared to call up federal troops if necessary to force South Carolina's compliance. Fortunately, Senator Henry Clay proposed a compromise that both sides could accept. Clay's compromise ended the crisis but the issues of states' rights and secession remained alive until the end of the Civil War.

John C. Calhoun

Conflict Over Slavery

As sectional differences became more defined and the nation's western expansion increased, the debate over slavery became more and more heated. As new regions became US territories and eventually states, they threatened to upset the balance of power between slave states and free states in Washington. Initially, compromises were reached to maintain peace. The **Missouri Compromise** of 1820 stated that all states admitted below 36°30' N would be slave states, while every state north of that mark would be free. It also admitted Missouri as a slave state and Maine as free, thereby maintaining the balance of power in the nation's capital.

Later, under the **Compromise of 1850**, Congress admitted California as a free state and declared the unorganized western territories free as well. The Utah and New Mexico territories, however, were allowed to decide the issue by **popular sovereignty** (the will of the majority). The people living in these areas would vote on whether or not to allow slavery. Attached to the compromise was the **Fugitive Slave**

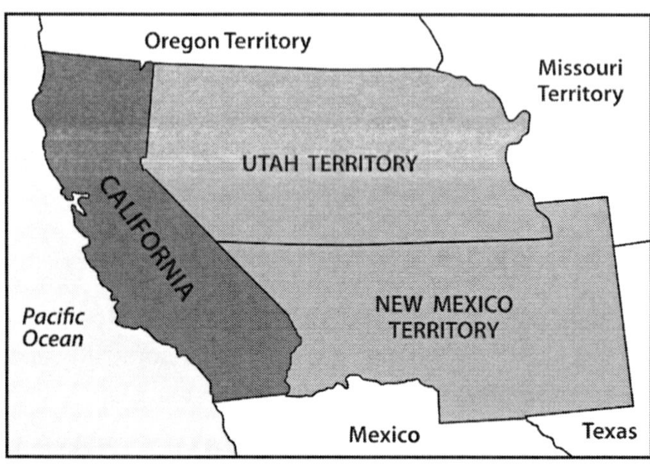

Map of California 1850

Law. This law required that northern states forcibly return escaped slaves to their owners in the South. Because the law was unpopular in the North, many northern citizens refused to obey it.

The Wilmot Proviso

David Wilmot

The war with Mexico reignited the slave debate. Victory in the war would mean new territories and the question of whether or not they should allow slavery. In the summer of 1846, a Pennsylvania congressman named David Wilmot put forth what would come to be known as the Wilmot Proviso. This *proviso,* or condition, proposed banning slavery from any land purchased from Mexico. It was embraced by Northerners but denounced in the South. It was voted down, but it reopened the debate about slavery and exposed serious sectional divisions in the country.

The Kansas-Nebraska Act

SOUTHERN CHIVALRY — ARGUMENT versus CLUB'S.

Brooks Attacks Sumner

In 1854, Congress passed the Kansas-Nebraska Act. This act allowed the previously free and unorganized territories of Kansas and Nebraska to choose whether or not to permit slavery. In so doing, it effectively repealed the Missouri Compromise and reignited the slavery issue. The territory became known as "bleeding Kansas" as armed clashes between pro-slavery forces and abolitionist settlers became commonplace.

In Washington, the act inspired emotional reaction. Charles Sumner, a fiery senator from Massachusetts who opposed slavery, strongly denounced the act and the senators who wrote it in a speech that spanned two days. A couple of days after the speech, Sumner was approached on the Senate floor by South Carolina congressman, Preston Brooks. Brooks was insulted by Sumner's words both because he was from the South and because he was related to one of the act's authors. Brooks beat Sumner with a heavy cane, almost killing him and causing him to be absent from the Senate for three years while he recovered from the attack. The Sumner-Brooks incident was a brutal example of how inflamed passions had become over the slavery issue. Meanwhile, two rival governments (one slave and the other free) formed in Kansas, leaving the territory in a state of civil unrest

Chapter 4

THE DRED SCOTT DECISION

Dred Scott

The 1857 case of ***Dred Scott v. Sanford*** threw the nation further into turmoil. Dred Scott, a slave in Missouri, was taken by his owner into free territory where he lived for four years. The owner later returned to Missouri, where he died. After his death, Dred Scott sued for his freedom. The Supreme Court ruled that Scott had no right to sue because, as a slave, he was not a citizen. It also declared that a slave owner could not be deprived of his "property" without due process of law. The decision also struck down the Missouri Compromise because it declared that it was a violation of the Fifth Amendment to declare slaves free of their owners without due process of law — even if that slave had entered a free state. The decision outraged both abolitionists and those who favored popular sovereignty.

JOHN BROWN'S RAID

In October of 1859, a group of radical abolitionists led by **John Brown** attacked the federal arsenal (location where weapons are made and stored) at Harper's Ferry, Virginia. They hoped to seize weapons and give them to slaves who could then rise up in armed rebellion. Their plan failed, however, when US troops under the command of Colonel Robert E. Lee surrounded the arsenal and forced Brown's surrender. Although the government hanged Brown, the failed raid intensified southern resentment of the abolitionist movement. Many southerners saw it as an affirmation that the South would have to shed blood to protect its way of life.

John Brown

FREE BLACKS AND SLAVES IN THE MID 1800S

Most African Americans in the South were slaves during the 1800s. If they were fortunate, slaves had masters who valued them at least as expensive property if not as human beings. In such cases, they were treated as well as a master might treat a prize horse. Still, they were forced to work long hours at whatever their task, could be whipped if their master thought it necessary, slave women were often sexually exploited by masters and their sons, and slaves usually lived in shacks providing only the bare necessities for shelter. Perhaps saddest of all, slave families were often separated. Slave marriages were not legally recognized, and only a couple of states forbade the selling of small children away from their mothers. As a result, the sale of slaves often tore loved ones apart. Their common suffering did, however, help slaves forge a close sense of community.

Slaves

Prior to the Civil War, there were some free blacks living in slave states, especially in the northern South. These African Americans were free either because they had purchased their own freedom or because their masters had freed them for one reason or another. Most worked as artisans, farmers, or simple laborers, but a few owned businesses, and some even owned black slaves themselves. Free blacks often wore badges so that whites would recognize that they were not slaves, and many of them were mulattos (people of color who had both black and white ancestry).

The Abolitionist Movement

Angelina Grimke Sarah Grimke
(Library of Congress)

In the 1830s, the **abolitionist movement** continued to grow. Among key white figures in this movement were William Lloyd Garrison and the Grimke sisters. Garrison founded an influential anti-slavery newspaper called *The Liberator* in 1831 and helped establish the American Anti-Slavery Society. Meanwhile Sarah and Angelina Grimke were members of a prominent slaveholding family in South Carolina who became abolitionists and won national acclaim for their passionate anti-slavery speeches.

Frederick Douglass

Important African-American abolitionists included **Frederick Douglass**. After escaping slavery in Maryland, Douglass educated himself and became the most prominent African American speaker for the abolition of slavery. He even helped John Brown plan — but did not participate in — the Harper's Ferry raid.

Harriet Tubman, herself an escaped slave, was also a hero of the abolitionist movement. She secretly returned to the South nineteen times in order to lead other slaves to freedom by way of the **Underground Railroad**. The Underground Railroad was not actually a railroad, but rather a network of people who helped slaves escape to the northern US and Canada.

Harriet Tubman

Uncle Tom's Cabin

Another activist was **Harriet Beecher Stowe**. Her 1852 novel, ***Uncle Tom's Cabin***, was a fictional account of the horrors faced by a slave family in the South. Though she was white and had never been a slave, her book motivated many people in the North to support the abolition of slavery.

Practice 4.1: States Rights and Slavery

1. Leaders in the South asserted which of the following in the years leading up to the Civil War?
   A. abolition
   B. the right of slaves to sue masters
   C. states' rights
   D. popular sovereignty

2. The term "bleeding Kansas" refers to which of the following?
   A. the violence that occurred as part of a nullification crisis
   B. the fighting that resulted between slaves and masters in Kansas
   C. the violence that resulted between anti- and pro-slavery forces after a federal act
   D. a book written by an abolitionist to show the brutality of slavery

3. Who is associated with the Underground Railroad?
   A. Harriet Beecher Stowe
   B. Harriet Tubman
   C. John C. Calhoun
   D. Frederick Douglass

4.2 The Republicans and Secession

In 1854, a coalition of northern Democrats (the party of Andrew Jackson) who opposed slavery, Whigs (the party that formed in opposition to Andrew Jackson), and Free Soilers (a party opposing slavery in new territories) came together and formed the **Republican party**. While the Republicans did not call for the immediate abolition of slavery, they did adopt the Free Soilers' position of opposing the extension of slavery into new US territories.

Election of 1860 and Southern Secession

Jefferson Davis

By the time of the **presidential election of 1860**, the country was at a boiling point regarding slavery. At its convention, the Democratic party split along sectional lines over the issue. The northern Democrats supported popular sovereignty and nominated Stephen Douglas. The southern Democrats, wanting federal protection of slavery in all US territories, nominated Vice President John Breckinridge of Kentucky. The Republicans chose a former Congressman and lawyer from Illinois named Abraham Lincoln. The South felt threatened by Lincoln's candidacy because, unlike Douglas who considered slavery a legitimate choice, Lincoln opposed its expansion. The southern states feared that Lincoln would seek not only to prevent slavery in the new territories, but to dismantle it in the South as well.

When Lincoln won the election, South Carolina responded by seceding (withdrawing) from the Union on December 20, 1860. By February 1861, six other states had seceded as well: Mississippi, Alabama, Georgia, Florida, Louisiana and Texas. In February of 1861, southern delegates from the seceded states met in Montgomery, Alabama to draft their own constitution. They elected **Jefferson Davis** as president of their new **Confederate States of America.**

FORT SUMTER

Fort Sumter

The day after his inauguration, President Lincoln learned that Union soldiers at **Fort Sumter** off the coast of South Carolina had only one month of supplies remaining. Wanting to uphold the Union without provoking war, he notified the governor of South Carolina that he was sending ships with food but no soldiers or munitions. On April 12, 1861, Confederate soldiers opened fire on the fort before the relief ships could arrive, forcing the Union troops to surrender the following day. In response, President Lincoln issued a call for 75,000 volunteers. The so-called border states were forced to decide whether to support the Union or the Confederacy. With a great deal of controversy and division, Kentucky, Missouri and Maryland remained in the Union, while Virginia, North Carolina, Arkansas and Tennessee joined the Confederacy. The capital of the Confederacy was then moved from Montgomery, Alabama to Richmond, Virginia. The Civil War began with lines clearly drawn between the North and South.

Practice 4.2: The Republicans and Secession

1. Why did the South fear the election of Abraham Lincoln?

   A. They knew that Lincoln was an adamant supporter of "popular sovereignty."

   B. Lincoln had run on a platform of abolishing slavery throughout the nation.

   C. Lincoln openly supported the Dred Scott decision.

   D. They feared that he would seek to end slavery.

2. Which of the following statements **best** describes the role of South Carolina in the decision of southern states to secede from the Union?

   A. It was the site of the Confederacy's first capital.

   B. It was the first state to secede and was where the first shots of the Civil War were fired.

   C. It was the first state to introduce Republican candidates for election.

   D. It was a border state that had to choose sides after other states seceded.

Chapter 4

4.3 The Civil War

Key Figures of the Civil War

Abraham Lincoln	Abraham Lincoln served as the president of the United States during the Civil War. He was the first Republican president in history. **Abraham Lincoln**
Ulysses S. Grant	Initially an effective general in the Union's western battles, Ulysses S. Grant eventually assumed command of the entire Union army in 1864. He defeated the South and accepted Robert E. Lee's surrender at Appomatox Courthouse. He went on to become the 18th president of the United States.  **Ulysses S. Grant**
William T. Sherman	 **William T. Sherman** Sherman was a Union general who took command of the western forces after Grant decided to remain with troops in the East. His capture of Atlanta in 1864 signaled to both the North and the South that the war was all but won for the Union and helped Lincoln win re-election in 1864. He is most remembered for his "march to the sea," in which he burned and destroyed southern cities and railways in an effort to disrupt the Confederate war effort and trap Lee between himself and General Grant.
Jefferson Davis	Jefferson Davis served as the First and only president of the Confederate States of America.  **Jefferson Davis**
Robert E. Lee	 **Robert E. Lee** General Robert E. Lee assumed command of the Confederacy's Army of Northern Virginia after General Joseph Johnston was injured. Despite winning several impressive victories during the course of the war, he did not have nearly enough men to sustain the war effort past early 1865. He eventually surrendered to General Grant.

Advantages for Both Sides

Northern Advantages

Both sides enjoyed certain advantages and weaknesses during the course of the Civil War. Ultimately, the Union's strengths proved to be too great for the Confederacy to overcome. **Northern Advantages** included more railway lines, which allowed supplies and troops to be transported to more locations and at a faster pace. The Union also had more factories for producing guns, ammunition, and supplies. In addition, it already had an established government and a standing military force with which to fight and administer a war. Finally, the Union states were home to two-thirds of the nation's population. Not only did this mean that the Union could send more soldiers into battle, but it also supplied the needed labor force to keep the northern economy and production of war supplies going.

Southern Advantages

Southern advantages existed too. The South initially had better military commanders. In fact, General Robert E. Lee, who eventually commanded the Confederate Army of Northern Virginia, was such a brilliant and respected commander that he was originally offered command of Union forces by President Lincoln. He declined, however, because he could not bring himself to fight against his homeland of Virginia.

Although the South had fewer men, it also did not need as many because it intended to fight a war of attrition. In other words, the South would fight a defensive war designed to inflict enough damage to wear down its enemy's will to fight. Much like the colonies during the American Revolution, the Confederacy believed it did not need to win the war; it only needed to resist long enough for the Union to give up.

Lastly, the South had the advantage of motivation. Southerners saw themselves as fighting for states' rights. Thus, they felt they were defending their homeland, their way of life, and the right to govern themselves. In this respect, they identified themselves with the founders of the United States who had fought for the same principles against the British.

Key Battles of the Civil War

The First Battle of Bull Run (July 21, 1861)

The First Battle of Bull Run (also known as First Manassas because Manassas was the nearest town) was the first confrontation between the two armies and a humiliating defeat for the Union forces. Because they were only thirty miles from Washington, DC, the victorious Confederates could have invaded the capital had they been better organized. Instead, they failed to pursue the retreating Union army and missed a golden opportunity.

First Battle of Bull Run

The battle made it evident that the war would be longer than expected and led Lincoln to adopt General Winfield Scott's **"Anaconda Plan."** This plan involved surrounding the Confederacy and cutting off all supply lines, much like an anaconda wraps around its prey and squeezes the life out of it. It restricted southern trade, transport, and communications by seizing control of the Mississippi River, cutting Confederate territory in half, and instituted coastal blockades (use of naval power to keep ships from entering or leaving enemy ports). Smugglers often used ships called "blockade runners" to get through these blockades and supply the South with goods.

Naval Battles

The Civil War saw innovations in naval technology. The Confederates created an ironclad (a warship shielded with iron to protect it from enemy fire) from an old wooden steamship called the *Merrimack.* (The South renamed this ship the *Virginia*, but it is better known as the *Merrimack.*) The Union navy's wooden ships found themselves powerless against this innovative weapon. In response, the Union finally built an ironclad of its own called the *Monitor.*

Battle of Ironclads

On March 9, 1862, the two ships met in a battle off the coast of Virginia. After several hours of fighting, the *Merrimack* withdrew with neither ship suffering much damage. Eventually, the South blew up the *Merrimack* to keep it from falling into enemy hands. The *Monitor* ultimately sank during a storm. While the two ships met only one time, their battle marked a new era in US naval warfare.

The Civil War also marked the first time that submarines (ships that remain entirely under water) were used as American weapons of war. The Union was actually the first to use a sub, but no Union submarine ever engaged in battle with a Confederate ship. The most notable Confederate sub was the *CSS Hunley.* The *Hunley* was intended to sink Union ships blockading Confederate harbors. On February 18, 1864, it became the first North American submarine to successfully sink an enemy ship. Unfortunately for the South, however, the *Hunley* also sank during the same battle.

Eastern Theater

SECOND BATTLE OF BULL RUN (August 29, 1862)

On land, the war was fought on two primary fronts, or theaters: eastern and western. In 1862, Robert E. Lee assumed command of the Army of Northern Virginia after General Joseph Johnston suffered an injury. One of Lee's first major victories came at the Second Battle of Bull Run (Second Manassas). The battle ended Union hopes of invading Richmond and emboldened Lee to attempt an invasion of the North.

ANTIETAM (September 17, 1862)

Battle of Antietam

Lee and his generals tried to maintain secrecy as they made preparations for their invasion. Meanwhile, General McClellan (the Union's commanding general), remained unaware of the Confederate army's whereabouts until a copy of Lee's orders were found wrapped around some cigars at an abandoned Confederate camp. Now aware of Lee's plans, McClellan saw to it that Lee met a prepared Union force at Antietam Creek, Maryland. The battle of **Antietam** proved to be the bloodiest single day of the war, halting the Confederate advance. McClellan hesitated to pursue, however, and Lee's army slipped away to fight another day.

CHANCELLORSVILLE (May 1 – 5, 1863)

The battle of Chancellorsville is known by many as "Lee's perfect battle" because of the great planning and good fortune that aided the Confederates. Thanks to the efforts of his most gifted general, Thomas "Stonewall" Jackson, Lee's army defeated more than 70,000 Union troops with only 40,000 Confederate soldiers. Unfortunately for the Confederacy, however, Jackson's own troops accidentally shot him as he was scouting the enemy's position at night. His left arm had to be amputated, leading to Lee's famous quote, "Jackson has lost his left arm, but I have lost my right." Although his injuries did not initially seem life threatening, Jackson died after contracting pneumonia during his recovery. As a result, Robert E. Lee was without his most talented and reliable commander at Gettysburg.

GETTYSBURG (July 1 – 3, 1863)

Fought just outside Gettysburg, Pennsylvania, the battle of **Gettysburg** was a key turning point in the war. Without Jackson to assist him, Lee's forces proved less aggressive than usual and failed to win valuable high ground early in the battle. Union forces under the command of General George Meade defeated Lee's army and ended any hope the South had of successfully invading the North. With more than 51,000 soldiers killed, wounded, or missing, Gettysburg was the bloodiest battle of the entire Civil War.

Battle of Gettysburg

Four months later, President Lincoln gave his famed Gettysburg Address at a ceremony dedicating a cemetery on the sight of the battlefield. Although a relatively short speech, it was a powerful affirmation of Lincoln's desire to see the Union survive and the nation reunited.

THE WESTERN THEATER

VICKSBURG (May 15 – July 4, 1863)I

In the late spring of 1863, the town of Vicksburg, Mississippi was the last Confederate obstacle to total Union control of the Mississippi river. Ignoring advice to withdraw, General Grant laid siege (a strategy by which an army surrounds its enemy, cuts off their supplies, and starves them into surrendering) to Vicksburg for almost two months. By the time the town finally surrendered on July 4, residents had been reduced to eating horses, mules, dogs, and even rats.

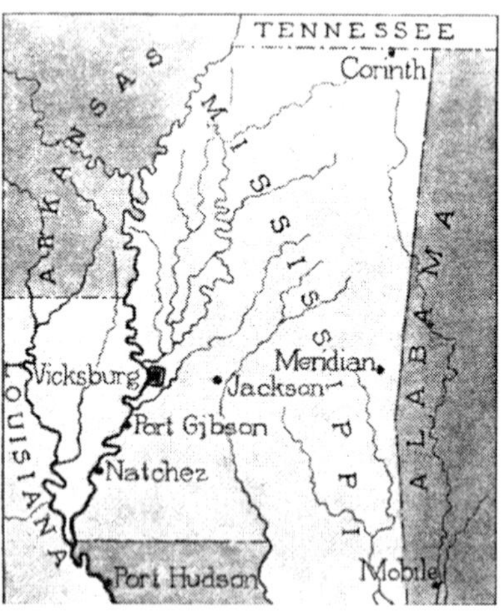

Vicksburg, Mississippi

SHERMAN'S MARCH (May – December, 1864)

Union forces under the command of **William T. Sherman** captured Atlanta in September of 1864, thereby helping President Lincoln to win re-election. After burning the city, Sherman continued his **"march to the sea"** destroying bridges, factories, and railroad lines. Union forces cut a nearly three hundred mile path of destruction across Georgia in route to the city of Savannah. Sherman then turned north into the Carolinas, intending to trap Lee's army between himself and the forces of Ulysses S. Grant.

William T. Sherman

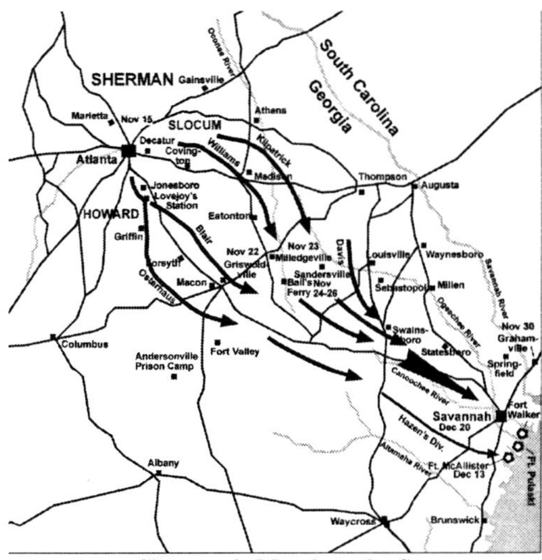

Sherman's March to the Sea

POLITICAL ISSUES OF THE WAR

As the battle lines were drawn, four slave states (Missouri, Kentucky, Delaware and Maryland) remained with the Union. Southern sympathizers, however, were common in these states. If Maryland joined the Confederacy, the Union capital of Washington, DC, would be surrounded by Confederate territory. Concerned that Confederate sympathizers might succeed in swaying Maryland to secede, President Lincoln took drastic action. He declared martial law in Maryland, suspended the **writ of habeas corpus** (the guarantee that a person cannot be imprisoned without being brought before a judge) and jailed the strongest supporters of the Confederacy. This allowed the Maryland legislature to vote in favor of remaining with the Union. Lincoln continued to use drastic measures when necessary throughout the war.

Another point of contention in the North was Lincoln's decision to establish a **draft**. A draft is a policy in which the government selects certain individuals for military service rather than waiting for them to enlist. Lincoln's draft was particularly unpopular among the poor and immigrants. They resented it because wealthy citizens could avoid military service by paying $300 or by hiring a substitute to serve in their place. In July 1863, draft riots broke out in New York City, killing more than one hundred people and resulting in the lynching of at least eleven African Americans by immigrants and poorer whites who blamed blacks for the war.

One group that was among Lincoln's most notable political opponents came to be called the **copperheads**. Named after a deadly snake, "copperheads" were Union Democrats who criticized Lincoln and the war. They played on northerners' fears and predicted that freeing southern slaves would mean huge numbers of African Americans migrating north to steal white jobs. Radical copperheads even encouraged Union soldiers to desert (abandon) the army, and called on citizens to resist the draft.

The Union Defending Against Copperheads
(Library of Congress)

The Emancipation Proclamation and African American Soldiers

The Union victory at Antietam gave President Lincoln the opportunity to issue the **Emancipation Proclamation**. This proclamation freed the slaves in states in rebellion against the Union, while maintaining slavery in the border states loyal to the Union (Lincoln still needed the support of these states both politically and militarily and could not afford to alienate them by outlawing slavery just yet). With this executive order, Lincoln hoped that Confederate states would return to the Union rather than risk losing their slaves. He also hoped to undermine the South's reliance on slave labor and ensure the support of England and France — both of which had already abolished slavery.

Storming Fort Wagner
(Library of Congress)

The Emancipation Proclamation encouraged free African Americans to serve in the Union army. Although originally not allowed to enlist, McClellan's early defeats led Congress to authorize accepting African Americans into the army in 1862. On warships, whites and blacks served side by side. In the army, however, African Americans served only in all black regiments under the command of white officers. These troops were often the object of racism and discrimination.

One of the most memorable African American units was the **54th Massachusetts**. Made famous by the motion picture *Glory*, this unit inspired its fellow white troops and won a place in history with their courageous assault on Fort Wagner near Charleston in July 1863. Seeing their battle as one to free their own people from the bonds of slavery, many African-Americans served notably during the war.

UNION VICTORY

Lee Surrenders to Grant

In March of 1864, President Lincoln put Ulysses S. Grant in command of the Union army. Grant, knowing he had far more men than Lee, began a campaign designed to crush the Confederate army in a series of head-to-head confrontations. Pushing south, Grant engaged Lee in a number of bloody battles. In less than two months, Grant's army suffered some 65,000 casualties. Still, the Union's overwhelming numbers meant that the Confederates were the ones on the retreat.

Finally, when Lee's army found itself surrounded in Virginia, the Confederate general elected to surrender rather than see more lives lost. On April 9, 1865, Robert E. Lee surrendered to Ulysses S. Grant at **Appomattox Courthouse**. Although some fighting continued afterwards, this effectively ended the war. Two weeks later, the largest and last major surrender of the war took place when General Joseph Johnston surrendered his Confederate army to General William T. Sherman at a farm house in Durham, North Carolina.

Practice 4.3: The Civil War

1. It was a major turning point in the war that ended the South's hopes of successfully invading the North. In addition, many believe that had General "Stonewall" Jackson been alive the South would have won this battle and, quite possibly, the war. Which battle was it?

   A. Gettysburg
   B. Antietam
   C. Vicksburg
   D. Chancellorsville

2. How did Sherman's taking Atlanta greatly impact the election of 1864?

   A. It allowed Lincoln to suspend the *writ of habeas corpus* in Georgia, thereby assuring that only Lincoln's supporters went to the polls.

   B. It inspired faith in military generals, thereby leading to General McClellan being nominated for president.

   C. It assured people in the North that victory was in sight, thereby increasing the popularity of President Lincoln and allowing him to win re-election.

   D. It led to Lincoln's defeat because he lost the support of Southerners whom Sherman had abused.

3. What was the Emancipation Proclamation, what impact did it have on the role of African-Americans in the Civil War, and why did it have this impact?

4.4 Southern Reconstruction

With the Union preserved, the nation entered a period known as **Reconstruction**. This was an era in which the government attempted to rebuild (and at times punish) the South. Lincoln did not want to make the South suffer. He wanted healing for both the Union and southern states. Sadly, however, Lincoln did not live to see his vision fulfilled. On April 14, 1865, just five days after the surrender at Appomattox Courthouse, a Confederate sympathizer named John Wilkes Booth assassinated Lincoln as he attended a play at Ford's Theatre.

John Wilkes Booth

Andrew Johnson and the Radical Republicans

With Lincoln's death, the presidency fell to **Andrew Johnson**. Johnson, himself a southerner and one time slave owner, proved sympathetic to the South. Taking office while Congress was in recess, Johnson pursued his own plan of reconstruction. It became known as **Presidential Reconstruction**.

Andrew Johnson

Johnson's plan was seen as far too lenient by many in the North, and conflict quickly arose between Johnson and the **Radical Republicans**. The Radical Republicans were members of the Republican party who favored a much tougher stance with the former Confederate states. Their stance came to be called **Radical Reconstruction**. They believed that Johnson's approach did not do enough because it failed to offer African Americans full citizenship rights. They also believed that Congress, not the president, should oversee Reconstruction and that the majority of each state's voting population rather than just 10% (the amount originally proposed by Abraham Lincoln) should have to pledge allegiance to the United States before a state could be readmitted to the Union. Republicans came to dominate southern governments during Reconstruction and set about drafting new state constitutions which reflected the party's ideals. As a result, Republican policies and leaders shaped the direction of southern states to a great extent in the years immediately following the Civil War.

Thaddeus Stevens

The Fourteenth Amendment and Federal Legislation

Prior to Lincoln's death, Congress passed the **Thirteenth Amendment** to the Constitution. Unlike the Emancipation Proclamation which only outlawed slavery in the Confederacy, the Thirteenth Amendment ended slavery throughout the United States.

Freed Slaves

The following year, Congress passed the Civil Rights Act of 1866 with the intent of giving citizenship rights to freed slaves. President Johnson opposed the measure, but Congress was able to override his veto. Concerned that the courts might strike down the new law as unconstitutional, Congress passed a new amendment to the US Constitution. The **Fourteenth Amendment** guaranteed that no person (regardless of race) would be deprived of life, liberty, or property without due process of law. It granted blacks the status of citizenship and was ratified in 1868. The Fourteenth Amendment meant that the Bill of Rights applied to state governments as well as the federal government.

Johnson's Impeachment

Edwin Stanton

The battle between Congress and President Johnson came to a head in 1868. Johnson tried to fire Secretary of War Edwin Stanton, who had been appointed by Lincoln, because he was closely tied to the Radical Republicans. This violated the Tenure in Office Act, which limited the president's power to hire and fire government officials and, in effect, gave Congress rather than the president power to command the armed forces.

Led by a fiery Radical Republican congressman named Thaddeus Stevens, Congress voted to **impeach** (charge with wrongdoing in order to remove from office) the president of the United States. On May 16, 1868, the Senate voted to spare Johnson's presidency by just one vote.

The Fifteenth Amendment

The last major piece of Reconstruction legislation was the **Fifteenth Amendment** to the Constitution. Ratified in 1870 during the presidency of Ulysses S. Grant, it guaranteed that no citizen may be denied the right to vote "by the United States or any state on the account of race, color, or previous condition of servitude." The amendment had great impact in the South by guaranteeing African Americans the right to vote in elections.

African Americans and Reconstruction

Farming and the Freedmen's Bureau

The Thirteenth Amendment freed the slaves. Now, **freedmen** (freed slaves) had to adjust to life after slavery. Although they had their freedom, they had no land or money. In order to survive, many turned to **sharecropping**. Under this practice, a family farmed a portion of a landowner's land in return for housing and a share of the crop. Many sharecroppers, unfortunately, fell victim to dishonest landowners who subjected them to a subtle form of slavery. Sharecroppers who were fortunate enough to have an honest landowner and good crops sometimes tried **tenant farming**. Tenant farmers paid rent to farm the land, owned the crops they grew, and were less at the mercy of white landowners than sharecroppers.

In 1865, Congress created the **Freedmen's Bureau**. As the first federal relief agency in US history, it served to provide clothing, medical attention, meals, education, and even some land to freed blacks and some poorer whites. Lacking strong support, however, it disbanded in 1869.

Education and the Church

The desire for freedom led to the rise of African American churches following the Civil War (the first new building constructed in Charleston, SC, following the war was a black church). As one of the few institutions truly controlled by African Americans, black churches became the centers for African American social and political life. Within these churches, African Americans could discuss issues relevant to the black community and organize strategies to meet the needs of freed blacks. As a result, African American ministers came to be seen not only as spiritual shepherds but as political/social leaders as well.

African American Church

(Library of Congress)

Blacks also sought education. Often with the help of the Freedmen's Bureau and/or the churches, the southern African-American community established the first black schools. Teachers were often African American soldiers who had acquired some education while in the service. Students included both children and adults.

Politics and Social Debate

African Americans also played a role in southern politics during Reconstruction. Allowed access to the political process by Republican policies, African American delegates often attended state political conventions. South Carolina's state convention actually had a black majority for a brief time. Some six hundred African Americans served in southern state legislatures, a few were elected to offices as high as lieutenant-governor, and one even served as acting governor of Louisiana when the white governor was charged with corruption. On a national level, a few blacks represented southern states in Congress.

New opportunities presented by Reconstruction also led to conflicts within the black community. Northern blacks and some "elite" southern blacks (usually considered elite because they had been raised free) tended to oppose policies designed to take land from private landowners and redistribute it to poorer freedmen (blacks freed from slavery after the war). Although they wanted political equality for all blacks, these "elitists" often saw themselves as socially superior to poorer, uneducated blacks who had only recently been emancipated. Meanwhile, southern blacks often resented the northern African Americans who came south and assumed positions of political influence that might otherwise have gone to southern blacks. Overall, however, African Americans' remained unified in their struggle to assert themselves in the post-war South.

James H. Young
African American Politician in North Carolina

Black Codes and the Ku Klux Klan

After Johnson took office and before Congress could convene to enact its own plan for Reconstruction, many states in the South passed **black codes**. These were laws meant to keep African Americans subordinate to whites by restricting the rights of freed slaves. For instance, blacks could not meet together after sunset, own weapons, or rent property anywhere other than in rural areas (this kept them working on the plantations). Blacks convicted of vagrancy (not working) could be whipped or sold for a year's labor. Black codes, in effect, continued the practice of slavery. It was in response to such laws that Congress ultimately passed the Fourteenth Amendment and the Civil Rights Act of 1866. Under Radical Reconstruction, these black codes lost much of their power.

Ku Klux Klan Members
(Library of Congress)

In response to Reconstruction, some whites advocated violence against freed blacks. Perhaps the most notorious group to use such tactics was the **Ku Klux Klan**. A secretive organization whose members often dressed in hooded white robes, the Klan used violence, murder, and threats to intimidate blacks and those who favored giving African Americans equal rights. The Klan practiced lynchings (mob initiated murders in which the victim is kidnapped and hanged) and other acts of violence against blacks throughout the remainder of the nineteenth and much of the twentieth century. Although some of their goals and tactics have changed and their numbers decreased over time, the Ku Klux Klan continues to exist today.

Chapter 4

Compromise of 1877 and the End of Reconstruction

Rutherford B. Hayes

Because of the bad economy and the many scandals surrounding President Grant, the Democrats were hopeful that their candidate, Samuel Tilden, could win the election of 1876. The Republicans nominated then governor of Ohio, Rutherford B. Hayes. Tilden received almost 300,000 more popular votes than Hayes, but the election was contested because officials disputed the results in some states. Congress appointed an electoral commission to settle the controversy, resulting in the **Compromise of 1877**. Under the conditions of this compromise, Democrats agreed to Hayes being president, and Republicans agreed to end Reconstruction. In addition, southern states received federal money, more power to govern themselves, and a promise to withdraw federal troops.

The Compromise of 1877 brought Reconstruction to an end and began the era of the **"Solid South."** The term refers to the fact that, for nearly a century after Reconstruction, Southerners remained distrustful of the Republican party and "solidly" supported Democratic candidates.

Post-Reconstruction

With the end of Reconstruction and the rise of groups like the Ku Klux Klan, African Americans soon lost whatever political position they gained in the years following emancipation. Southern states soon began passing **Jim Crow laws** that required blacks and whites to use separate public facilities. Many states also tried to avoid upholding the Fifteenth Amendment by requiring citizens to pass **literacy tests** or pay **poll taxes** in order to vote. Literacy tests required that a citizen prove he could read/write, while poll taxes required voters to pay a set amount of money in order to vote. Since most African Americans in the South tended to be poor and uneducated, the new laws prevented many of them from voting. In order to keep these laws from hindering poor and illiterate whites, some states instituted **grandfather clauses**. These were clauses that exempted citizens from restrictions on voting if they, or their ancestors, had voted in previous elections. Since whites had enjoyed the right to vote for years, grandfather clauses allowed poor and illiterate whites to vote while excluding African-Americans.

Segregation

Sign
(Library of Congress)

Following the end of Reconstruction, states began to pass Jim Crow laws. These were laws that established racial **segregation** (separation based on race) in restaurants, hospitals, schools, public transportation, etc. There are two kinds of segregation: De jure and de facto. *De jure segregation* is segregation based on law. *De facto segregation* is segregation that is not officially instituted by law but rather evolves due to economic or social factors (ie, when members of different races tend to live in different neighborhoods because one race tends to be more economically disadvantaged than the other). In 1896, the Supreme Court upheld de jure segregation in the case of ***Plessy v. Ferguson***. The case involved a 30 year old man named

Homer Plessy. Plessy, who was one-eighth African-American, was jailed for sitting in a "whites only" railway car. Under Louisiana law at the time, Plessy was guilty of a crime. He sued, claiming the law was unconstitutional. After considering the case, the Supreme Court ruled that segregation was lawful as long as the separate facilities and services were equal. The case set the precedent that segregation was legal so long as separate facilitates held to the standard of "separate but equal." In reality, however, the facilities for whites were usually far superior to those of blacks.

Notable African Americans of the Post Reconstruction Period

Booker T. Washington

Booker T. Washington

A number of notable African Americans emerged in the years following reconstruction. One of these was a former slave named **Booker T. Washington**. Washington founded the Tuskegee Institute in Alabama. Tuskegee served to train African Americans in a trade so that they could achieve economic freedom and escape the oppression often suffered by uneducated blacks. Washington taught his students that if blacks excelled in teaching, agriculture and blue collar fields (trades requiring manual labor), they would eventually be treated as equal citizens.

While Washington's school became an important center for technical education in the South, some blacks found his philosophies controversial. Washington, for instance, saw no problem with segregation. In a famous speech given in Atlanta in 1895, Washington stated, "In all things that are purely social we (whites and blacks) can be as separate as the fingers, yet one as the hand in all things essential to mutual progress."

W.E.B DuBois

Another key African-American leader of the day was **W.E.B. Du Bois**. Du Bois was the first black Ph.D. graduate from Harvard University and adamantly disagreed with Booker T. Washington. He was offended by the ideas expressed in Washington's Atlanta speech and viewed Washington as someone who had sold out to try and please the white community. For this reason, he labeled the speech the "Atlanta Compromise." Instead of accepting segregation and "settling" for achieving in blue collar fields, Du Bois argued that blacks should pursue occupations in the humanities and in white collar (managerial or professional) fields. Du Bois, unlike Washington, believed that blacks must be politically, legally and socially active in order to obtain true equality.

W.E.B. Du Bois

Du Bois helped to organize a group of black intellectuals known as the Niagara Movement. Their goal was to outline an agenda for African-American progress in the United States. In 1905, these leaders met on the Canadian side of Niagara Falls after being denied hotel accommodations in the US. In 1909, Du Bois was instrumental in founding the National Association for the Advancement of Colored People (NAACP). The organization devoted itself to the progress of the African-American community. It also founded an official magazine called *The Crisis*, which featured journalism, editorials calling for social reform, and even poetry. Today, the NAACP continues to be a prominent political voice among the African-American community.

Ida Wells-Barnett

Ida Wells-Barnett was one of the most influential African American women of the post Reconstruction era. At a time when groups like the Ku Klux Klan were terrorizing southern blacks, she boldly led a campaign against lynching that made many northerners aware of some of the crimes happening in southern states. She also played an active role in the women's movement. She gained notoriety for her refusal to march at the end of suffrage parades simply because she was black. Wells-Barnett also helped DuBois and others organize the NAACP.

Practice 4.4: Efforts at Racial Reform

1. Which of the following would be supported by the decision in *Plessy v. Ferguson*?

   A. It is OK to have separate schools for blacks and whites, if both have qualified teachers.

   B. It is illegal to separate people by race because it violates the spirit of the Constitution.

   C. African Americans cannot be denied the right to vote.

   D. Segregation is not acceptable based on the US Constitution.

2. On which of the following points would W.E.B. Du Bois likely **disagree** with Booker T. Washington?

   A. what occupations African Americans should pursue in US society

   B. the need for African Americans to take steps to better themselves and become economically independent

   C. the need for African Americans to be better trained and educated

   D. the belief that whites enjoy certain advantages in society

3. Why did the Radical Republicans oppose Johnson's plans for Reconstruction, and what two pieces of legislation did they push through Congress between 1866 and 1868 to help ensure the civil rights of African Americans?

4. What were the conditions of the Compromise of 1877 and what is meant by the term, "Solid South?"

5. Describe the role of African Americans in southern politics during the days of Reconstruction. How did this role change after Reconstruction?

CHAPTER 4 REVIEW

Key TermsFreedmen's Bureau

Civil War
secession
states' rights
South Carolina Nullification Crisis
John C. Calhoun
Missouri Compromise
Compromise of 1850
popular sovereignty
Fugitive Slave Law
Dred Scott v. Sanford (Dred Scott decision)
John Brown
abolitionist movement
Frederick Douglass
Harriet Tubman
Underground Railroad
Harriet Beecher Stowe
Uncle Tom's Cabin
Republican party
presidential election of 1860
Confederate States of America
Fort Sumter
Abraham Lincoln
Ulysses S. Grant
William T. Sherman
Jefferson Davis
Robert E. Lee
northern advantages
southern advantages
Anaconda Plan
Antietam
Gettysburg
march to the sea
writ of habeas corpus
draft
copperheads
Emancipation Proclamation
54th Massachusetts
Appomattox Courthouse
Andrew Johnson
Presidential Reconstruction
Radical Republicans
Radical Reconstruction
Thirteenth Amendment
Fourteenth Amendment
Fifteenth Amendment
sharecropping
tenant farming
Freedmen's Bureau
black codes
Ku Klux Klan
Compromise of 1877
Solid South
Jim Crow Laws
literacy tests
poll taxes
grandfather clauses
segregation
Plessy v. Ferguson
Booker T. Washington
W.E.B. Du Bois
Ida Wells-Barnett

1. Which of the following describes the abolitionist movement?

   A. It did not include southern whites.

   B. Religion had little influence on the movement.

   C. African Americans and whites from both the North and the South took part.

   D. Because of sexual discrimination, no women were abolitionists.

2. A southern politician in the 1800s would have been **most** supportive of which of the following?

   A. popular sovereignty

   B. abolition

   C. tariffs

   D. states' rights

3. Why was the issue of slavery in new US territories so politically heated in the 1800s?

   A. Most politicians knew that they could not win enough votes to stay in office if they did not openly oppose slavery.

   B. Settlers in new territories opposed slavery and did not like the fact that Congress was requiring them to allow the practice.

   C. Southern pro-slavery leaders and northern anti-slavery leaders both wanted to maintain their power in Washington.

   D. Nearly every new state allowed slavery while almost all politicians in Washington, DC opposed slavery.

4. Which of the following **best** describes southern reaction to John Brown's raid on Harper's Ferry?

   A. alarmed, because they saw it as a violent threat to the southern way of life

   B. encouraged, because it showed that some men were willing to go to extreme measures to protect states' rights

   C. amused, because they dismissed it as an isolated incident led by a fool

   D. saddened, because Brown was a southern hero and news of his death was disheartening

> *"I cannot say enough about such bravery. Why, one could count on one hand the number of men who would take such risk — much less women. To return to the land in which she was held captive solely to help lead others to the same freedom she now possesses (but would surely lose if she were caught), is no doubt an exploit that will be eternally celebrated in heaven, if not in this life. The same can be said for those who provide shelter and sanctuary for her and her band of fleeing souls as they make their way north."*

5. The above quote is **most** likely talking about who?

   A. a white abolitionist

   B. Harriet Beecher Stowe

   C. Elizabeth Cady Stanton

   D. Harriet Tubman

6. Which of the following describes the Republican Party's official stance on slavery in the 1850s?

   A. The party officially supported the total abolition of slavery.

   B. The party was in favor of popular sovereignty.

   C. The party opposed the extension of slavery into new US territories.

   D. The party rejected the stance of the Free Soilers in favor of supporting states rights.

7. Which of the following **best** describes South Carolina's reason for seceding from the Union?

   A. They did not trust Lincoln to protect the rights of states to permit slavery.

   B. They feared that Lincoln was not truly an abolitionist.

   C. They knew he favored popular sovereignty.

   D. They believed that Lincoln intended to ship more military supplies to Fort Sumter in preparation for an invasion of the South.

- The bloodiest single day of the war
- stopped Lee's first attempt to invade the North
- gave Lincoln the opportunity to issue the Emancipation Proclamation
- good example of why you should never wrap your cigars in the general's top secret orders

8. Which battle is the above list referring to?

   A. Gettysburg

   B. Antietam

   C. First Battle of Bull Run

   D. Chancellorsville

9. Someone who believes strongly in civil rights would have been **most** upset with Lincoln for which of the following?

   A. opposing slavery in the new territories

   B. failing to leave General McClellan in command of the Union forces

   C. suspending the *writ of habeas corpus*

   D. issuing the Emancipation Proclamation

10. Although it was considered brutal by the South, it showed that Union victory was in sight and helped President Lincoln win re-election. What was it?

    A. Lincoln's suspension of habeas corpus

    B. the siege of Vicksburg

    C. Sherman's victory at Atlanta and "march to the sea"

    D. Grant's assault on Appomattox

11. Who of the following would have **most** likely been the quickest to give power back to state governments in the South?

    A. Andrew Johnson

    B. Thaddeus Stevens

    C. the Radical Republicans

    D. Edwin Stanton

12. Reconstruction ended predominantly for what reason?

    A. The South had been rebuilt and no longer needed to be reconstructed.

    B. New laws ensured the welfare of freed slaves, and a new generation of southern leaders were ready to continue Union policies.

    C. Reconstruction was too expensive to continue.

    D. A compromise put a Republican candidate in the White House in exchange for withdrawing Union forces from the South.

13. Which of the following statements is inaccurate regarding African Americans in the South after the Civil War?

    A. African American churches arose as centers of life and politics for the African American community.

    B. Blacks were unable to vote or serve in public office at any point during Reconstruction.

    C. Some blacks were elected to Congress during Reconstruction.

    D. At times, there was conflict within the African American community over the issue of social status.

14. The Fifteenth Amendment guaranteed which of the following to blacks?

    A. freedom from slavery

    B. the status of citizenship

    C. the right to vote

    D. the right to education and land ownership

15. Which of the following ended slavery in the United States?

    A. Thirteenth Amendment

    B. Fourteenth Amendment

    C. Fifteenth Amendment

    D. Emancipation Proclamation

16. Which of the following guaranteed citizenship and extended the Bill of Rights to state governments?

    A. Presidential Reconstruction

    B. Fifteenth Amendment

    C. Thirteenth Amendment

    D. Fourteenth Amendment

Chapter 5
Expansion, Industrialization, and Reform

This chapter addresses the following standard(s):

New Indicators	4.1, 4.2, 4.3, 4.4, 4.5, 4.6
Old Indicators	3.1, 5.1, 5.2, 5.3, 5.4, 5.5, 5.6, 5.7

5.1 Western Expansion

After the Civil War, territorial expansion continued at a rapid rate. White settlers claimed land originally occupied by Native Americans. The availability of land and precious metals like gold and silver drew many Americans west in hopes of finding wealth, happiness, and prosperity.

Railroads

Railroads had great economic impact and proved crucial to western expansion. It was the railroads that allowed farmers and ranchers to ship their products to eastern cities, thereby still having access to the nation's most profitable markets. Railroads also contributed to the rapid growth of population and the development of western cities by allowing people to migrate west much easier than before.

In 1862, Congress coordinated an effort among the railroad companies to build a **transcontinental railroad**. Union Pacific (an eastern rail company) and Central Pacific (a rail company from Sacramento, California) joined their tracks at Promontory, Utah, in 1869. As a symbol of their union that now linked the nation east to west, representatives drove a gold spike to mark the occasion.

The demands for land and gold meant that the US government often forced Native Americans to give up territories they had occupied for generations. As a result, western expansion negatively impacted Native Americans.

Chapter 5

Impact on Native Americans

The Plains Indians greatly depended on the **buffalo** for their livelihood. They used the buffalo for food, clothing, fuel, and shelter. As settlers and fur trappers came into the region, they killed great numbers of buffalo for their hides and to make way for ranchers and their herds of cattle. By 1889, only about one thousand buffalo were left on the continent. As a result, the Plains Indians could no longer continue their way of life.

Buffalo

Many Native American tribes were forced to relocate to **reservations** (parcels of land set aside by the federal government for the Native Americans). Often the government forcibly removed the tribes again each time gold was discovered or whites needed land. Large numbers of Native Americans died as a result of being forced to travel great distances and settle on reservations in lands to which they were not accustomed.

Important Battles Between US Troops and Native Americans

The Sand Creek Massacre and the Battle of Little Bighorn

Crazy Horse leads his people to surrender
(Library of Congress)

On a number of occasions, Native American peoples chose to resist white settlement rather than accept being moved off of their land. In 1861, US officials forced the Cheyenne to give up claims to land that they had been promised by the government. In retaliation, Cheyenne warriors launched several raids on mining camps and local settlements. In response, US forces surprised five hundred Cheyenne at Sand Creek., killing 270 Native Americans — most of whom were women and children.

Chief Red Cloud

Under the leadership of chiefs Red Cloud and Crazy Horse, the Sioux Indians also resisted. In 1876, a US commander named George Armstrong Custer attempted to surprise and defeat the Sioux at the Battle of the Little Bighorn**.** Custer greatly underestimated the size of his enemy's forces, however, and recklessly rushed into battle. Sioux warriors quickly surrounded the outnumbered US troops, killing Custer and more than 200 of his men. The battle became

Gen. Custer

known as "Custer's last stand." It would be the last great victory for Native Americans. By 1877, both the Sioux and Cheyenne surrendered to US troops and were forcibly expelled to reservations in the Dakotas and Oklahoma.

Wounded Knee

Sitting Bull

The last notable armed conflict between US troops and Native Americans occurred in 1890 at **Wounded Knee.** It happened after a Sioux holy man named Wovoka developed a religious ritual called the Ghost Dance. The Sioux believed that this dance would bring back the buffalo, return the Native American tribes to their land, and banish the white man from their land. Believing that the Sioux leader, Sitting Bull, was using the Ghost Dance to start a Native American uprising, the government sent in the US Army. When soldiers tried to arrest Sitting Bull, a gunfight resulted in the deaths of fourteen people, including Sitting Bull. Soldiers then pursued the Sioux to Wounded Knee Creek. When a shot rang out (no one is sure who fired it), the soldiers started firing. Before it was over, more than 150 Native American men, women and children — most of whom were unarmed — lay dead.

The Dawes Act

In 1887, Congress passed the **Dawes Act**. This act abolished tribal organizations and divided up reservations for the purpose of allotting land to individual Native American families. After twenty-five years, ownership of the land would go to the Native Americans who would become US citizens.

The Dawes Act turned out to be a huge failure. Most Native Americans did not want to give up their tribal identity nor be assimilated into white culture. Many had no interest in farming either. Even those who wished to farm often did not receive land suitable for growing crops. In the end, the Dawes Act accomplished little as the Native American population decreased due to poverty and disease.

Practice 5.1: Western Expansion

1. Railroads had which of the following impacts on Native Americans?

   A. They helped Native Americans thrive because they opened new markets.

   B. They made Native Americans wealthy because railroad companies paid them for their land.

   C. They hurt Native Americans by altering their way of life and disrupting their culture.

   D. They had little effect on Native Americans because Native Americans did not ride trains.

2. What was the Dawes Act? Why did it fail?

5.2 The Rise of Big Business

Inventions and Natural Resources

Alexander Graham Bell

In the years following the Civil War, the United States continued to become an industrialized society. This was especially true of large urban centers in the North. A number of inventions helped to contribute to this trend. Samuel B. Morse's telegraph and Alexander Graham Bell's telephone made it possible for individuals and businesses to communicate much more easily and on a broader scale than ever before.

Thomas Edison's light bulb had great impact because it enabled factory work to continue after sunset. Expanding upon Edison's work with electricity, **George Westinghouse** developed the first alternating current system in 1886. Combined with the invention of an alternating current motor, this innovation allowed businessmen to build and locate factories wherever they wanted rather than being limited to areas with waterfalls or accessible deposits of coal necessary for generating power. As a result, people worked longer hours, the number of US factories increased, and industries produced more goods.

Other key inventions included the typewriter, vacuum cleaner, refrigeration cars for trains, elevators which made tall buildings practical, and innovative machinery for farming (ie, threshers, mowers, mechanical planters, etc.).

Mass Production

Mass production is the process of producing goods in large number. By selling more, producers can charge consumers less money and still make a profit. Industrialization made mass production possible.

Model T

By the start of the first world war, Henry Ford improved upon the earlier invention of the automobile when he began to mass produce his Model T. Ford's innovative assembly line allowed him to produce more cars at less cost, thereby allowing him to sell them at an affordable price for average consumers. As a result, more people started buying cars, and the nation was on its way to being transformed into a commuter society.

Industrialization also increased due to the availability of **natural resources** (resources formed by nature that are used to produce goods). The Appalachian Mountains provided rich reserves of coal and iron ore. In western Pennsylvania and the Southwest, oil was abundant. In the South, lumber provided by the vast forest regions provided a profitable enterprise due to the need for new housing, and running water from rivers and streams produced needed hydroelectricity.

GIANTS OF EARLY US INDUSTRIALIZATION

With industrialization came new opportunities and chances to make money. It was during this period that a handful of Americans became extremely wealthy as entrepreneurs (people who start businesses). They forever changed US business.

The Railroad Industry

The railroad industry was the first to take off in the years following the Civil War. Railroads made life out west possible by allowing farmers, ranchers, and other settlers access to eastern markets and resources. They also made it easier for people to move west and populate territories at a rapid rate.

A few men got rich developing the railroad industry. Because some of them were known to be crooked in their dealings, they collectively came to be called **"robber barons"** (a name that soon came to be identified with wealthy entrepreneurs in other industries as well). One key figure in the railroad industry was **Cornelius Vanderbilt**. In 1869, he extended his New York Central railroad to reach Chicago, Illinois. Travelers could go from New York to Chicago without having to transfer trains multiple times. This greatly helped the railroad industry by making travel faster and much easier for passengers and businesses shipping goods.

Vanderbilt

OIL

John D. Rockefeller became one of the nation's richest and most powerful businessmen. Rockefeller's company, **Standard Oil**, was the nation's first **trust**. A trust is a business arrangement under which a number of companies unite into one system. In effect, trusts serve to destroy competition and create **monopolies** (a market in which there is only one supplier of a product and no market competition).

John D. Rockefeller

Through the trust, Rockefeller was able to dictate prices, eliminate competition, and control the US oil industry. Much of Rockefeller's success was due to his masterful use of vertical integration (a business strategy in which one corporation owns not only the company that produces the finished product, but also the companies that provide the materials necessary for production). Rather than pay other producers to supply the materials he needed, Rockefeller's company made what it needed itself (ie, its own barrels, cans, etc.). In the words of Rockefeller, he was determined to "pay nobody a profit."

Chapter 5

STEEL

Andrew Carnegie

In the late 1850s, a man named Sir Henry Bessemer developed a new method for making steel known as the *Bessemer process*. Using this process, manufacturers could make steel much cheaper than ever before. Increased production of steel meant faster expansion of railroads and more construction of buildings. Steel became very important to the nation's economy.

Andrew Carnegie came to control this industry. Like Rockefeller, Carnegie used vertical integration. He owned not only the steel mills, but also the necessary iron ore, coal mines, railroads, and ships used for transporting supplies. In this way, Carnegie was able to form a monopoly.

Carnegie was also a great philanthropist (someone who gives money to public / charitable causes) who gave much of his wealth to finance public projects. Citing what he referred to as the "Gospel of Wealth," Carnegie believed that it was the responsibility of the wealthy to make sure their money was put to good use serving others, rather than being spent on frivolous pursuits.

FINANCE CAPITALISM

With the expansion of US business came a new kind of business leader—the finance capitalist. These were bankers who exerted economic influence through companies' stocks and bonds. The most powerful and influential of the early finance capitalists was **J.P. Morgan**. Morgan eventually exercised control over banks, insurance companies, and various stock market operations. By 1913, Morgan and his associates had assets of over $22 billion! The amount was equal to three times the estimated value of all the real estate in New York City at the time. Morgan was so rich that he eventually bought out Carnegie's steel company to form a new company — US Steel. He paid Carnegie nearly $500 million, making Carnegie the richest man in the world. Carnegie later commented, "I should have asked for more," to which Morgan casually responded, "I'd have paid it."

J.P. Morgan

INTERLOCKING DIRECTORATES AND TARIFFS

It was the era of big business, as industrial leaders established power through monopolies, trusts, and **interlocking directorates**. These directorates allowed directors of one company to serve as directors for other companies also. As a result, they could control entire industries, thereby increasing their economic gains and limiting competition.

Business leaders also received aid from the government in the form of **protective tariffs**, which taxed foreign imports and made it easier for US businesses to sell their products at higher prices.

Social Darwinism and the Gilded Age

Herbert Spencer

In the mid-1800s, an English philosopher and political theorist named Herbert Spencer introduced a concept which came to be known as **Social Darwinism**. Basing his ideas on the theories of Charles Darwin, Spencer believed that life was a battle for "survival of the fittest:" Many business leaders were drawn to this philosophy and made it the basis of their belief in laissez-faire capitalism (the belief that the government should not interfere with the market or regulate business, but rather let the market take its natural course). Borrowing from Darwin's observations about animals in the wild and the beliefs of Spencer, these businessmen reasoned that business was also a battle for survival and that it was best for the economy if only those industries and industrialists who were "the strongest" survived. Therefore, they believed that the natural economic laws of supply and demand should dictate business practices without the "unnatural" disturbance of government interference.

Charles Darwin

Many in society had nothing but the greatest admiration for these men and bought into their view of business/success. People believed that just about anyone, no matter how poor, could "pull themselves up by their bootstraps" and become rich.

However, not everyone agreed. As businesses grew and business leaders acquired more economic control, concerns began to grow as well. Some saw the wealth enjoyed by the few as being at the expense of the many who remained in poverty. They felt that while business leaders grew rich, their laborers were left with harsh working conditions and inadequate pay. The period from 1877 until the early 1900s came to be called the **Gilded Age**. The phrase comes from writer Mark Twain, and refers to a time in which it appeared that a thin layer of prosperity was covering the poverty and corruption that existed in much of society.

Cultural, Economic and Political Impact

Capitalism fueled industrial growth in the United States. **Capitalism** is an economic system in which means of production (factories, machines, and so on) are privately owned. Producers provide goods and services in response to market demand. As a result, producers tend to supply goods and services that people want and are willing to pay for. In a capitalist system, different producers are free to produce the same goods or services. This creates market competition. Market competition leads to lower prices as producers compete for consumers. The desire to sell goods for less encourages mass production and leads to industrialization.

1891 Kodak Ad

Industrialization had numerous effects on the United States. For individual citizens, increased production and new inventions meant that consumer goods were more affordable and available than ever before. Thus, the demand for goods increased. As a result, people's **standard of living** tended to rise in the second half of the 1800s due to new products and the availability of new jobs created by the growth of business.

In addition, technological advances like the electric trolley fueled the rise of a new middle class and suburbs by allowing people to live further out while commuting into the cities for work and entertainment.

Meanwhile, US businesses thrived not only at home but in **international markets** also. As business leaders increased their profits, they began to invest in other countries. The desire to deal internationally eventually led to calls for territorial expansion and led the nation into international conflicts.

Electric Trolley

As urban populations increased, so did **democracy**. Poorer citizens, immigrants, other "common people" gradually won greater say in their government. More offices required direct election from the people. As the role of urban governments increased, so did their power. Politicians sought to provide services and favors that would win the support of the people. Unions, ethnic groups, and other organized groups often voted for candidates together.

Practice 5.2: The Rise of Big Business

1. George Westinghouse and Thomas Edison are connected in which of the following ways?

   A. Their inventions made it much easier for businesses to communicate on a broader scale.

   B. They both made important strides in inventing ways to harness the power of electricity.

   C. Edison invented the first telephone, and Westinghouse later improved on his invention.

   D. Edison discovered electricity, and Westinghouse figured out a way for factories to use it.

2. Which of the following men became rich and powerful as a finance capitalist who exerted influence over a number of different types of businesses?

   A. Andrew Carnegie
   B. Buck Duke
   C. J.D. Rockefeller
   D. J.P. Morgan

3. What is a monopoly and how did trusts and interlocking directorates help encourage their existence?

4. How did railroads effect US business and Native Americans?

5.3 Farmers and Populism

Throughout the South and West, farming remained an important part of life. However, in the 1870s and 1880s, it became a very costly industry. Farmers borrowed from banks in order to purchase the latest machinery. Mechanization helped make farming easier and enabled farmers to produce more goods. While this initially benefitted farmers because they could sell more, it ultimately resulted in **overproduction** (too many agricultural products) and caused farm prices to drop drastically. This meant farmers were getting less money for their products at the same time that their costs were increasing.

Farmers in Late 1800s

As farmers slipped further and further into debt, many of them blamed politicians and big business for their plight. They wanted the government to regulate railroads which they believed overcharged them to ship their goods. Eventually, in 1887, President Grover Cleveland signed into law the Interstate Commerce Act. This law provided for the creation of an Interstate Commerce Commission and regulated railroad rates in the name of public interest.

Farmers also wanted **subsidies.** They wanted the government to pay them money to cover their losses due to over-production. Farmers also wanted to see more money pumped into the nation's economy. For this reason, they supported the circulation of more **greenbacks** (paper money). Farmers wanted to put more money in the hands of consumers, thereby promoting inflation and increasing farm prices.

The Grange

To deal with the financial crisis, many farmers began banding together to protect their interests by collectively standing up to railroads and other industries. Through a cooperative called **the grange**, local farmers pooled their resources to purchase new machinery and supplies, as well as to sell their produce without paying other distributors. By 1874, farmers joined over fourteen thousand national grange associations. They later formed other alliances too.

Chapter 5

Populism (The People's Party)

Tom Watson

The concerns of the farmers eventually gave rise to the **Populist Movement**. Populism was a political movement that embraced what farmers wanted. It supported the circulation of greenbacks and increased government regulation of business (particularly railroads and warehouses).

In 1892, under the official name of the People's Party, the Populists met in Omaha, Nebraska and formally adopted many of these stances in what came to be called the Omaha Platform. Politically, Populism appealed to the "common man." It was a movement that praised agriculture as the backbone of the country and favored the farmers of the South and West. It was also revolutionary in that it sought to break down racial divisions between white and black farmers. If only for political gain, Populists preached that the two groups must unite if they hoped to overcome the "oppression" of big business and corrupt politicians.

The Election of 1896

William Jennings Bryan

William McKinley

As the country approached the presidential election of 1896, it was experiencing one of its worse economic depressions ever. This made President Cleveland vulnerable and seemed to present an opportunity for any candidate who could win the support of the Populists. As the depression deepened in 1894, more and more people blamed President Cleveland for the worsening condition. Cleveland, blaming the silver standard for the nation's economic woes, returned the US to a strictly gold standard, meaning that the dollar could only be backed by gold.

Many people argued that the dollar should be based on silver too. By backing the dollar with silver as well as gold, money would become more plentiful. More money would give consumers more to spend. This would increase the money supply and raise prices on farm products and other goods.

The position that supported backing the dollar with silver became known as **bimetallism**. Miners in the West backed bimetallism. Eventually, Populists agreed to support bimetallism too along with greenbacks. They hoped their alliance with miners and other bimetal supporters would help strengthen them politically and make it easier for the Populists to win approval of their policies.

The silver question became the major issue of the 1896 campaign. When the Democrats met for their convention that year, they nominated a fiery speaker named **William Jennings Bryan**. Bryan backed bimetallism and won the support of the Populists. In his address to the Democratic Convention, Bryan made his famous "Cross of Gold" speech. In it he stated, "You shall not press down upon the brow of labor this crown of thorns; you shall not crucify mankind upon a cross of gold!"

Despite his abilities as a public speaker and a national campaigner, Bryan could not overcome splits in the Democratic party to win enough votes. Republican William McKinley won the presidential election of 1896. Populism faded soon after.

Practice 5.3: Farmers and Populism

1. Which of the following was a problem faced by farmers in the late 1800s?

    A. Falling railroad prices interfered with their ability to ship products.

    B. High farm prices caused financial problems because few people could afford their products.

    C. Overproduction of agricultural products led to falling farm prices and made it hard to make a profit.

    D. Because there was too much money in circulation, it was impossible for farmers to get the price they needed for their goods.

2. Which of the following statements **best** describes reasons for joining the grange?

    A. The grange provided a means by which farmers could protect their interest collectively.

    B. The grange was a political movement which farmers and low income workers felt represented their needs.

    C. The grange gave a voice to railroad industrialists who felt unfairly criticized by angry farmers.

    D. The grange provided a place where farmers could fight to protect laissez-faire economics.

3. What was bimetallism and why did people support it?

5.4 Urbanization

From the end of the Civil War until the beginning of the twentieth century, the size of US cities increased rapidly. In the West, new towns grew out of nothing as railroads and western settlements took hold. Many of these towns grew into bustling cities. Meanwhile, in the East, established cities grew in population due to industrialization and the job opportunities it created.

Migration to the Cities

As industrialization continued in the US, many people left their farms and migrated (moved) to the cities where they could earn higher wages. Rising farm costs and declining prices for agricultural products meant that fewer individuals could make a living farming. Out west, cities like San Francisco began to grow and thrive. Denver, Kansas City, and Omaha also transformed from frontier "villages" into booming urban areas. Even the South began to see an increase in urban life as industries like tobacco, iron production, and textiles contributed to the rapid growth of places like Birmingham, Houston, and Durham. However, it was the northeastern cities like New York that saw the greatest numbers of population growth.

All over the US, people were making their way to the cities. As for African Americans, most southern blacks tended to either farm, move west, or migrate to cities within the South. Not until the early twentieth century did mass numbers of African Americans migrate to northern cities due to the economic opportunities created by World War I.

Immigration

Immigrants

The second half of the nineteenth century also saw a dramatic increase in **immigration** to the United States. In the East, most of these new arrivals came from Europe, while on the west coast, many immigrated from China in hopes of making money working on US railway lines. Some immigrants came seeking a better life, others fled hardships like famine, and still others hoped to escape political persecutions. By the end of the 1880s, nearly 80% of New Yorkers were foreign born.

Industrialization was largely responsible for the flow of immigrants. As industry grew and the need for labor increased, the US became a land of promise much like it had been for the first colonists nearly three hundred years before.

ELLIS ISLAND

To handle the large numbers of people arriving in the country, the federal government opened **Ellis Island** in 1892. A tiny island near the Statue of Liberty, it became a well known reception center for immigrants arriving by ship.

Ellis Island

As more and more people immigrated to the US, the nation's population became very diverse. Such diversity inspired the phrase, "melting pot." In a melting pot, people mix different ingredients together as they cook and prepare an appetizing final product. In the same way, many envisioned the United States as a place where people of all backgrounds could come and be assimilated into American society. In reality, however, most immigrants did not want to fully assimilate (become like the US mainstream). They wanted to maintain many of their traditional ways. The nation, particularly the large cities, began to experience a great deal of **cultural pluralism** (presence of many different cultures within one society).

PROBLEMS AND CONCERNS CAUSED BY IMMIGRATION

Inner City Ghetto

While immigration had positive effects, such as greater diversity and providing much needed labor for the nation's factories, it also presented problems. Many US citizens looked on immigrants negatively. They felt that immigrants took jobs away from natives (people born in the US), and they often mistrusted foreigners whose cultural ways they could not understand. People who strongly opposed immigration became known as **nativists**.

Nativists were suspicious of **ethnic ghettos** in inner cities. Ghettos were neighborhoods where immigrants from a certain region or country tended to live together due to their common culture, language, and heritage. Many natives saw this as a sign of disloyalty to the United States. Religious differences were also a source of tension. Most US citizens were Protestants, while many of the arriving immigrants were Catholics. As a result, an immigrant's religious practices often conflicted with those of native-born citizens.

Even among immigrants themselves, problems existed. As people from different nations and ethnic groups lived in ghettos that were in close proximity to one another, conflicts arose. People from one nation or ethnic group developed rivalries with those of another.

Nativism and Restrictions on Immigration

As feelings of **nativism** (opposing immigration) grew, anti-immigrant groups grew. Nativism often meant that foreign immigrants were the victims of violence and discrimination. Eventually, the government reacted to nativist concerns by attempting to pass legislation restricting immigration. A number of such efforts failed when they were vetoed by US presidents. Legislation did pass, however, restricting immigration from China. The Chinese Exclusion Act of 1882 prohibited Chinese immigrants from legally coming to the US and was not repealed until 1943.

Nativism

Living and Working Conditions

For poor, unskilled citizens and newly arrived immigrants, urban life could be hard and challenging. Whole families tended to work because wages were low, and no one person could earn enough to support a whole household. Men, women, and children worked in mills and factories; usually at least twelve hours/day, six days/week. Women tended to be limited to running simple machines and were given almost no opportunity for advancement. Meanwhile, **child labor** became a common practice. Children —some as young as five years old — had to leave school in order to work from an early age. This not only meant that they missed out on a childhood, but without an education they were inevitably caught in an endless cycle of poverty as well.

Child Labor

Although industrialization did create some opportunities for African Americans in the 1800s, they were extremely limited. Even many labor unions would not accept African American workers among their membership. It was an age in which most workers feared losing their job at a time when Social Security and unemployment benefits did not exist.

Factory Workers

Working conditions were often difficult. Factories relied on the work of specialized laborers with machines that performed the same task over and over. Work was often monotonous and left employees feeling very little sense of pride. Also, work hours were long, wages were low, and factory conditions were often very dangerous. **Sweatshops** were also hazardous. These were makeshift factories set up by private contractors in small apartments or unused buildings. Since factories often needed more production than they had room to produce, they would hire these contractors and then pay them by production. Often poorly lit, poorly ventilated, and unsafe, sweatshops relied on poor workers (usually immigrants) who worked long hours for little pay.

Cliff Dwellers **by George Bellows**
depicts an Urban Slum

To house the overwhelming numbers of migrants and immigrants, **urban slums** (poor, inner-city neighborhoods) consisting of **tenements** (overcrowded apartments that housed several families of immigrants or poor laborers) arose in the cities. Overcrowded and impoverished, these slums often had open sewers that attracted rats and other disease-spreading pests. The air was usually dark and polluted with soot from coal-fired steam engines and boilers. The individual tenements were often poorly ventilated and full of fire hazards. Often, they were occupied by more than one family crammed together into a small, sometimes one room, apartment.

The New Urban Lifestyle and Entertainment

As the urban population grew and transformed, urban life transformed with it. Transportation evolved as **electric trolleys** allowed people to live outside the inner city while still working and pursuing leisure activities within it. As a result, the nation began to see the development of its first suburbs. Increased divisions in economic classes developed as those of the middle and upper classes moved further out and left the inner city to the poorer classes and immigrants.

Vaudeville Theater

On the farm, people tended to work by production. They worked until the work was done. Leisure time was limited and reserved for only certain celebrations and seasons. Urban factory workers, on the other hand, worked by the clock. Once the work hours ended, people looked for ways to amuse themselves. To meet this need, new means of **leisure and entertainment** began to grow in the cities.

Among men, saloons became popular places to drink, socialize, forge bonds, and engage in politics. Women enjoyed dance halls and cabarets where they could watch musical shows and try the latest dances. For families, there were amusement parks and vaudeville shows (inexpensive variety shows). It was during this time that the moving picture industry was born, and spectator sports (boxing, horse racing, and especially baseball) became popular. The period also saw a number of city parks come into being. Most notable was New York's Central Park.

Political Machines

The fast growth of the urban population meant that government had to improve police and fire departments, transportation systems, public services, sewage systems, and so on. This meant more public money and a greater role for government. It also gave the government more power and made the battle for government positions more intense.

The **political machine** was an unofficial entity meant to keep a certain party or group in power. It was led by a *boss*, who may or may not hold a political office himself. During this period, graft (the use of one's political position or job to gain wealth) became a common practice. Poor workers and immigrants proved to be an important source of political power for the machines. Often times, it was the machine that took the initiative to help immigrants adjust to life in the US when they arrived. By intervening on behalf of such individuals, the machine was able to secure votes in exchange for political favors, financial help, and promises of aid.

Perhaps the most notorious political boss was New York City's Boss William Tweed. Tweed ran Tammany Hall, a political club that controlled the city's Democratic party. Over time, Tweed stole over $100 million from the city treasury. Even after Tweed's fall from power, Tammany Hall continued to dominate New York City politics.

Boss Tweed

Practice 5.4: Urbanization

1. Between the late 1860s and the early 1900s, which of the following **best** describes the changes that occurred in urban population?

   A. The number of African Americans living in the inner city of Northern urban areas more than doubled.

   B. Many farmers migrated to the cities, while foreign immigrants did not start to come until just after 1900.

   C. Urban areas of the North became culturally diverse as more immigrants arrived.

   D. The US middle class declined as people tended to be either rich businessmen or poor laborers.

2. Which of the following statements would be **most** supported by a nativist?

   A. "Since the US is suppose to be the land of the free and the country of opportunity, then let all those who desire freedom and a better life come to the United States."

   B. "Immigration is bad for this country. Immigrants take jobs that otherwise would go to those born here. Their ways pollute our way of life. We need laws to prevent immigration."

   C. "Cultural diversity is a good thing. It is our differences and the way foreigners hold on to their traditional ways that make our nation great."

   D. "God bless the Irish, the German, and the Italian immigrant. Give 'em a home here, I say. But blast the Chinese. Keep 'em out by all means."

3. What were some of the living and working conditions faced by poor laborers and immigrants to the US in the big cities?

4. How did industrialization and urban growth affect lifestyle in the late 19th and early 20th centuries?

5.5 The Rise of Labor Unions

Labor Unions arose out of the challenging conditions that faced industrial workers. Unions are organizations of workers formed to protect the interests of its members. During this period, a number of notable unions and union leaders arose.

The **Knights of Labor** formed in 1869 and hoped to organize all working men and women into a single union. It also recruited and included African Americans. The Knights pursued social reforms such as equal pay for equal work, the eight hour workday, and an end to child labor. After initial success, a series of failed strikes led to the group's decline and eventual disappearance in the 1890s.

Samuel Gompers

In 1886, the **American Federation of Labor (AFL)**, led by **Samuel Gompers**, formed. It focused on the issues of wages, working hours and working conditions. The AFL used the economic pressures of **strikes** (refusal of employees to work until employers meet certain demands) and **boycotts** (refusal to buy or pay for certain products or services in the hopes of forcing producers to change their policies or actions). The AFL also believed in collective bargaining. Collective bargaining is a process through which employees negotiate as a united group rather than as individuals, thereby increasing their bargaining power.

To increase their ability to negotiate with business owners, the AFL pressed for "**closed shop**" workplaces in which employers could hire only union members. "Closed shops" forced employers to deal with the union because they could not look elsewhere for workers.

Eugene Debs

One of the most influential union leaders in history was **Eugene Debs**. Debs organized the American Railway Union in 1893, and went on to lead the famed Pullman Strike of 1894. He ran for president several times as leader of the American Socialist Party.

Employer Response to Unions

Employers hated the unions. Many of them forced employees to sign contracts, which forbade workers from even joining. Others placed union workers on blacklists (lists of workers who employers would refuse to hire). At times, they would also institute lockouts in which employees were not allowed to return to work.

Lockout **by Kyra Markham**

When strikes occurred, employers often hired scabs (replacement workers) to take over the jobs left vacated. As time went on, employers and business leaders came to realize that they had the support of government when it came to breaking strikes (ending strikes by force). Employers would ask for **injunctions**. These were court orders that forbade strikes because they violated the law or threatened public interests. When all else failed, some employers used violence and intimidation to deal with labor unrest.

STRIKES AND CONFRONTATIONS

The first major case of nationwide labor unrest occurred in 1877. Upset by a proposed wage cut, railway workers responded with violence throughout the Midwest and eastern United States. Alarmed by the violence and concerned about the disruption to the nation's railways, President Rutherford B. Hayes sent in federal troops on two separate occasions to put down the protest. Known as the "**Great Strike**," it showed employers that they could appeal to the federal government for help in dealing with striking workers.

Haymarket Riot

In May of 1886, workers mounted a national demonstration in support of an eight hour workday. On May 4, many of them held a rally at Chicago's Haymarket Square. During the rally, a group of radicals exploded a bomb that killed or wounded several police officers. A riot immediately broke out with gunfire that killed both police and striking workers. The **Haymarket Riot** turned public opinion against the unions as many in the nation began to identify strikes with anarchy and violence.

The **Homestead Strike** broke out among steel workers in 1892 at the Carnegie Steel plant in Homestead, Pennsylvania. While Carnegie was in Europe, his partner, Henry Frick, hired a private police force known as the "Pinkertons" to put down the strike. Strikers and Pinkertons eventually engaged in a shootout that left several people dead or wounded. The Pinkertons eventually surrendered and left. But the public once again perceived the striking workers as instigators of the violence. In the end, the union had no choice but to call off the strike.

Like the first of the great strikes, the last involved the railroad industry. In 1894, a delegation of employees went to railroad car industrialist, George Pullman, to protest the laying off of workers. Pullman responded by firing three of the labor representatives, leading the

Shootout Between Pinkertons and Strikers
(Library of Congress)

local union to go on strike. Pullman then closed the plant rather than negotiating with union leaders. Led by Eugene Debs, the American Railway Union called for a boycott of Pullman cars nationwide.

By June, roughly 120,000 workers had rallied to the strike. The federal government responded with a court injunction against the union, and President Cleveland sent in federal troops to make sure that it was enforced. Days later, the strike was over. The **Pullman Strike** established a precedence for factory owners appealing to the courts to end strikes.

Pullman Strike

Practice 5.5: The Rise of Labor Unions

1. Which of the following contributed to the rise of unions?

   A. increased numbers of workers in urban areas

   B. child unemployment

   C. unsafe farming techniques

   D. government policies giving more power to workers

2. How did the public often perceive unions as the result of events like the Haymarket Riot and the Homestead Strike?

   A. The unions were viewed as champions of the common man.

   B. The unions were viewed as persecuted and victims of harsh treatment by employers.

   C. The unions were viewed as promoting violence and anarchy.

   D. The unions were viewed as being treated unfairly by the government.

3. What role did the federal government and the courts play in early labor disputes?

5.6 Social Reform

Upton Sinclair

As the 1800s came to a close, only a handful of people enjoyed wealth and prosperity. Immigrants and poor laborers continued to live and work under harsh conditions. Meanwhile, the country was riddled with government corruption at all levels.

Many citizens and government officials demanded reforms in government, business, and society in general. The turn of the century marked the beginning of the **Progressive Movement** and was a time of political, social, and economic change in the United States.

The Muckrakers

Ida Tarbell

A number of leading intellectuals and writers came on the scene during the Progressive Period. Many of these writers wrote stories exposing abuse in government and big business. President Theodore Roosevelt labeled these journalists the **"Muckrakers."**

Among the Muckrakers were a number of respected writers. Lincoln Steffens exposed political corruption in St. Louis and other cities. Ida Tarbell revealed the abuses of the Standard Oil trust.

Perhaps the most famous muckraker was **Upton Sinclair** who published a novel called *The Jungle* in 1906. The book horrified readers as it uncovered the truth about the US meat packing industry. Its impact helped lead to the creation of a federal meat inspection program.

Jane Addams

Hull House

Jane Addams (nicknamed the "mother of social work") opened Hull House as a settlement house in Chicago. Settlement houses were houses established in poor neighborhoods where social activists would live and from which they would offer assistance to immigrants and underprivileged citizens. By 1910, there were more than hour hundred settlement houses in the United States. Hull House also served as a launching pad for investigations into economic, political, and social conditions in the city.

Temperance

During the Progressive Period, momentum continued to grow for the **temperance movement**. This was a movement that originally wanted to limit and, eventually, advocated eliminating alcohol.

Famed Temperance Activist Carrie Nation

Ratified in 1919, the **Eighteenth Amendment** prohibited the making, selling or transporting of any alcoholic beverage in the United States. Commonly referred to as "Prohibition," this amendment later proved to be a failure and was repealed.

Women's Suffrage

Women's Suffrage Supporters

Even more lasting in its impact than the temperance movement was the **women's suffrage movement**. Ever since the Seneca Falls Convention of 1848, women had demanded suffrage (the right to vote). By the 1870s, Susan B. Anthony was arguably the most recognized leader of this movement. Along with Elizabeth Cady Stanton and others, Anthony helped establish the National American Woman Suffrage Association (NAWSA) which she led until 1900. Initial attempts to win a constitutional amendment granting women the right to vote failed, although women did win the right to vote in a few states.

Carrie Chapman Catt and **Alice Paul** played a major role in passage of the **Nineteenth Amendment** (constitutional amendment that gave women the right to vote). Catt served as president of the NAWSA and founded the League of Women voters. Paul served as national chairwoman for the NAWSA's congressional committee. She led many of the efforts in Washington to convince Congress to support the Nineteenth Amendment and send it to the states for ratification.

Finally, in 1920, Congress passed the Nineteenth Amendment and sent it to the states for ratification. On August 21, Tennessee became the last state needed to make the "Anthony Amendment" part of the Constitution. At last, women had the right to vote nationwide.

Theodore Roosevelt

Theodore Roosevelt

In 1901, **Theodore Roosevelt** became the youngest man ever inaugurated president of the United States. He proved to be a progressive president who pursued a number of reforms. The first evidence of this came during the Anthracite Coal Mine Strike in 1902. Roosevelt called both sides to the White House and threatened to send in armed troops if a settlement could not be reached. When the strike was over, the miners had received a wage increase and Roosevelt was seen as a national hero for making sure that the nation got coal.

Although Roosevelt was not opposed to big business, he did believe that some regulations were necessary. He was especially concerned about trusts and the monopolies they created. Roosevelt felt that monopolies were harmful and he was determined to take them on. Roosevelt brought suit against the Northern Securities Company and its railroad monopoly in the Pacific Northwest. In 1904, the Supreme Court ruled in *Northern Securities **v. US*** that the company's existence did violate federal law and therefore must be broken up. Roosevelt was praised as a reformer and he later went after a number of other large trusts.

Woodrow Wilson

Woodrow Wilson won election as president in 1912. He ran for president as a candidate who opposed both big business *and* big government. He desired to enforce antitrust laws without threatening free economic competition. In 1913, he supported Congress in passing the **Federal Reserve Act**. This act established a Federal Reserve to oversee banking in the United States. The Federal Reserve gave the federal government greater control over the circulation of money and helped prevent bank failures.

Woodrow Wilson

Wilson also signed the Clayton Antitrust Act in 1914. This act served to make strikes, peaceful picketing, and boycotts legal. It also meant that employers could no longer use antitrust laws to put down strikes or break up labor unions.

During Wilson's first term, he nation ratified two new amendments to the Constitution. The **Sixteenth Amendment** gave Congress the power to collect taxes on the incomes of businesses and individuals. Since most of the money was in the hands of big business, this was seen as a progressive move. Meanwhile, the **Seventeenth Amendment** established that US senators would be elected directly by the people, rather than by state legislatures.

Practice 5.6: Social Reform

1. President Theodore Roosevelt would **most** likely use the term "muckraker" to apply to which of the following?

   A. a woman demanding the right to vote

   B. a supporter of the temperance movement

   C. a journalist writing about abuses by businesses

   D. a woman with a hatchet attacking saloons

2. Which of the following **best** describes Hull House?

   A. It provided a place for immigrants to live.

   B. It was a place where social workers lived and helped immigrants.

   C. It was a government-run school for the poor.

   D. It was where the woman's suffrage movement began.

3. Who of the following is **most** associated with the women's suffrage movement?

   A. Jane Addams

   B. Theodore Roosevelt

   C. Carrie C. Catt

   D. Woodrow Wilson

4. What was established by the Nineteenth Amendment?

Chapter 5 Review

Key Terms

transcontinental railroad
reservations
Wounded Knee
Dawes Act
light bulb
George Westinghouse
mass production
Henry Ford
natural resources
robber barons
Cornelius Vanderbilt
John D. Rockefeller
Standard Oil
trust
monopolies
Andrew Carnegie
J.P. Morgan
interlocking directorates
protective tariffs
Social Darwinism
Gilded Age
capitalism
standard of living
international markets
democracy
overproduction
greenbacks
the grange
Populist Movement
bimetallism
immigration
Ellis Island
cultural pluralism
ethnic ghettoes
nativism
child labor
sweatshops
urban slums
tenements
electric trolleys
leisure and entertainment
political machine
labor unions
Knights of Labor
American Federation of Labor (AFL)
Samuel Gompers
strikes
boycotts
closed shop
Eugene Debs
injunctions
Great Strike
Haymarket Riot
Homestead Strike
Pullman Strike
Progressive Movement
Muckrakers
Upton Sinclair
Jane Addams
temperance movement
Eighteenth Amendment
women's suffrage movement
Carrie Chapman Catt
Alice Paul
Theodore Roosevelt
Woodrow Wilson
Federal Reserve Act
Sixteenth Amendment
Seventeenth Amendment

Chapter 5

Review Questions

> *"He was an incredible business man and a generous humanitarian. Why, I bet he gave away almost as much money as he made. Meanwhile, he made the steel industry what it is today. When he sold his business to old Morgan, it made him the richest man in the world."*

1. Who is the above statement referring to?

   A. Cornelius Vanderbilt
   B. Andrew Carnegie
   C. John D. Rockefeller
   D. Tammany Hall

2. It was the nation's first trust.

   A. Vanderbilt's New York Central Railroad
   B. J.P. Morgan's bank
   C. E.C. Knight's sugar plantation
   D. John D. Rockefeller's Standard Oil

3. The impact of railroads on Native Americans can **best** be described as

   A. beneficial.
   B. harmful.
   C. neutral
   D. unnoticeable

4. Which of the following individuals would be considered a "robber baron?"

   A. an urban politician
   B. a union leader
   C. a leader of industry
   D. an industrial worker

5. Which of the following methods would be embraced by a union leader?

   A. court injunctions
   B. collective bargaining
   C. lock outs
   D. trusts

6. The government's role in early labor disputes can **best** be described as what?

   A. supportive of business out of concern that strikes could adversely affect the nation

   B. supportive of workers out of concern that business owners were failing to protect civil rights

   C. restrained, choosing to let labor and business owners work out their own solutions

   D. disinterested, because labor disputes were a matter of private enterprise

7. Which of the following fueled the rise of Populism?

   A. rising agricultural prices

   B. the use of the silver instead of greenbacks

   C. calls for racial segregation

   D. the inability of farmers to pay off their debts

8. Which of the following individuals would have been **most** likely to become a nativist?

   A. an Italian immigrant who arrived in the US via Ellis Island

   B. an Irish immigrant who did not want to compete for work against other immigrants

   C. a Protestant worker born in New York City

   D. a Catholic priest born and raised in the United States

> *"The place smelled horrible. All those people forced to live together in such a confined place. Why, they were practically sleeping on top of one another. It was two whole families from Ireland, plus a couple of young men that weren't related to either one. Each one of 'em — women and children included — work in the factories by day and return to that mouse hole to eat and sleep."*

9. The above quote is **most** likely talking about what?

   A. the appearance of an urban slum

   B. life in a tenement

   C. conditions in a sweatshop

   D. aftermath of an industrial accident

10. Writers who exposed corruption were referred to as

    A. Pinkertons.

    B. Muckrakers.

    C. Bull-moosers.

    D. Suffragists.

11. Who of the following was praised for opposing monopolies?

    A. John D. Rockefeller

    B. Alice Paul

    C. Andrew Carnegie

    D. Theodore Roosevelt

12. What amendment did Progressives support because they wanted the rich to pay more taxes?

    A. Sixteenth

    B. Seventeenth

    C. Eighteenth

    D. Nineteenth

Chapter 6
International Expansion and Conflict

This chapter addresses the following standard(s):

New Indicators	5.1, 5.2, 5.3, 5.4, 5.5
Old Indicators	6.1, 6.2, 6.3, 6.4

6.1 The US Looks Outward

Reasons for Expansion

Economics

Toward the end of the nineteenth century, a growing number of people in the US believed in **imperialism**. They believed that the United States needed to look beyond its own borders to acquire overseas colonies. Some were motivated by capitalism. Business leaders and politicians believed that US expansion was important because it would provide the country with more economic markets and greater potential for economic growth.

Defense

Alfred T. Mahan

There was also a growing sense among many that the United States needed to expand (or at least be capable of expansion) in order to maintain **national security**. In 1890, Captain (later to be Admiral) Alfred T. Mahan wrote *The Influence of Sea Power Upon History.* In his book, Mahan made a convincing case that the United States must build a powerful navy if it ever hoped to be a world power and protect its interests abroad. Just ten years later, in large part due to Mahan's influence, the United States had one of the most powerful navies in the world.

Chapter 6

NATIONALISM AND "DESTINY"

F. J. Turner

Many in the country felt that it was the pioneer spirit of the early settlers that had made the US great. With the West conquered, some argued that the country needed to look abroad with a new sense of adventure and purpose. One of these people was historian Frederick Jackson Turner. In a famous speech given in 1893, Turner proclaimed that the frontier had played a vital role in forming the American character. He appealed to **nationalism** (national pride) and argued that expansion was essential to maintain the US spirit and keep the country strong.

Some leaders harkened back to Manifest Destiny. They saw it as the responsibility and destiny of whites in the US to civilize and take democracy to the rest of the world. They often appealed to **Social Darwinism** to justify US imperialism. This was ideology that taught "survival of the fittest." Many whites in the US believed it was only natural that the United States exercise control over "less fit" and "inferior" races of people.

In response to the United States' conquest of the Philippines during the Spanish-American War, British writer Rudyard Kipling wrote his famous poem, ***The White Man's Burden***. Although some argued that the poem was intended to be a warning to the United States concerning the cost of imperialism, most considered it to be an endorsement of the belief that white westerners have a moral obligation to "civilize" and help "lesser peoples."

ISOLATIONISM

While more and more US citizens and leaders were advocating imperialism, others preached **isolationism**. They believed it was not in the best interest of the United States to acquire and exercise control over foreign territories. They felt that such acquisitions would inevitably pull the US into foreign conflicts of which isolationists wanted no part. While some pointed to domestic concerns and believed that it was not economically nor politically wise to expand, others made the case that expansion contradicted the very principles of freedom and self-government on which the United States was founded.

THE PACIFIC

Cartoon: Seward's Folly

(Library of Congress)

Initially, most expansionists turned their attention towards the Pacific. Both political leaders and businessmen saw the Pacific as crucial because it was the pathway to the promising foreign markets of China and Southeast Asia. To promote unthreatened access to these markets, Secretary of State William Seward negotiated the purchase of Alaska from Russia in 1867. Most people in the US thought it was a foolish move and labeled the transaction "**Seward's Folly**."

Seward, however, wanted the Russians away from the North American coast. He was also concerned about British influence in Canada and correctly saw Alaska as a land rich in natural resources and full of great economic potential for the United States.

While many US citizens could not see the wisdom in buying Alaska, **Hawaii** was a different story. Not only were the islands home to Pearl Harbor (a potentially important naval base), they were economically important as well. During the 1850s, business leaders in the United States began investing in sugar plantations in Hawaii. As time passed, these owners gained economic control over the islands and struggled for power with the Hawaiian monarchy. In 1893, the wealthy white plantation owners rebelled against Queen Liliuokalani, who opposed the increasing control of the owners. With the help of US troops from a nearby ship, the plantation owners seized the islands and deposed the queen. After attempts to annex the islands were initially blocked in Washington, the United States finally annexed Hawaii and made it a US territory in 1898.

Queen Liliuokalani

(Library of Congress)

Practice 6.1: The US Looks Outward

1. Someone who favored US imperialism supported which of the following?

   A. the United States acquiring foreign territories

   B. the United States staying out of foreign conflicts

   C. the United States strengthening the economies of foreign countries

   D. the United States focusing on economic interests rather than military strength

2. What were some of the arguments used to support US expansion?

3. Someone who opposed US expansion and involvement in foreign affairs is known as what?

   A. an imperialist

   B. an isolationist

   C. an expansionist

   D. a militarist

Chapter 6

6.2 THE SPANISH - AMERICAN WAR

Theodore Roosevelt

In the late 1800s, the island of **Cuba** was still under Spanish rule. In 1895, the Cuban people rebelled. Spain sent 150,000 troops to restore order. As part of their strategy, the Spanish relocated thousands of Cuban citizens to concentration camps. These camps had miserable conditions, and many Cubans died.

As pressure mounted for the US to intervene, competing newspapers printed stories about the Spanish abuses against the Cubans. Often exaggerated and untrue, these stories were meant to sell papers rather than accurately report the facts. They also served to ignite the emotions of the US public. This brand of journalism became known as "yellow journalism," and it contributed to calls for war with Spain.

One of the many voices calling for war was that of Assistant Secretary of the Navy, **Theodore Roosevelt**. When war finally came, Roosevelt resigned his position in the administration to become a Lt. Colonel and command a group of volunteers known as the Rough Riders.

The **Spanish-American War** officially began as a result of what happened on February 15, 1898. A US battleship, the *USS Maine*, exploded while anchored in a Cuban harbor. Immediately, the newspapers blamed Spain, and US citizens demanded war. Although it was later determined that the explosion was most likely an accident, Congress adopted a resolution declaring war on Spain in April 1898.

Commodore Dewey

USS Maine

Upon hearing of the declaration of war, US Commodore George Dewey set sail for another Spanish colony — **the Philippines**. Destroying the Spanish fleet there, Dewey quickly seized control of the Philippine Islands.

Meanwhile, in Cuba, Roosevelt led the Rough Riders in bold charges up Kettle and San Juan Hills. This became the most famous incident of the war and helped the United States achieve victory over the Spanish.

In less than three months, the United States had defeated Spain in both Cuba and the Philippines. To people in the US, it seemed like a relatively easy victory. John Hay, the future secretary of state and good friend of Theodore Roosevelt, captured what most people felt regarding the entire conflict when he referred to the taking of the Philippines as "a splendid little war."

Rough Riders in Cuba

Cuba, Puerto Rico, and Guam

The Spanish-American War officially ended with the signing of the Treaty of Paris. Attached to Congress' 1898 war resolution with Spain was the **Teller Amendment**, which promised that the United States would allow for Cuban independence by not annexing the territory. However, to protect US business interests, President William McKinley installed a US military government for three years to restore stability.

In 1900, when the Cubans began drafting their own constitution, the United States continued to exercise its influence by insisting that the document include the **Platt Amendment**. This amendment put limits on what the Cuban government could do, gave the US two naval bases in Cuba, and allowed for US intervention in the region whenever the United States believed it was necessary. The Platt Amendment stayed in effect until the early 1930s. Meanwhile, Puerto Rico became a US territory which US leaders hoped to use as a base to ward off foreign threats in the Caribbean, while Guam became a US territory in the Pacific.

The Philippines

Of all the territory involved in the Spanish-American War, none caused more controversy or division than the Philippines. People in the US clearly understood reasons for occupying Cuba during the war; but the Philippines were all the way on the other side of the world and seemed to many to have little to do with events in the Caribbean. Those who opposed expansion argued that annexing the Philippines would undermine democracy and increase the likelihood of future wars in the Pacific. Some even joined the **Anti-Imperialist League** financed by Andrew Carnegie.

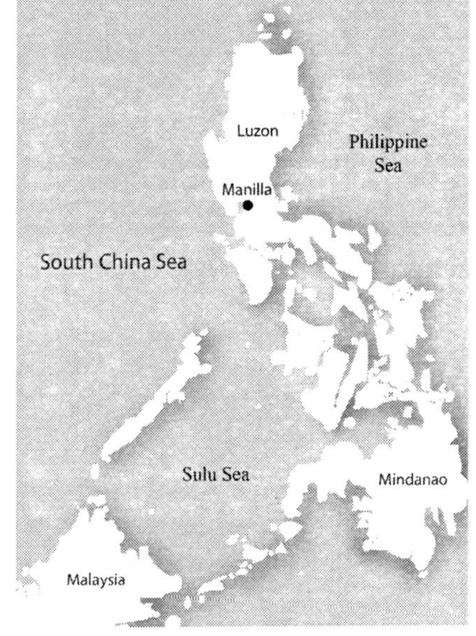

Roosevelt and others, however, saw the Philippines as crucial for protecting US economic interests in Southeast Asia. While debate raged in Washington, Filipino resistance to the US occupation resulted in warfare that lasted more than two years. Finally, in 1902, the Philippines became an "unorganized territory" of the United States. Later, in 1946, the Philippines officially became an independent nation.

Practice 6.2: The Spanish – American War

1. What happened to Cuba after the Spanish-American War?
   - A. It remained part of Spain.
   - B. It became part of the United States.
   - C. It rebelled against US intervention.
   - D. It became an independent country

2. Why did expansionists want to annex the Philippines? What arguments did anti-imperialists give for opposing this action? How was the issue of the Philippines ultimately settled?

6.3 Foreign Policy After the War

China and Japan

Boxer Rebellion

The end of the 19th century marked a new era in US foreign policy (how the US approaches its relationships with other countries). In addition to protecting its newly acquired territories, the US entered the twentieth century hoping to expand its trade with China. Fearing that European imperial powers would try to gain control over Chinese exports and markets, the United States insisted on an **Open Door Policy** that would leave China open for US trade and commerce.

Some Chinese nationalists, however, wanted to bring an end to foreign influence in China altogether. Known as the "Boxers," these nationalists massacred three hundred foreigners and Chinese Christians in 1900 to launch the Boxer Rebellion. The US and other imperial powers sent troops to fight the nationalists and eventually put down the rebellion. The US, fearing that other imperialist nations would use the rebellion as an excuse to seize more Chinese territory, strongly reaffirmed its devotion to keeping an Open Door Policy in the region.

Meanwhile, as the US was dealing with Spain, Japan began asserting its influence in Southeast Asia. Between 1894 and 1905, the Japanese successfully launched wars against both China and Russia. As a result, President Theodore Roosevelt distrusted Japan and felt that US interests in the Pacific were potentially threatened. In 1907, Roosevelt sent the US Navy (by now second in strength only to Great Britain's) to sail around the world. The president's main goal was to show the Japanese the strength of the US fleet and make them think twice before moving against more of China or the Philippines.

Cruiser *USS Newark*

THE PANAMA CANAL

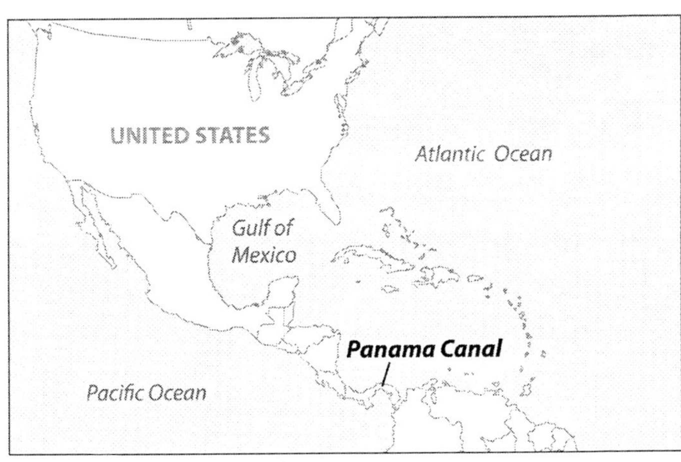

Panama Canal

Following the assassination of President William McKinley in 1901, Theodore Roosevelt became the 26th president of the United States. In order to enable US ships to move more quickly between the Atlantic and Pacific Oceans, Roosevelt envisioned a canal across the isthmus of Panama. This canal would serve US military and economic interests by allowing ships to travel between US territories in the Pacific (the Philippians, Hawaii, and Guam) and those in the Atlantic (ports in Cuba and Puerto Rico) without having to go around South America. Unfortunately for the president, the Colombian government which controlled the territory refused to sell or lease the land necessary for the project.

Then, in 1903, the Panamanian people revolted against the Colombians. Roosevelt responded by providing US naval support that helped the Panamanians win their independence. In return, the Panamanians allowed the US to lease the land needed for the canal. Construction got underway in 1905. In 1914, workers completed construction of the **Panama Canal**.

THE ROOSEVELT COROLLARY ("BIG STICK" DIPLOMACY)

By the 1900s, the United States was becoming a major player in world affairs. In 1904, President Roosevelt issued Roosevelt's Corollary. It was a statement which expanded upon the Monroe Doctrine. Monroe had said that the US would not allow European powers to colonize newly independent nations in the western hemisphere, nor would the US interfere with such nations. Roosevelt modified this by saying that the US had the right to intervene in the region *if* a nation had trouble paying its debts. Roosevelt wanted to make sure that imperialist nations did not use debt collection as an excuse to occupy territories in the Caribbean or Latin America.

This doctrine came to be known as Roosevelt's "**big stick diplomacy.**" The name came from a West African proverb which said, "Speak softly and carry a big stick; you will go far." It meant that the US did not intend to be a threatening presence in the Western Hemisphere, but neither would it hesitate to forcefully protect its own interests.

William Howard Taft and "Dollar Diplomacy"

Following Roosevelt, President William Taft sought to "substitute money for bullets" and promoted a foreign policy known as **"dollar diplomacy."** He believed that the US could best maintain order in nations abroad by increasing US foreign investments. As a result, his administration encouraged US bankers to invest in Latin America and the Caribbean and wired US financial help to China to finance railroads. Unfortunately, Taft's policy sometimes meant huge losses for US businesses. It also created enemies among some Latin American peoples who opposed US involvement and resented US efforts to "buy influence" in the region.

Taft

Woodrow Wilson's "Moral / Missionary Diplomacy"

Woodrow Wilson

In 1913, President **Woodrow Wilson** succeeded Taft and renounced dollar diplomacy. Instead, he advocated what came to be known as **"missionary diplomacy"** (sometimes referred to as **"moral diplomacy"**). Wilson based his foreign policy on the idealistic view that it was the role of the US to promote democracy and moral progress in the world. For this reason, he opposed imperialism and proclaimed that the US would not, "...seek one additional foot of territory by conquest."

Unfortunately for Wilson, however, events abroad soon tested his convictions. In 1915, when a series of revolutions and assassinations rocked the nation of Haiti, Wilson sent in the US Marines to protect US property and banking interests which had been established under dollar diplomacy. Fearing that the US intended to make the country a US territory, many Haitians responded violently. Following a series of bloody skirmishes, the Haitian government ended the violence by signing a treaty that made Haiti a protectorate — but not a territory — of the United States.

Practice 6.3: Foreign Policy After the War

1. *"Speak softly and carry a big stick..."* is associated with the foreign policy of which US president?

   A. Theodore Roosevelt
   B. William Taft
   C. Woodrow Wilson
   D. William McKinley

2. What did Wilson hope to see flourish as a result of his "missionary diplomacy?"
   A. US business interests in Haiti
   B. federal protection of citizens in New Mexico
   C. democracy in the Western Hemisphere
   D. US investments in Latin America

3. What was meant by the term "Open Door Policy," and how did this policy lead to US troops being involved in the Boxer Rebellion?

4. What were the basic differences in Roosevelt's "big stick diplomacy," Taft's "dollar diplomacy," and Wilson's "missionary / moral diplomacy?"

6.4 Beginnings of World War I

The Roots of War

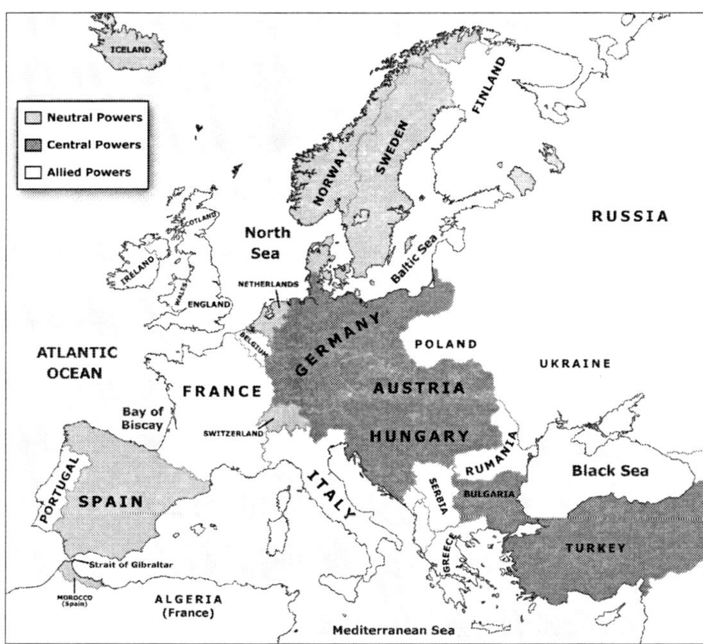

In 1914, **World War I (WWI)** broke out in Europe. Although it originally began as a conflict between European powers, it eventually involved the United States and a number of other nations as well.

The causes of this great conflict were in place long before the first shots were ever fired. In the years leading up to WWI, a spirit of **nationalism** (pride in one's own country or nationality) was sweeping across Europe. This nationalism resulted in countries being far more concerned with their own interests than with those of Europe as a whole. It also took the form of certain ethnic groups (groups with different racial/cultural backgrounds) within existing countries wanting to establish their own independence.

In order to protect their self interests, many nations adopted a policy of **militarism** (the process by which a nation builds up its military might for the purpose of intimidating and deterring other countries). This led to an arms race in which countries continually tried to produce more advanced weapons. Countries also formed **alliances**. Alliances are agreements between nations to help each other in the event of war. If one country in an alliance is attacked, then the other countries in the alliance agree to come to that nation's defense. This means that an attack against one nation can actually drag several into war, thereby setting up a domino effect. By 1914, almost no nation in Europe could become involved in military conflict without the whole continent being pulled in with it.

THE WAR BEGINS

Archduke Ferdinand

The spark that ignited the "Great War" finally happened on June 28, 1914. Archduke Francis Ferdinand, the heir to the throne of Austria-Hungary, was visiting the province of Bosnia. Operating within the province was a Serbian nationalist group known as the "Black Hand." Members of this group were radicals who believed that Bosnia belonged to Serbia rather than Austria-Hungary. During his visit, one of these nationalists assassinated the Archduke and his wife. Austria-Hungary accused Serbia of being involved in the assassination and threatened to go to war. Russia, which was allied with Serbia, mobilized (prepared for war) and vowed to intervene if Austria-Hungary attacked. This brought Germany into the mix because of their alliance with Austria-Hungary. Within two months the dominos fell. Due to the existing alliances, Europe was divided and at war. Great Britain, France, and Russia formed an alliance called the Triple Entente. Meanwhile, Germany and Austria-Hungary lined up against them as the Central Powers.

THE US REMAINS NEUTRAL

President Wilson

At first, the United States did not get involved in the war. On August 4, 1914, President Woodrow Wilson officially declared the United States neutral (not backing either side).

Many in the United States believed in isolationism and did not see a war in Europe as being of any concern to the US. Many citizens became peace activists during this period. Others supported a policy of preparedness, which advocated neutrality while taking steps to prepare for war just in case it became necessary. US policy towards the war became the key issue in the 1916 election. Wilson narrowly won a second term running on the slogan, "He kept us out of war!"

The US Enters the War

Kaiser Wilhelm II

Despite Wilson's original desire for neutrality, a number of factors eventually led to US involvement in the war. While many recent immigrants to the US were of German descent and tended to favor the Central Powers, most of the country's public opinion supported the Triple Entente. This was in large part because US bankers had loaned large amounts of money to Great Britain and had a vested interest in Britain winning the war. In addition, the British had managed to cut the main lines of communication from Germany to the United States. As a result, images of the war that reached the United States predominantly came from Great Britain. As time passed, people in the US came to see Kaiser Wilhelm II, the leader of Germany, as a ruthless aggressor out to destroy democracy and freedom.

The Lusitania

One of Germany's fiercest weapons in WWI was their dreaded **U-boats** (submarines). Hidden under water, these U-boats wreaked havoc in the Atlantic during the war. The Germans warned all nations that they would attack any ships entering or leaving British ports. President Wilson rejected the warning, arguing that no warring party could be allowed to disrupt neutral shipping on the high seas.

The *Lusitania* sinks

In reality, however, the US was not entirely neutral. Unknown to passengers, the US had begun shipping military supplies to Great Britain aboard commercial cruise liners. One of these liners, the ***Lusitania***, was torpedoed by a German U-boat in 1915. Twelve hundred people died in the attack, including 128 US citizens.

People in the US were furious! A wave of anti-German feeling swept across the country. Not wanting to pull the United States into the war, Germany agreed not to attack US passenger ships. However, in 1917, the Germans resumed their attacks on merchant and commercial ships, moving the United States closer to war.

The Zimmerman Telegram

In 1917, the US also intercepted the **Zimmerman Telegram**. Arthur Zimmerman, the German Foreign Minister, sent a telegram to the German embassy in Mexico. In his telegram, Zimmerman told embassy officials to ask Mexico to attack the US if it declared war on Germany. In return, Germany promised to help Mexico win back land the US had acquired as a result of the Mexican-American War.

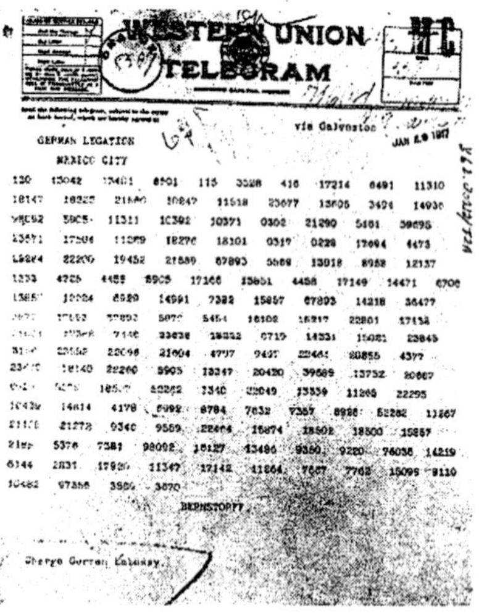

Zimmerman Telegram

News of this communication did not go over well in the United States. Anti-German sentiment increased even more, and President Wilson chose to break off diplomatic relations with Germany. Likewise, the sinking of US ships meant that the United States could no longer stay neutral. In March 1917, Wilson made an idealistic case for war and proclaimed that "the world must be made safe for democracy." Wilson wanted the US public to see the war as a battle between good and evil; he wanted the people to view it as a fight between democracy and tyranny. Congress passed a war resolution soon afterwards, and in April 1917, the United States officially entered World War I.

Practice 6.4: Beginnings of the Great War

1. Isolationists would have likely backed which of these actions?

   A. sending military troops to aid the British because of business interests in Great Britain

   B. staying out of the conflict in Europe because it is someone else's fight

   C. being prepared to intervene on the side of the Triple Entente if it appeared they were about to lose the war

   D. sending weapons and financial support to Austria-Hungary

2. Which of the following contributed **least** to the start of World War I?

   A. strong feelings of nationalism in Europe

   B. strong feelings of isolationism in the United States

   C. alliances among nations in Europe

   D. the desire of certain groups to see Bosnia as part of Serbia

3. What factors caused the US to abandon neutrality and enter the war?

6.5 US Involvement in World War I

The war featured new technology like the machine gun (mechanical gun that could fire lots of rounds very rapidly), hand grenades (hand-held explosives that could be thrown at the enemy) and mustard gas (poisonous gas first used by the Germans). These advanced weapons significantly transformed warfare, and leaders on both sides had great difficulty adjusting their tactics. As a result, the European powers found themselves at a virtual stalemate (neither side with an advantage) and their armies mired in **trench warfare**. Trenches were long ditches in which soldiers would take cover while they fired on the enemy. Since they could not advance without being exposed to fire and suffering heavy losses, both sides lived for long periods of time in wet, dirty, rat-infested trenches.

Hand-to-Hand Fighting

American Soldiers in Trenches

The United States was not prepared to send a large army to Europe right away. In order to boost the number of US soldiers, Congress passed the **Selective Service Act** authorizing a draft of young men for military service. Many of these draftees, as well as volunteers, went oversees to fight as part of the American Expeditionary Force (AEF) and became known as "doughboys." No one is certain as to the origins of the nickname, but there is no doubt that these soldiers played a vital role in helping the Triple Entente and its allies defeat the Central Powers.

Poster Depicting the Harlem Hellfighters

Among their number was the 369th Infantry Regiment. Known as the **"Harlem Hellfighters,"** the 369th was an all African American unit that served so admirably in combat that it was given France's highest medal for bravery and distinguished service during the war.

Chapter 6

Turning Points in the War

Russia Pulls Out

By early 1917, the Russians were tired of fighting. They had lost almost two million lives, not to mention the countless sick and wounded. Many of their people were starving while the nation's resources went to support the war effort rather than to feed the hungry.

Vladimir Lenin

In March 1917, the **Russian Revolution** took place. Those supporting democracy removed Czar Nicholas II from power and established a new republic. This republican government did not last long. By November, the Bolsheviks, under the leadership of Vladimir Lenin, took over the country and established a communist regime. Having received assistance from Germany in exchange for a guarantee of peace, the Bolsheviks pulled Russia out of the war. With the Russians no longer involved, the Germans did not have to worry about fighting anyone to the east of them and could focus on fighting their enemies to the west.

US Troops Save Paris and Help Turn the War

Now that Russia was no longer a concern, Germany concentrated all of its efforts on taking Paris. Within two months, the German forces were within fifty miles of the French capital. Then, in early June, US Marines helped fight off the advancing Germans and turn the tide of the war. With Paris saved, the Allies (countries fighting against the Central Powers) used a new weapon, the tank (armed ironclad vehicles), to push through the German lines. Sensing that the war had turned against them, the Germans had no choice but to seek terms of peace. Finally, in late 1918, they signed an **armistice** (cease-fire or agreement to stop fighting) ending hostilities.

Captured German Guns in Paris
(Library of Congress)

After the War

Once the fighting had ceased, the leaders of the warring nations met together for a peace conference in Paris. President Wilson went to the conference with no desire to punish Germany, nor did he hope to acquire territory for the United States. Wilson's goal was to help establish peace and stability in Europe. He put forth a peace proposal known as the **"Fourteen Points."** Among other things, Wilson's plan called for a reduction in armaments (weapons) and the right of self-determination (power to govern oneself) for ethnic groups like those in Austria-Hungary.

Big Four

Wilson also proposed the founding of the **League of Nations**. The purpose of the League would be to provide a place where countries could engage in diplomacy (negotiate peaceful solutions to their differences rather than go to war).

The ideals behind the League of Nations were ones which Wilson had held for some time. Even before the United States entered the war in 1917, Wilson had alluded to them in a speech he gave to the US Senate. In his speech, Wilson stated that the only lasting peace would be a peace that united nations. He called for a **"peace without victory,"** and stated that a peace imposed by a victor upon a loser would only give birth to resentment that leads to conflict. The only lasting peace, Wilson believed, would be a peace agreed upon by "equals." This belief was at the heart of Wilson's peace plan, and the League was meant to be the institution through which such a peace could be reached.

A number of nations joined the League of Nations. Ironically, the United States was not one of them. Isolationism grew strong again in the US after the war, and the United States Senate would not ratify the Treaty of Versailles which ended the war and sanctioned the League of Nations. Opponents feared that commitment to an international organization would lead to binding alliances that might drag the nation into another costly war.

THE TREATY OF VERSAILLES

Treaty of Versailles

While Wilson wanted peace and stability, many of his European allies wanted retribution. The European countries had suffered longer and lost far more lives than the US (over twenty million Europeans died in WWI). In June 1919, the Allies forced Germany to sign the **Treaty of Versailles**. The treaty made Germany take total responsibility for the war and made it pay reparations (money to compensate for losses from the war) to the Allies. These conditions ultimately led to economic depression and great bitterness on the part of most Germans. Wilson's predictions about "peace" imposed by victors upon the defeated proved to be true. The resentment felt by the German people ultimately made it possible for a young, charismatic leader named Adolf Hitler to rise to power and plunge Europe back into war.

In the meantime, Wilson's plea for the United States to ratify the treaty and join the League of Nations fell on deaf ears. Despite his masterful diplomacy in Paris, Wilson failed to convince his own country to sign the treaty ending World War I.

Chapter 6

Government Actions at Home

Wartime Propaganda

Although the fighting had taken place overseas, World War I had a huge effect on life in the US as well. For starters, the war in Europe meant an increased role for government in the United States. Using powers granted to him by Congress, Woodrow Wilson helped establish the **War Industries Board** to regulate the nation's economy as it sought to obtain supplies for the US military and its allies. Wilson also set up the **Committee on Public Information (CPI)** for the purpose of encouraging public support for the US war effort. Through various forms of propaganda, the CPI painted a picture of the Germans as evil monsters that it was the nation's duty to fight and defeat.

In 1917, Wilson appointed future president Herbert Hoover to head the Food Administration. Hoover's task was to encourage the US population to conserve food that could be used in the war effort. The government also launched efforts to conserve fuel nationwide. This led to the idea of daylight savings time. By having citizens turn their clocks ahead one hour during certain months, people would have more daylight and have to burn less fuel.

The federal government also passed a number of laws limiting civil liberties. In the name of protecting national security, Congress passed the **Espionage** and **Sedition Acts**. These acts made it illegal to interfere with the draft, obstruct the sale of Liberty Bonds, or make statements considered disloyal to, or critical of, the government, the Constitution, or the US military. Socialist leader, Eugene Debs, was actually sentenced to ten years in prison under these laws for criticizing the US government. Just a few years earlier, he had been a candidate for president.

1920 Election

Warren G. Harding

After World War I, people in the United States wanted a return to the security they'd felt before the war. In 1920, they elected **Warren G. Harding** president of the United States. Harding won much of his support by stating that the nation needed a **"return to normalcy."** As things turned out, however, the 1920s ended up being a decade of great change and innovation prior to one of the most challenging chapters in US history.

Practice 6.5: US Involvement in World War I

1. Why were the European Allies more interested in retribution than the United States after the war?

2. Which of the following could have been an accurate newspaper headline in the US regarding the war?

   A. "Russia Switches Sides: Helps Germany Attack Allies"

   B. "German Troops Conquer Paris"

   C. "American Black Soldiers Honored by France"

   D. "United States Senate Ratifies Treaty Ending the War"

3. What were the effects of the Treaty of Versailles on Germany and how did the conditions in this treaty conflict with the principles set forth in Wilson's "Peace Without Victory" speech?

4. For which of the following reasons did the US fail to join the League of Nations?

   A. President Wilson refused to join because the European powers had changed too many of its conditions.

   B. Isolationist sentiment in the US kept the United States Senate from ratifying the treaty that would have made the US a member.

   C. European nations would not accept US membership because the United States had not suffered as much as they had during the war.

   D. It could not afford the dues.

5. What actions did the US government take at home as a result of the war?

CHAPTER 6 REVIEW

Key Terms

imperialism
national security
nationalism
The White Man's Burden
isolationism
Seward's Folly
Hawaii
Cuba
Theodore Roosevelt
Spanish-American War
the Philippines
Teller Amendment
Platt Amendment
Anti-Imperialist League
Open Door Policy
Panama Canal
big stick diplomacy
dollar diplomacy
Woodrow Wilson
missionary/moral diplomacy
World War I
nationalism
militarism
alliances
U-boats
Lusitania
Zimmerman Telegram
trench warfare
Selective Service Act
Harlem Hellfighters
Russian Revolution
armistice
Fourteen Points
League of Nations
peace without victory
Treaty of Versailles
War Industries Board
Committee on Public Information
Food Administration
Espionage and Sedition Acts
Warren G. Harding
return to normalcy

Chapter 6 Review Questions

1. Which of the following would be **least** likely to agree with imperialism?

   A. President Theodore Roosevelt

   B. someone associated with jingoism

   C. an isolationist

   D. an expansionist

2. Of the following, which territory became the center of greatest debate between expansionist and isolationists after the Spanish-American War?

   A. Cuba

   B. the Philippines

   C. Guam

   D. Puerto Rico

> *"What a leader! What a man of conviction! He advocated war and then, when it came, he left his comfortable office in Washington to go to the front and lead in the fighting. Not only that, but he led his volunteers in a heroic charge that helped win the war. Without hesitation, I support him as he becomes our next vice president."*

3. The above quote is talking about whom?

   A. William McKinley

   B. Commodore George Dewey

   C. Theodore Roosevelt

   D. William Taft

4. The Open Door Policy was meant to ensure trade with which country?

   A. Spain
   C. the Philippines

   B. China
   D. Hawaii

5. Which of the following president's official foreign policy would have been the **most** likely to advocate exerting influence over other nations by economic means?

   A. William McKinley
   C. William Taft

   B. Theodore Roosevelt
   D. Woodrow Wilson

6. Which US president would have been the **most** likely to oppose expansion on ideological grounds?

   A. Theodore Roosevelt
   C. William Taft

   B. Woodrow Wilson
   D. William McKinley

7. Which president advocated "big stick" diplomacy?

   A. Woodrow Wilson
   C. William McKinley

   B. William Taft
   D. Theodore Roosevelt

8. Leaders from three different countries meet together and agree that if one is attacked, the other two will go to war to protect it. This is an example of what?

   A. nationalism
   C. militarism

   B. internationalism
   D. alliances

9. "He kept us out of war!" proved to be a successful slogan for Wilson in 1916, in large part due to which of the following?

   A. Theodore Roosevelt had led the nation into war with Spain years earlier

   B. the strong desire for alliances that would keep us out of war

   C. the desire of many citizens to only enter the war once it appeared that Germany was beaten

   D. the fact that isolationism was a common sentiment in the US at the time

10. A diplomat stands before an international group of leaders and argues that the only lasting peace will be a peace agreed on by *all* nations involved in a conflict, rather than one imposed on weaker nations by stronger ones. This diplomat's views are consistent with which of the following?

    A. the views of an isolationist

    B. the principles put forth in Wilson's "Peace Without Victory" speech

    C. the conditions laid out in the Treaty of Versailles

    D. the conditions agreed upon at the Paris Peace Conference

11. The United States Senate refused to approve US membership in the League of Nations. The Senate's reasoning for not joining the League can **best** be described as which of the following?

    A. A militaristic spirit that viewed the US as superior to other countries and therefore wanted to use the threat of US military strength to intimidate and control other nations.

    B. A spirit of nationalism that felt the League of Nations did not do enough to grant concessions to the US following WWI.

    C. A spirit of isolationism and fear that such an organization would bind the US in alliances that could easily lead to future conflicts.

    D. A spirit of politics in which the Republican controlled Senate was not about to let a Democratic president get the credit for creating a successful international body.

Chapter 7
Roaring 20s and the Great Depression

This chapter addresses the following standard(s):

New Indicators	6.1, 6.2, 6.3, 6.4
Old Indicators	7.1, 7.2, 7.3, 7.4, 7.5

7.1 Scientific Innovations and Cultural Transformation

The 1920s proved to be a period of transformation. The economy boomed as new machinery and innovative approaches to production fueled market growth and created jobs and income. Meanwhile, new social ideas and trends greatly changed the American way of life.

Life in 1920s

New Scientific Ideas and Discoveries

Darwin

During the 1870s, many people began to question and re-examine traditionally held beliefs in light of new scientific theories and discoveries. Charles Darwin's theories about **evolution** (the idea that all life on earth, including human life, evolved over time) challenged the idea that the Bible's account of creation was literally true. Meanwhile, scholars introduced **"higher criticism"** which proposed that the Bible should be studied as any other work of literature or history to determine its validity and relevance. Such radical ideas alarmed many traditionalists who felt that their beliefs were under attack.

The "Monkey Trial"

Some interpreted scientific discoveries to be contradictions of traditional religious views. Others looked at world events like World War I and questioned the existence of God in a world with such suffering. Still others were directly attacking the legitimacy of the Bible in the name of scholarly study. As a response to such views, **fundamentalism** gained momentum during the early part of the century. Fundamentalists believe that the Bible is literally true and, because it is from God, cannot contain contradictions or errors. The debate between fundamentalism and scientific theory gained national attention during the **Scopes Trial** in 1925.

Nicknamed the "monkey trial," it centered around a science teacher named John Scopes. Scopes was arrested for violating a Tennessee law that forbade teaching Darwin's theory of evolution instead of the Bible's account of creation.

Clarence Darrow and William Jennings Bryan
Scopes Trial

Fundamentalist and former presidential candidate, William Jennings Bryan, volunteered to prosecute Scopes. Meanwhile, former Eugene Debs attorney, Clarence Darrow, went to Tennessee to represent the accused teacher. The trial reached a climax when Darrow put Bryan himself on the stand and got him to admit that even he did not interpret everything in the Bible literally. Scopes was ultimately found guilty and the law against teaching evolution remained in effect.

New Technology

There were innovations in business as well. Although he was not the first to invent the automobile, **Henry Ford** was the first to perfect and successfully market it. In 1907, Ford sold 30,000 of his first, mass-produced car — the Model T.

Henry Ford

What truly set Ford apart was his vision for **mass production**. He decided to produce enough automobiles that he could afford to sell them at greatly reduced prices, thus allowing "ordinary people" to be able to afford his cars. To achieve this goal, Ford relied on the **assembly line**. Assembly lines had existed before; but Ford's was innovative because it had the employees stay in one spot while the assembly line brought the parts to them. Up until that time, parts remained stationary while employees moved from station to station.

Ford also saw his **workers as consumers**. He wanted those who made his cars to also be able to buy them. For this reason, Ford paid his workers an unheard of $5 per day wage.

From 1907 until 1926, Ford built half the automobiles in the world (16,750,000 cars). The automobile greatly changed the face of US culture by allowing people to become more mobile, live further away from where they worked, and attend activities and events that otherwise would have been inaccessible. His cars, along with the advent of public transportation (electric trolleys, etc.) helped give rise to the new middle class and the US suburb.

While Ford revolutionized the auto industry, the **airline industry** came into being as well. In 1903, brothers Orville and Wilbur Wright successfully conducted the first flight at Kitty Hawk, North Carolina. Soon after, airplanes were used for military service and to carry the US mail. In 1926, the nation saw the birth of commercial air travel that carried passengers across country for business and pleasure faster than ever before. One of the industry's greatest boosts came in 1927 when US pilot, Charles Lindbergh, became the first person to fly solo and non-stop across the Atlantic Ocean.

Wright Brothers' First Flight

New Appliances and Forms of Entertainment

The increased availability of electricity in homes allowed a variety of **new appliances** to become more common in the 1920s. Refrigerators meant that more food could be bought at one time and then stored for longer periods without fear of it spoiling. Meanwhile, sewing machines, vacuum cleaners, and washing machines greatly reduced the amount of time needed to do traditional chores around the house. As a result of technological advances, people began finding themselves with more time for leisure activity.

Advances in transportation and the use of electric power also gave birth to a bustling **nightlife**, in which people ventured into the city after dark to attend shows, have dinner, or take part in evening social events.

Simultaneously, a new **mass media** formed. National magazines allowed news stories and businesses to reach people nationwide. **Radio** became an important medium for entertainment and communication, as people across the nation began enjoying the same shows and hearing the same news reports. It also transformed politics by giving leaders direct access to larger numbers of people.

Between 1910 and 1930, the **movie industry** boomed in the United States. First to silent pictures, and then to movies with sound (called "talkies"), people flocked to be entertained by the big screen. The fashions and lifestyles portrayed in the movies helped define a national culture. People all over the nation wanted to wear the clothes they saw in the movies, drive the cars they saw on screen, and take part in the fads popularized by Hollywood. As a result, movie stars became national icons.

Poster for the First Full-Length "Talkie"

The New Consumerism

Innovative techniques of mass production (producing large amounts of a product) meant that producers could afford to sell their goods at less cost to consumers. Advertisers convinced US citizens that they not only wanted but *needed* certain products. Innovations like the **installment plan** transformed the consumer market. Under these plans, producers and businesses offered easy credit that allowed consumers to pay a little at a time rather than all at once. People could purchase more expensive items (like cars and refrigerators) much sooner than normal. This caused sales of such products to boom during the twenties.

For the first time, the United States became a **consumer society**. In the past, people had concentrated on saving money. Now, as people began to measure their social status by how much they could buy and own, they began to save less and spend more. While this initially meant growth for the economy, it also meant that peoples' debt increased as their savings became less.

WOMEN IN THE 20S

As the decade progressed, the role and expectation of women in society continued to change drastically. Economic necessity and advances in technology led more women than ever into the US workforce. Although this was a major shift in the roles they had traditionally held, women still faced obstacles. Generally, employers only hired single women. They believed that married women would eventually have children and quit. Since there was no such thing as maternity leave in those days, this usually turned out to be the case. Therefore, women were rarely trained for or given positions of leadership.

As women's place in the US workforce increased, they began to change their dress and behavior. Women's hair got shorter and hemlines higher as women sought clothes that were comfortable and hairstyles that were more manageable. Socially, women began going out on dates instead of entertaining male visitors at home under the supervision of a chaperone. These "new women" were sometimes called **"flappers"** and they tended to be more rebellious and "fun-loving" than women of the past. They challenged the traditional gender roles in society and often caused more traditional citizens (men and women alike) great concern.

Flapper

INTELLECTUAL RESPONSES

While the decade of the twenties was mostly an era of prosperity, there were those who were disturbed by what they saw. A number of these people are remembered for their literary and artistic accomplishments. Sinclair Lewis critiqued society through stories like *Main Street, Babbit,* and *Elmer Gantry*. In 1930, he became the first US citizen in history to win the Nobel Prize for literature.

Ernest Hemingway

One group of writers became known as **"The Lost Generation"** because they felt lost in a society of greed and moral corruption. Among their number were F. Scott Fitzgerald, who authored *The Great Gatsby*, and Ernest Hemingway, who wrote of the lost generation in his novel, *The Sun Also Rises*.

The twenties also saw great cultural accomplishments within the African American community. **Jazz** became a popular form of music after World War I, as musical artists from Louisiana and Mississippi brought their talents to the northern cities. Its fast pace rhythm inspired new dances like the "Charleston" and helped create a thriving nightlife. Crossing ethnic boundaries, jazz found a receptive audience among both blacks and young whites. Louis Armstrong, a trumpeter and singer from New Orleans, was among the most noted jazz musicians.

An increase in black racial pride and awareness led many black intellectuals to write works portraying the daily lives of working class African Americans. Langston Hughes wrote memorable poetry and short stories about the black experience and reminded black Americans of their African heritage. Meanwhile, female writer, Zora Neal Hurston, gained fame for her novel *Their Eyes Were Watching God.* Many other black painters, dancers, and musicians also produced enduring works of art. Because much of this cultural movement took place in New York City, it became known as the **Harlem Renaissance**.

Zora Neal Hurston

Practice 7.1: Scientific Innovations and Cultural Transformation

1. Evolution and "higher criticism" played an important role in what?

   A. the debate that existed between new ideas and traditional beliefs

   B. cultural pursuit among African Americans

   C. innovative ideas introduced by Henry Ford

   D. the roles of women in the 1920s

2. Which of the following would be considered a "flapper?"

   A. a fundamental criticizing evolution

   B. a woman of the 20s challenging traditional gender roles

   C. a writer rebelling against the materialism of the decade

   D. an urban male enjoying the city's nightlife

3. What are some examples of how advances in technology impacted society in the 1920s?

4. What was the Harlem Renaissance and who were some of its key figures?

7.2 Social Conflicts of the 1920s

The "Red Scare" and Immigration

Initially, the Russian Revolution encouraged people in the United States. US citizens were glad to see a monarch like the czar replaced with a republican form of government. But, when the Bolsheviks took over and instituted **communism** (a political and economic philosophy in which the government owns all property and individual rights mean little compared to the welfare of the state) US citizens grew concerned. People feared that such a revolution might occur in the United States. This led to a period known as the **"Red Scare."**

When anarchists (those who want to bring down *any* form of government) attempted to assassinate Attorney General A. Mitchell Palmer and Standard Oil icon John D. Rockefeller, many associated the attacks with communism. In response, Palmer authorized the **Palmer Raids**, in which suspected communists and other "subversives" (those believed to pose a threat to the US government) — many of whom were immigrants who had committed no crimes — were arrested and jailed. More than five hundred immigrants were deported back to their countries of birth as a result of Palmer's actions.

Sacco and Vanzetti

Sacco and Vanzetti

The association of immigrants with communism and anarchy eventually resulted in one of the most controversial trials in US history. In 1920, two Italian immigrants believed to be anarchists were accused of murder in Massachusetts. Although the evidence against them was disputable and many felt they had been targeted due to their political beliefs, the court convicted Nicola Sacco and Bartolomeo Vanzetti. They were executed in 1927.

Immigration Restrictions

The new rise in **nativism** (opposition to immigration) after World War I led to efforts to restrict immigration. The government placed **quotas** (limitations) on the number of immigrants that could enter the US annually from different parts of the world. Congress passed a temporary limit to the number of immigrants who could come to the US in 1924 and permanent bans beginning in 1929. Racist in nature, many of the laws were designed to allow more immigrants from Western Europe into the country than from Eastern Europe or the Far East.

Because few laws addressed immigration from nations in the Western Hemisphere, however, the number of Hispanic Catholic immigrants (both legal and illegal) increased drastically during this time period and made Latin Americans the fastest growing minority in the United States.

Resurgence of the Ku Klux Klan

Fear of communism and mistrust of immigrants also contributed to resurgence of the **Ku Klux Klan**. Originally only targeting blacks, the Klan grew in numbers as it expanded to attack Jews, Catholics, and immigrants. Large numbers of people in the North and the South flocked to join the organization. Using intimidation and fear, Klansmen burned crosses outside people's homes, sent hate letters, and put pressure on employers to fire black or immigrant workers. When this was not enough, Klan members resorted to lynchings and other forms of violence against those they persecuted.

1920s KKK Members

Prohibition

Al Capone

In 1919, the states ratified the Eighteenth Amendment which outlawed alcoholic beverages. Congress then passed the Volstead Act which defined "intoxicating" and enforced the amendment. This ban on alcohol became known as **Prohibition**. Prohibition gave rise to a new form of outlaw, known as the bootlegger. Bootleggers were criminals who sold illegal alcohol. Their name came from the old practice of drinkers hiding flasks of liquor in the leg of their boots. Many people wanted their alcoholic drinks despite the law, so they turned to bootleggers to supply them. Some people would also go to illegal bars called speakeasies. Organized crime grew as gangsters like Al Capone used violence, intimidation, and bribes to dominate bootlegging and control public officials. Eventually, even many of those who supported the intent of Prohibition came to realize that it was a failure. The **Twenty-first Amendment** repealed (ended) Prohibition in 1933.

Practice 7.2: Social Conflicts of the 1920s

1. The phrase "Red Scare" refers to what?

   A. the fear African Americans and immigrants felt concerning the Ku Klux Klan

   B. the nation's fear that communist revolution could occur in the US

   C. the fear immigrants felt concerning postwar nativism

   D. the fear many reformers felt when Prohibition was repealed

2. Which of the following statements **best** describes Sacco and Vanzetti?

   A. They were immigrants accused of murder and believed to be anarchists.

   B. They were bootleggers who got rich off of Prohibition.

   C. They were reformers who supported Prohibition.

   D. They were nativists executed for a crime many thought they never committed.

3. How did Congress respond to the postwar wave of nativism that existed and why did the Ku Klux Klan grow in numbers during the 1920s?

7.3 The Great Depression

Prosperous Beginnings

After President Harding died in 1923, Vice President Calvin Coolidge became president. The following year, Coolidge won a full term. Coolidge supported big business and believed in *laissez-fair* economics. One of Coolidge's most famous quotes was, "The business of the American people is business." He strongly believed that the government should not interfere with the growth of business and that the natural business cycle would fix any problems in the economy.

For most of the 1920s, it appeared Coolidge was right. The stock market did very well as prices reached new highs and continued to climb. People tried to take advantage of the prosperity by buying stock on **speculation** (made high-risk investments in hopes of making high returns on their money). Many investors also engaged in something called "**buying on margin**." Under this practice, investors purchased stocks for only a portion of what they cost. They then borrowed the difference and paid interest on the loan. Many believed that the stock market was doing so well that they could still make money, even while paying such interest.

Calvin Coolidge

Technology also helped produce a booming economy. Henry Ford's mechanized assembly line revolutionized the auto industry and was starting to transform other industries as well. **Mechanization** (increased use of machinery for production) meant that products could be produced in far greater numbers and more efficiently. This increase in production meant that manufacturers could afford to charge less money. As a result, more people purchased cars, clothes, appliances, and other goods. Money kept pouring into the economy, companies did well, and jobs were created.

Farmers in the 1920s

Farmers did not enjoy the same prosperity. New machinery, such as tractors, allowed farmers to produce far more. However, this resulted in **overproduction** and caused agricultural prices to drop drastically in the 1920s. Although Congress made attempts to pass bills designed to increase farm prices, President Coolidge vetoed them. He saw them as unconstitutional efforts at price fixing. As a result, the agricultural industry was unable to recover, and many farms went into foreclosure.

Eventually, overproduction had devastating effects on the environment as well. In an attempt to take advantage of high demand for their products during WWI, midwestern farmers unknowingly stripped much of the land and left it damaged by poor farming techniques. This damage combined with a massive drought served to create a disaster in the early 30s.

Dust Bowl

The **Dust Bowl** was a series of storms that hit the Midwest, causing enormous clouds of dust to be created by the high winds. These black clouds would blanket farms, and even entire cities, as they destroyed areas and left them uninhabitable. The ruthless storms displaced hundreds of thousands of farmers, forcing them to become homeless migrants.

The Beginning of the Great Depression

Black Tuesday

Republican Herbert Hoover became president in 1929. Like Coolidge, Hoover opposed government interference in business. Unfortunately for Hoover, he took office at a time when the US economy was about to collapse. On October 29, 1929, a date known as **Black Tuesday**, the stock market crashed! Prices dropped drastically. Many who bought stock on speculation or invested by buying on the margin lost everything. Others were financially ruined as brokers and banks began to call in loans that people had no money to pay. The disaster marked the beginning of the **Great Depression**.

Herbert Hoover

Chapter 7

HARD TIMES

New York Stock Exchange

Following the stock market crash of 1929, the US economy unraveled. People rushed in mass to withdraw money from banks, causing them to close. People stopped investing in the stock market, causing stock prices to fall even further. Wealthy families suddenly found themselves with nothing. At one point, roughly a quarter of the nation was unemployed. Countless numbers of people became homeless. Many people had to rely on soup kitchens and breadlines that provided food for the poor in order to have anything to eat.

HOOVERVILLES

In larger cities, many of the homeless would gather together to live in homemade shacks. These makeshift villages came to be called **"Hoovervilles."** People named them after the president whom they blamed for their woes.

Hooverville
(Library of Congress)

FDR

In 1932, the nation elected Democrat **Franklin Delano Roosevelt** (known to millions of US citizens as "**FDR**"), president of the United States by an overwhelming majority. With a broad smile and optimistic demeanor, FDR served as a much-needed image of hope for a nation battered by the Great Depression. He became the first president to effectively use radio to his advantage. Speaking directly to the nation in a series of "**fireside chats**," he helped instill confidence and even succeeded in getting many people to redeposit their money in banks.

FDR

Unlike his predecessors, Roosevelt was also ready to experiment with government actions to deal with the nation's crisis. Roosevelt believed that the country needed the government to provide **direct relief** (federal help to those hurting from the financial crisis). Many economists and politicians argued that the economy would eventually be good if government left it alone. Roosevelt believed that this policy had already proven to be a failure and was willing to engage in **deficit spending** (government spending of borrowed money) to help get the US economy moving in the right direction.

Roosevelt introduced new legislation and a number of programs known collectively as the **New Deal**. The period from FDR's inauguration in March 1933 through the following June became known as the first hundred days. During this time, Roosevelt pushed program after program through Congress in an effort to provide economic relief and recovery.

Roosevelt's First New Deal

The following programs were part of what came to be known as Roosevelt's **New Deal.**

Civilian Conservation Corps (CCC)	Established in 1933, the CCC provided employment for unmarried men between the ages of 17 and 23. These young men worked in the national parks installing electric lines, building fire towers, and planting new trees in deforested areas.
Agricultural Adjustment Act (AAA)	Passed in 1933, this act approved government loans to farmers and paid farmers not to grow certain crops in order to increase the price of agricultural products.
Federal Deposit Insurance Corporation (FDIC)	The FDIC was established in 1933 under the **Federal Reserve Act** to insure bank deposits of up to $100,000 in case of bank failure. This insurance was intended to prevent people from withdrawing their money out of panic.
National Industrial Recovery Act (NIRA)	Passed in 1933, this law sought to bolster industrial prices and prevent US business failures. One part of the NIRA was the **Public Works Administration (PWA)**. The PWA launched a number of public works such as the construction of dams, highways, and bridges. These projects helped provide citizens with desperately needed jobs.
Tennessee Valley Authority (TVA)	Established in 1933, the TVA built hydroelectric dams to create jobs and bring cheap electricity to parts of the South that had previously been without power. The southern Appalachians were historically one of the poorest areas in the nation. With the help of the TVA, this region prospered as never before.
National Labor Relations Act (NLRA)	Also known as the Wagner Act, this act was passed in 1935 and created a board to monitor unfair management practices such as firing workers who joined unions.
Social Security Act (SSA)	**Social Security** passed in 1935. This act established retirement income for all workers once they reach the age of sixty-five. The Government passed it intending to provide income to those who were too old or disabled to work. Today, Social Security is the lone remaining program from the New Deal. One of its architects was Frances Perkins. As Roosevelt's secretary of labor, she was the first woman in history to be appointed to a US president's cabinet.
Revenue Act of 1935	This law raised taxes on those making above $50,000/year as well as corporate and estate taxes. It won the favor of many on the left and was nicknamed the "soak the rich tax."

Chapter 7

Effects of the New Deal

Although FDR's New Deal was a revolutionary approach to government, it actually failed to end the Great Depression. In fact, some historians agree that it made the crisis last longer. On the eve of World War II, much of the nation was still unemployed, and the economy was still hurting. The new Deal did, however, provide some relief and enabled the nation to stay afloat until the onset of war caused the economy to boom in the 1940s.

Labor

John L. Lewis

The New Deal helped the **labor movement** in a number of ways. The NIRA required industries to recognize workers' rights to organize/unionize. As a result, union membership increased and a powerful new union, the Committee for Industrial Organization (CIO) arose under the leadership of United Mine Workers president, John L. Lewis.

In 1937, the Supreme Court upheld the Wagner Act, causing businesses to comply even more with federal guidelines regarding unions. Due to the advances made by organized labor during the New Deal era, unions became consistent supporters of the Democratic party.

Women

Overall, **women** and minorities did not benefit from the New Deal as much as white males. Federal programs tended to show favoritism towards men on the grounds that they were the breadwinners of their families. They also allowed businesses to pay women less money than male employees. The New Deal did nothing to regulate domestic work (such as housekeepers) which was still the largest female occupation during the 1930s.

Employment Poster

Minorities

As for **minorities**, many of them still worked as farmers and migrant workers. Their lack of government payroll records often excluded them from programs like Social Security. In addition, New Deal work programs sanctioned racial segregation, maintaining the idea that it was acceptable to treat minorities and whites differently.

Laundry Day
(Library of Congress)

Throughout the Great Depression, African Americans experienced the highest ratio of unemployment among US citizens. However, most African Americans credited

FDR and his policies for the jobs they did acquire. As a result, the African American community began to shift its political loyalty from the Republican party of Lincoln to the Democratic party of Roosevelt during the mid 1930s.

Practice 7.3: The Great Depression

1. Someone who buys stock for less than what it is worth, then borrows the difference in the hopes of making money is said to be doing what?

   A. undermining *laissez-faire* economics

   B. engaging in mass production

   C. buying on margin

   D. purchasing tariffs

2. Roosevelt's plan for economic relief and recovery was called what?

   A. deficit relief

   B. the first hundred days

   C. fireside chats

   D. the New Deal

3. What was the purpose of Social Security?

4. Why did African Americans and unions drift towards the Democratic party during the Great Depression?

CHAPTER 7 REVIEW

Key Terms, People, and Concepts

evolution
higher criticism
fundamentalism
Scopes Trial
Henry Ford
mass production
assembly line
workers as consumers
airline industry
new appliances
nightlife
mass media
radio
movie industry
installment plan
consumer society
flappers
Lost Generation
jazz
Harlem Renaissance
communism
Red Scare
Palmer Raids
nativism
quotas
Ku Klux Klan
Prohibition
Twenty-first Amendment
speculation
buying on margin
mechanization
overproduction
Black Tuesday
Great Depression
Hooverville
Franklin Delano Roosevelt (FDR)
fireside chats
direct relief
deficit spending
New Deal
Federal Reserve Act
Public Works Administration (PWA)
Social Security
labor movement
women
minorities

1. How would someone associated with big business have **most** likely responded to the news that Calvin Coolidge had been elected to a full term as president?

   A. Upset, because he feared that Coolidge would regulate businesses with his *laissez-faire* policies.

   B. Upset, because he feared that Coolidge would support legislation to aid farmers rather than businessmen.

   C. With optimism, believing he would finally propose government programs to pump more money into business.

   D. With optimism, because he believed that Coolidge would not regulate business at all.

2. Which of the following contributed to booming economic times in the 1920s?

   A. higher stock prices

   B. Roosevelt's New Deal

   C. Social Security benefits from the government

   D. the overproduction of farm products

3. Which of the following statements **most** accurately describes the plight of US farmers during the 1920s?
   - A. They enjoyed prosperity like much of the nation.
   - B. They maintained the same level of economic stability they had during the war years.
   - C. They suffered because of falling prices caused by overproduction.
   - D. They suffered because of Congress' refusal to pass Coolidge's programs.

4. What was significant about FDR's "fireside chats?"
   - A. They marked the first time that a president effectively used radio.
   - B. They sparked controversy by suggesting that the nation was in a depression.
   - C. They called for an end to direct relief and deficit spending.
   - D. They helped FDR defeat Calvin Coolidge.

> *"The best day of my life was when they passed Prohibition. Before that, I was struggling to make enough money to even eat. But now... I can't count it all, the money rolls in so fast. Hey, a man's gonna drink. All I do is supply what people want. Can I sleep with myself at night? You bet I can."*

5. The above quote is **most** likely from whom?
   - A. a speakeasy
   - B. an athlete
   - C. a bootlegger
   - D. a fundamentalist

6. The work of Zora Neal Hurston **best** demonstrates what?
   - A. Women can serve effectively in a president's cabinet.
   - B. Working women benefitted greatly from Roosevelt's New Deal.
   - C. the plight of Midwest farmers in the 20s and 30s
   - D. Women played a substantial role in the Harlem Renaissance.

7. Which of the following was meant to protect bank deposits?
   - A. TVA
   - B. FDIC
   - C. Wagner Act
   - D. PWA

8. A fundamentalist could **best** be described as which of the following?

   A. a critic of FDR's New Deal because it tramples on the fundamental principles of freedom

   B. a Christian who believes that the Bible is God's word and not to be questioned

   C. a progressive who looks to science for fundamental truths

   D. an economist who opposes direct relief

9. Which of the following statements **best** describes the political loyalties of the African American community after the Great Depression?

   A. It was with the Republicans because it was the part of Lincoln.

   B. More African Americans were leaving the Democrats to support Republicans.

   C. African Americans switched loyalties from the Republicans to the Democrats.

   D. African Americans were neutral because neither party helped them enough.

10. The notion that government should spend money to provide programs to help the economy is known as

    A. fundamentalism.

    B. free economy.

    C. direct relief.

    D. buying on margin.

Chapter 8
World War II and the Early Cold War Era

This chapter addresses the following standard(s):

New Indicators	7.1, 7.2, 7.3, 7.4
Old Indicators	8.1, 8.2, 8.3, 8.4

8.1 World War II Begins

Foreign Aggression

Hitler and Germany

During the 1920s and 1930s, totalitarian dictators rose to power throughout much of Europe. In Germany, **Adolf Hitler** and his Nazi Party assumed control. Hitler's goal was to establish an empire he called the "Third Reich." In addition to ruling Germany with an iron fist, he wanted to conquer other parts of Europe and ultimately the Soviet Union. In 1936, Hitler's troops invaded the Rhineland. A few years later Germany annexed Austria and parts of Czechoslovakia as well.

Hitler

British and French leaders met with Hitler in Munich to express their concern. However, instead of answering Hitler's aggression with military force, Britain and France chose **appeasement**. This is an approach in which an aggressor nation is allowed to keep regions it has conquered in hopes that it will "appease" the country's leaders and prevent future aggression. Britain and France signed the Munich Pact, an agreement that agreed to let Germany keep the territories it had taken in exchange for a pledge not to invade anymore countries. Hitler broke the pledge in 1939 when he invaded Poland.

Stalin in the Soviet Union

In the Soviet Union, **Joseph Stalin** gained control of the Communist Party and became the country's leader. Stalin executed many of his rivals and political opponents. He tolerated no political opposition and strictly limited the Soviet people's freedom.

Mussolini in Italy

Benito Mussolini

Benito Mussolini rose to power as early as 1922. Mussolini was a fascist. Although the government did not own all the businesses and property the way it would under a communist regime, Mussolini's government certainly controlled all aspects of business and politics. Mussolini, like other dictators, did not allow political opposition.

In 1935, Mussolini's forces invaded Abyssinia in North Africa. (Today, Abyssinia is known as Ethiopia). The League of Nations condemned Mussolini's actions. Mussolini withdrew Italy from the League of Nations. Italy and Germany then became allies.

Tojo in Japan

Hideki Tojo

Beginning in the 1920s, Japan began expanding its territory. It used its military to conquer regions in China, Korea, and other parts of Eastern Asia. In 1941, a military officer named **Hideki Tojo** became Japan's prime minister. Although the country had an emperor, Tojo and his fellow generals truly controlled the government. Under their leadership, Japan continued on a course to invade more Asian nations.

Japan eventually signed an agreement with Germany and Italy. The three countries became allies. They formed an alliance that came to be called the **Axis Powers**.

The US Remains Neutral

As the Axis Powers became increasingly militaristic, the United States remained neutral. Many US citizens still believed in **isolationism**. The devastation of WWI left many in the US unwilling to become involved in another international conflict, while the economic effects of the Great Depression meant many US citizens wanted their government concerned with fixing problems at home rather than abroad. Responding to this isolationist sentiment, Congress passed the **Neutrality Act** in 1935. This act prohibited the sale of weapons to warring nations. Anti-war feeling was so strong that an amendment to the Constitution was introduced in 1937 requiring a national vote before the US could declare war. It failed by a narrow margin.

Hitler's Aggression

The Fall of Poland and France

On September 1, 1939, German forces invaded Poland starting World War II in Europe.

Then, in Spring 1940, Germany conquered Denmark, Norway, Belgium, the Netherlands, and eventually France. On June 14, German troops entered the city of Paris. Hitler made France sign an armistice yielding half the country to German control, with the remaining half to be ruled by a French, pro-German government known as the "Vichy regime" because its political center was in Vichy, France.

As a symbol of redemption for Germany's defeat in WWI, and in an attempt to humiliate the French, Hitler insisted that France sign the armistice in the very train car where Germany had been forced to sign the armistice ending the first world war years before.

Britain's Resistance

A few months later, Hitler's air force launched an air campaign against Great Britain. Hitler knew that he had to destroy Britain's mighty Royal Air Force before he could cross the English Channel and launch an invasion. In the Battle of Britain that raged from July – October 1940, thousands of German planes bombed British airfields and cities. During the almost nightly air raids, residents of London slept in subways for cover and woke up to find more and more of their city reduced to smoke and rubble.

Winston Churchhill

Churchill, however, proved to be a great leader who inspired the British people with a strong sense of nationalism and hope. Thanks to the heroism of their Royal Air Force, the British were able to fight off the German assault and resist long enough to force Hitler to give up his plans of invading Great Britain.

The United States Enters the War

Lend-Lease

Roosevelt and Churchill

In 1940, Franklin Delano Roosevelt became the only US president ever elected to a third term. Although the majority of US citizens favored neutrality, Roosevelt was already convinced that the United States could not afford to stay out of the war much longer. As Britain struggled in its fight against Germany, Roosevelt proclaimed to the United States public, "If Great Britain goes down, all of us in the Americas would be living at the point of a gun. We must be the great arsenal of democracy."

In March 1941, Congress passed the **Lend-Lease Act**. Under this act, the president could send aid to any nation whose defense was considered vital to the United States' national security. If the country had no resources to pay for the aid, the US could send it and defer payment until later. Roosevelt helped win public support for this policy by offering the analogy of a neighbor's house being on fire. "If your neighbor's house is on fire," Roosevelt reasoned, "you don't sell him a hose, you give it to him. Then, you take it back after the fire is out. This helps your neighbor and makes sure that the fire doesn't spread to your own house."

Chapter 8

PEARL HARBOR

While Hitler steamrolled through Europe, the United States also had one eye on Japan. Like other countries, Japan had been hurt by the worldwide depression. As a small series of islands, Japan also lacked many of the natural resources it needed. The Japanese military saw aggressive expansion as the answer to Japan's problems. When the United States responded to Japan's aggression by imposing an embargo (refusal to ship certain products to a country) on oil and steel, many in Japan's government felt that the time had come for Japan to take what it needed by force. After conquering Manchuria and much of China, Japan set its sights on the rich natural resources of Southeast Asia and the Dutch East Indies.

Pearl Harbor

Japan realized, however, that it could not make the advances it wanted without being threatened by the US naval fleet anchored at **Pearl Harbor**, Hawaii. Although he doubted Japan's ability to win a war with the United States, Japanese Admiral Isoroku Yamamoto knew that his country was determined to expand. He developed an all but impossible plan to sail six aircraft carriers (huge ships that carry war planes) across the Pacific undetected and launch a surprise attack on Pearl Harbor. Maintaining radio silence the entire way, the Japanese ships reached their destination as planned. US intelligence knew that the Japanese were planning an attack of some kind; they just didn't know where. Believing that the waters of Pearl Harbor were too shallow for planes to drop torpedoes (explosive devices that hit the water and then are propelled towards a target), they focused on the Philippines and the threat of sabotage (people trying to damage US military equipment, such as planes parked in hangers).

A few minutes before 8 a.m. on December 7, 1941, Japanese airplanes began the first wave of bombings on the Pacific fleet at Pearl Harbor. United States military personnel actually detected the incoming planes on radar but, thinking that they were US planes flying in from the mainland, dismissed them as nothing to be concerned about.

Meanwhile, US intelligence had finally determined that an impending attack was coming. By the time word reached Admiral Kimmel at Pearl Harbor, however, it was too late. In less than two hours, the Japanese forces sank or seriously damaged a dozen naval vessels, destroyed almost two hundred warplanes, and killed or wounded nearly three thousand people. The next day, President Roosevelt emotionally described December 7 as "a day which will live in infamy." Both houses of Congress approved a declaration of war against Japan and later against Germany and Italy as well. Suddenly, the US was plunged into the middle of World War II.

Practice 8.1: The World Goes to War

1. Why did FDR want to see the United States get involved in the war?

   A. He believed that communism was a threat and was concerned that Hitler had aligned himself with Stalin.

   B. He believed that if Great Britain fell to Hitler, it would be a threat to US democracy also.

   C. He hated the Japanese and wanted an excuse to fight them.

   D. He wanted to protect US business interests in France.

2. Why did President Roosevelt refer to December 7, 1941 as, "a day which will live in infamy?"

   A. It was the day Hitler invaded Poland and started World War II in Europe.

   B. It was the day that Japan invaded Manchuria and started worldwide aggression.

   C. It was the day German planes attacked London, putting Great Britain in jeopardy.

   D. It was the day Japanese planes bombed Pearl Harbor, pulling the US into war.

3. Why did the Japanese decide to attack Pearl Harbor?

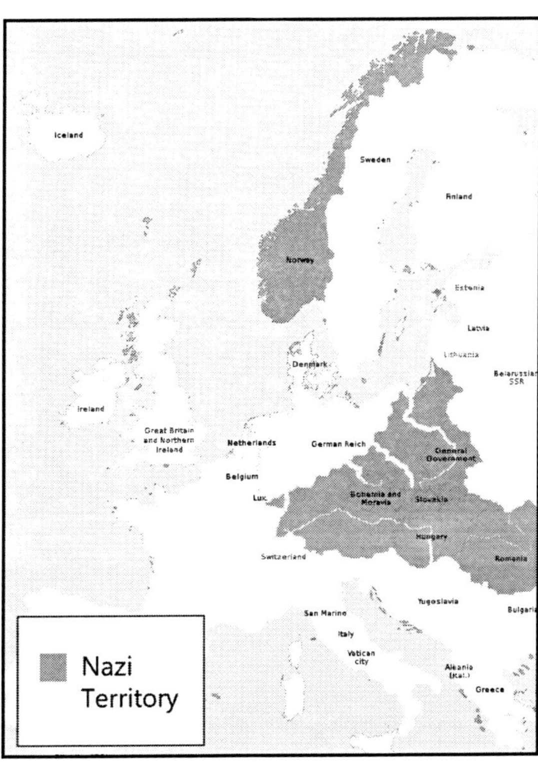

4. Which leader conquered the areas pictured on he map by the end of 1940?

   A. Benito Mussolini

   B. Joseph Stalin

   C. Adolf Hitler

   D. Winston Churchill

8.2 The Course of the War

Disagreement among Allies

Serious disagreements arose between the Soviet Union and its western allies, the United States and Great Britain. The United States and Britain did not want to launch an invasion of Western Europe until the allies first drove enemy forces from North Africa. Roosevelt and Churchill believed it was important to secure access to the Suez Canal in Egypt.

Eventually, the British and Americans succeeded in taking North Africa. Roosevelt and Churchill met in Casablanca, Morocco to discuss what to do next. They invited Stalin, but he did not attend. Together, Roosevelt and Churchill elected to invade Italy next.

Stalin resented his allies' reluctance to invade France and create a western front. He even later accused the two countries of intentionally stalling because they wanted to see the Soviet Union weakened as much as possible since it was a communist nation. While the western allies secured southern Italy, Stalin did his best to hold off advancing Germans in the East.

D-Day

D-Day

Roosevelt, Churchill, and Stalin finally met for the **Tehran Conference** in December 1943. Stalin desperately wanted the Allies to launch an invasion of France and create a second front against Hitler. In Tehran, the reluctant British finally agreed. US General Dwight D. Eisenhower was made the Supreme Allied Commander of Operation Overlord.

Dwight D. Eisenhower

On June 6, 1944, the western allies launched the **D-Day invasion**. Hitting the beaches at Normandy, France, the first soldiers ashore received overwhelming gunfire. Despite suffering heavy losses, it took the Allies less than a week to get over 500,000 troops ashore. From their established foothold, these forces were able to advance further into France. On August 25, 1944, the Allies fought their way into Paris, liberating the city from four years of German occupation.

Victory in Europe

Anticipating Germany's defeat, the **Big Three** (Roosevelt, Churchill, and Stalin) met in February 1945 at the city of Yalta and conducted the **Yalta Conference**. There, they discussed military strategy and postwar policies. During the negotiations, Stalin restated his promise to declare war on Japan after the defeat of Germany. He also agreed to allow free elections to establish democratic governments in eastern European countries freed from German occupation. In return, Roosevelt and Churchill agreed that the USSR would retain land in Poland (the US and Britain considered this only temporary) and have special rights to certain islands and Chinese lands presently under Japanese control.

Big Three at Yalta
(Library of Congress)

Because of the tremendous losses inflicted on the USSR by the war, Allies agreed that the Soviet Union would receive half of the war reparations from Germany. The resolutions of the conference included a provision for Germany being divided into four zones to be administered by the Allies following the war. In addition, the leaders scheduled a conference in San Francisco for the following April to establish the United Nations as a permanent peace-keeping organization.

German Soldiers Surrender

In the face of certain defeat, Hitler committed suicide on April 30, 1945 as Soviet troops overran Berlin. One week later, Germany surrendered unconditionally, ending the war in Europe. Sadly, President Franklin Roosevelt died on April 12 and never saw the day of victory. After many long years of war, people in the Allied countries finally celebrated V-E Day (Victory in Europe Day) on May 8, 1945.

Funeral of FDR
(Library of Congress)

Chapter 8

War in the Pacific

Within hours of the attack on Pearl Harbor, Japanese warplanes attacked Clark Field in the **Philippines**, destroying nearly half of the US airplanes stationed there. A few days later, Japanese forces invaded and eventually took the Philippines as well.

Gen. Douglas MacArthur

Battle of Midway and the US Offensive

Admiral Yamamoto, considered a military genius for orchestrating the attack on Pearl Harbor, felt that the remainder of the US Pacific Fleet must be destroyed if Japan had any hope of winning the war. He believed that US Admiral Chester Nimitz would be determined to protect the island of Midway because it was key to preventing an invasion of Hawaii.

The **Battle of Midway** in June 1942 proved to be a turning point in the war. This time, it was the Japanese who failed to detect the location of its enemy's aircraft carriers and US planes were able to attack the Japanese carriers as they were still attempting to load bombs onto their planes. The US victory at Midway forced the Japanese to assume a more defensive war strategy. Midway proved to be their last offensive operation of the war.

Island Hopping

Iwo Jima

The United States then began a process of **island hopping**. Its forces attacked and conquered one group of islands, then move on to the next as its forces made their way to Japan. In the south, General Douglas MacArthur retook the Philippines.

Meanwhile, forces under Admiral Nimitz won key battles at Guadalcanal, Iwo Jima, and Okinawa.

President Truman

Soon after entering the war, the US began work on developing the **atomic bomb**. The top secret endeavor was called the **Manhattan Project** and was headed by J. Robert Oppenheimer.

On July 16, 1945, scientists tested the new weapon in the desert of New Mexico. The flash was blinding and the explosion so great that it shattered windows 125 miles away.

J. Robert Oppenheimer
(Library of Congress)

The new president, **Harry S. Truman**, was at the Potsdam Conference discussing postwar policies with Prime Minister Churchill and Joseph Stalin. While there, the allied leaders restated their policy of "**unconditional surrender**." When the Japanese refused to surrender until they were given a guarantee that the position of the Emperor would be protected, Truman authorized the use of the bomb.

On August 6, 1945, a specially equipped B29 bomber called the *Enola Gay* dropped the first atomic bomb on the Japanese city of **Hiroshima**. The blast leveled the city and killed thousands of civilians and military personnel. Many more died later from radiation released in the blast. Two days later, the Soviet Union declared war on Japan and invaded Manchuria. When Japan delayed in issuing its surrender, the US dropped another bomb on August 9 on the city of **Nagasaki**.

In the face of the massive death and destruction caused by these attacks, and with the Soviet Union now involved in the fighting, Japan finally surrendered on August 14, 1945. The next day the US celebrated V-J (Victory over Japan) Day. Although the world was shocked by the power of the atomic bomb, Truman defended the decision to use it. He pointed out that by dropping the bomb, an invasion of Japan had been avoided, thereby saving the lives of Allied soldiers.

Practice 8.2: Major Points of the War

1. The "Big Three" refers to which of the following?

   A. Roosevelt, Churchill, and Stalin

   B. Hitler, Mussolini, and Tojo

   C. Germany, Italy, and Japan

   D. The United States, Great Britain, and France

2. What was D-day and what impact did it have on World War II?

3. What was the Manhattan Project and what effect did it have on the war?

8.3 The War at Home

Home Front
(Library of Congress)

Most US citizens never experienced any fighting in World War II firsthand. However, the war still impacted people in the United States in many ways. In 1940, Congress authorized the first peacetime draft in US history when it passed the **Selective Service Act**. This provided a pool from which young men were selected to serve in the armed forces. Following the Pearl harbor attack, a large number of volunteers enlisted in the military as well.

Chapter 8

National Morale, War Industry, and Citizen Sacrifice

National Support

The government realized that it needed to maintain strong public support for the war effort. It also knew that a sense of patriotism and national morale would be crucial. The government paid artists to design patriotic war posters, and movie theaters began playing newsreels depicting the US war effort in a positive light. Ads depicting patriotic themes in magazines and on radio broadcasts also became common.

Economic Impact

War meant that the United States' economy had to switch from peacetime to wartime as quickly and efficiently as possible. To oversee this transformation, President Roosevelt established the **War Production Board (WPB)**. This board re-directed raw materials and resources from the production of civilian consumer goods to the production of materials needed for waging war against Germany and Japan.

The economic result of the war was that the US economy boomed and people's standard of living increased. Unemployed men now found themselves employed either as soldiers or in industries producing goods needed for the war effort. Others began migrating to northern cities and out west to fill the jobs needed for wartime production.

Citizen Sacrifice

War Bonds Poster
(Library of Congress)

In order for the United States to have the money and resources available to win the war, it called on sacrifices from citizens. The number of people required to pay income taxes greatly increased during the war years. To make sure these taxes were collected, the government introduced the idea of *withholding income tax.* For the first time, the government required employers to withhold taxes from employees' paychecks and give it to the government immediately.

Another means of raising money was through the sale of war bonds. By buying bonds, citizens loaned money to the government in return for interest. Thus, **war bond drives** to promote the purchase of such bonds became common as advertisements, posters, even movie stars encouraged people to buy bonds as part of their patriotic duty. Through bonds, the government raised more than sixty million dollars.

In addition to money, the government also called on people to sacrifice resources. People started growing **victory gardens** of their own so that more food could be sent to feed the soldiers. The government also started a program of **rationing** by which it could control how certain resources were distributed. In 1941, the government began rationing tires. Two years later, certain items were assigned points values. Once a citizen used up all their points, they could no longer obtain these items until they acquired more points. In this way, the government forced the public to conserve resources that were needed to support the war effort.

Victory Gardeners
(Library of Congress)

The Role of Women

"Rosie the Riveter"

With so many US men going off to fight, women became an important part of the workforce at home. Women of all cultural and racial backgrounds stepped forward to take on jobs traditionally held by men. A popular song of the day was called ***Rosie the Riveter***. The song described a woman who worked in the factory as a riveter while her boyfriend served in the marines. *Rosie the Riveter* became the symbol of those women who entered the workforce to fill the gap left vacant by men serving in the war.

Rosie the Riveter

Women in Uniform

It was not just white males who served heroically in the US military in World War II; women and minorities also served with honor. By the end of the war, almost 275,000 women had volunteered to serve in the armed forces. Although nearly every branch had a division for women, the **WAC** (Women's Army Corps) was by far the largest. Due to personnel shortages and a great sense of need, the US military had women serving both at home and abroad in just about every role except combat.

WAC Poster
(Library of Congress)

Chapter 8

African Americans in Uniform

Minorities also played a crucial role in the US war effort. Nearly 1 million African Americans volunteered or were drafted. At first, these troops found themselves prohibited from combat roles. Eventually, however, the numbers of casualties and the shortage of soldiers led to a change in policy.

The **Tuskegee Airmen** served as an all black squadron of fighter pilots. They successfully protected every bomber they escorted during the war.

Tuskegee Airmen

Native Americans and Mexicans

Native Americans also served valiantly in the armed forces. The United States Marines even developed a code for communicating based on the Navajo language. This code proved effective, and the Japanese were unable to break it. Some three hundred Navajo marines served as radio operators known as **"code talkers"** during the war against Japan. Meanwhile, Mexican Americans who served in the US military won seventeen Congressional Medals of Honor.

Japanese Americans

The 442nd

Finally, there were the Japanese Americans who served. Originally, Japanese Americans could not enlist, but this changed in 1943. One Japanese American unit, **the 442nd**, served so valiantly in Europe that it became the most decorated unit in United States history. The contributions of the Japanese American troops were remarkable considering the racism and discrimination that many of their families endured ay home during the war.

Minorities at Home

The boom in war industry jobs revived African American migration. Large numbers of blacks moved to the cities and out west, whereby California, Oregon, Washington, and Utah became among the top five states in African American population growth during the 1940s.

The increased access of blacks to the nation's available jobs, as well as black men fighting and dying overseas just like white men, fueled cries for social justice. Many African Americans advocated what they called the **"double V"** —victory at home, as well as abroad; and proclaimed that the war should be against "Hitlerism" (prejudice and racism) as well as against Hitler. As a result, the period marked the beginnings of more open and bold challenges on the part of African Americans to the racial injustices that existed in US society.

Hispanic Farm Workers
(Library of Congress)

Nearly one-fourth of the Native American workforce was employed in the war defense industry during World War II. The availability of jobs meant that many Native Americans were able to leave the reservations for better opportunities in urban areas and began to integrate more with the rest of US society.

Meanwhile, as more and more citizens made their way to urban areas to work in industry, rural areas experienced labor shortages on farms. To fill this need, the US government encouraged more Mexican immigrants to cross the border to work in agriculture. The government even went so far as to sign a formal agreement with Mexico promising not to draft Mexican immigrants for military service and to pay them a reasonable wage in exchange for increased immigration and labor. The result was a rapid rise in the **Hispanic population** that sometimes created racial conflict.

Internment of Japanese Americans

The Japanese attack on Pearl Harbor fueled suspicion and fear of Japanese people in the United States. On February 19, 1942, President Roosevelt signed Executive Order 9066, ordering all Japanese Americans away from military facilities. Under authority of this order, the US military forced more than 100,000 Japanese Americans from their homes and businesses during the war and placed them in **internment camps**. These camps tended to be located in remote areas owned by the federal government. Many of these Japanese American citizens lost everything as a result. Many of them were US citizens who had lived in the United States for several generations. Others had been born in the US to parents who had immigrated from Japan.

Internment Camp

In 1944, a Japanese American named Fred Korematsu challenged the executive order on the grounds that it violated his civil rights. But the Supreme Court ruled that the government internment of Japanese Americans was not unlawful because "the military urgency of the situation..." justified it.

Practice 8.3: The War at Home

1. Which of the following statements is **true** regarding the role of women and minorities in the military during World War II?

   A. Women served in combat.

   B. The Tuskegee Airmen were notable African American fighter pilots.

   C. Mexican Americans won Congressional Medals of Honor for their service as "code talkers."

   D. Native American men who fought in the war were nicknamed "WACs."

2. "Rosie the Riveter" was a symbol of what?

   A. women's new role in the US workforce during the war

   B. women's new role in the US military during the war

   C. the government's call for economic sacrifice to help the war effort

   D. the need for citizens to purchase war bonds as part of their patriotic duty

3. What were some of the social effects of the war on Japanese Americans?

8.4 The Aftermath of World War II

The Holocaust and War Crime Trials

The invasion of Europe by the Allies not only brought an end to the war, but it also exposed the horrible atrocities committed by the Nazis against people they labeled as socially inferior and unfit to live. Among the groups so targeted, no group suffered in such great numbers as the Jewish people.

Hitler ascended to power in large part due to anti-Semitism (prejudice against Jewish people). He successfully portrayed the Jews as a major reason for Germany's financial problems and began implementing laws and policies that were discriminatory against Jewish citizens. Eventually, this progressed to what Hitler called the "Final Solution" to the "Jewish problem." The Nazis set about attempting to exterminate the Jewish race through mass genocide (murder of a race of people). Under Hitler's regime, Jews were rounded up, separated from their families, and either killed or shipped to **concentration camps**. In the camps, Jews and other prisoners were either immediately put to death or forced to provide slave labor before finally being executed or dying of disease or starvation.

As Allied soldiers began liberating areas of Europe formerly held by the Nazis, they encountered the camps that housed tortured and starving people, most of whom were Jews. They found gas chambers for conducting mass executions and ovens for burning bodies. Troops also uncovered mass graves where victims had been thrown after they'd been killed or left to die in the camps. Roughly six million Jews died during this horrible episode in history known as the **Holocaust**.

NUREMBERG

Defendants at the Nuremburg Trials
(Library of Congress)

When the world became aware of the Holocaust, there was an outcry for justice. Hitler was dead, but there were others in the Nazi regime who could be punished. The **Nuremberg Trials** began in November 1945 and placed more than twenty Nazi leaders on trial for "crimes against humanity." The court sentenced several of the defendants to death, while others received long prison terms. Some Nazi leaders escaped to countries like Argentina. Many remained in hiding until their death. Others, like Adolf Eichmann (architect of the "Final Solution"), were eventually found, put on trial, and executed years later.

Meanwhile, the world did not forget Japanese atrocities, either. During the war, the Japanese treated prisoners of war and conquered people harshly. After the war, this led to the trials of a number of Japan's military leaders. As a result, the Allies executed seven Japanese leaders, including Tojo Hideki. Between Japan and Europe, more than 2,000 war crime trials took place after the war.

LASTING IMPACT OF SCIENTIFIC AND TECHNOLOGICAL DISCOVERIES

THE NUCLEAR AGE

Atomic Bomb
(Library of Congress)

The war years produced **advancements in technology** that greatly changed society and had lasting impact. Arguably, the greatest change coming out of World War II was the introduction of the **nuclear age**. Not only did the atomic bomb end the war, but it also changed how future wars would be fought. Both Truman and Stalin were aware of this. Because of their differences in political ideology (Truman a strong believer in democracy and capitalism; Stalin a dictator and devout communist), the two never trusted one another. They had only forged an alliance because the war forced them to. With the war now over, each viewed the other as the new enemy. When Truman learned in Potsdam that the atomic bomb had been successfully tested, he could not wait to tell the Soviet leader that the US now had a new weapon of unprecedented power. In fact, some believe Truman chose to use the bomb as much to intimidate Stalin as to defeat Japan.

When Truman told Stalin about the "new weapon," Stalin calmly expressed his hope that it would end the war. In reality, Soviet spies had already told Stalin about the bomb. He was indeed concerned and determined to see his own country develop a similar weapon. As a result, a **nuclear arms race** between the United States and the USSR began. Over time, both sides continued to develop even more powerful weapons, including nuclear missiles capable of destruction thousands of times greater than that experienced at Hiroshima and Nagasaki.

Radar and Sonar

Another invention that had great military importance was radar (radio detection and ranging). Radar uses sound waves to detect the approach of enemy planes while they are still a long way off. It was invented by the British and helped them defeated Germany's air force by giving the Royal Air Force advanced notice of German attacks. Today, radar is used for commercial (i.e., commercial airlines) as well as military purposes. Similarly, the war also saw advances in sonar (sound navigation and ranging), which uses similar technology to detect the location of objects under water.

Radar

Microwave Technology

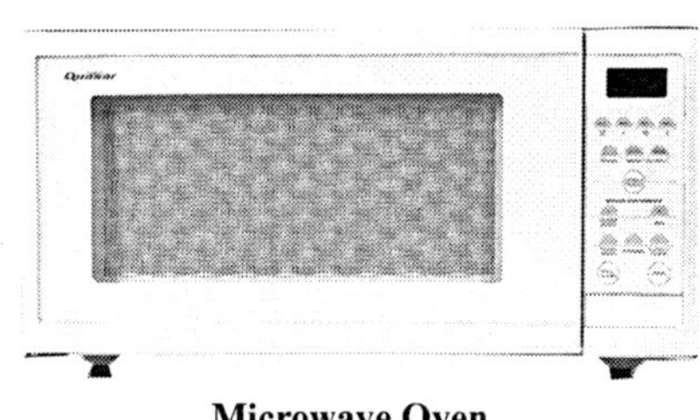

Microwave Oven

An American engineer named Percy Spencer discovered microwave technology by accident. While working on radar technology for the war effort in 1945, Spencer noticed that the candy bar in his pocket had melted. Upon further testing, he discovered that the technology he was working with could be used to cook food much faster than conventional ovens.

By the 1950s, the first home unit microwave ovens were on the market. By the 1970s, affordable countertop models were available, contributing to the change in women's roles by providing more freedom and less time in the kitchen.

Computers

Laptop Computer

During the war, the need for devices that could make fast calculations and decode enemy messages became critical. Computer technology proved important. The first computers were huge and took up entire rooms. Within a relatively short amount of time, technological advances led to their size decreasing as their abilities increased.

Additional Innovations

World War II saw other inventions and innovations as well. New **medical technology** appeared in the form of antibiotics, such as the use of penicillin to treat bacterial diseases. Meanwhile, new methods for isolating blood plasma were also introduced. Advances in **agriculture** also took place as farmers enjoyed a rise in demand for their products due to the government's need to feed both its military and the nation. New technology and equipment made farming more productive, efficient and economical.

Oil Pipelines

Radios became smaller and more portable, thereby making them more popular. Radios soon became standard features in cars. The accessibility of radio eventually helped spread a nationwide youth culture during the 1950s and 60s.

Practice 8.4: The Aftermath of World War II

1. What was the Holocaust and how did the world respond to it after the war?

2. Which of the following statements is **true** regarding technological advances that occurred during the war years?

   A. Few technological and scientific advances occurred during the war because nations had to focus most of their efforts on achieving military victory.

   B. Military commanders stopped using radar in favor of more advanced sonar.

   C. Important strides were made in medical and computer technology.

   D. Computers were invented by accident as scientists studied microwave technology.

3. What impact did the atomic bomb have on future military weapons?

Chapter 8 Review

Key Terms

Adolf Hitler
appeasement
Joseph Stalin
Benito Mussolini
Hideki Tojo
Axis Powers
Neutrality Act
Lend-Lease Act
Pearl Harbor
Tehran Conference
D-day
Big Three
Yalta Conference
Philippines
Battle of Midway
island hopping
atomic bomb
Manhattan Project
Harry S. Truman
Hiroshima
Nagasaki
Selective Service Act
War Production Board
war bond drives
victory gardens
rationing
Rosie the Riveter
WAC
Tuskegee Airmen
code talkers
the 442nd
double V
Hispanic population
internment camps
concentration camps
Holocaust
Nuremburg Trials
advancements in technology
nuclear age
nuclear arms race

Chapter 8

1. Why did the United States hesitate to become involved in World War II after Hitler invaded Poland?

   A. The United States supported Hitler and wanted him to have time to withdraw.

   B. The United States was at war with Japan and did not want to fight Germany too.

   C. Isolationism was widespread in the United States, and citizens did not want war.

   D. US forces were not strong enough to fight a war and needed more time to train.

2. What happened on December 7, 1941 that greatly changed the course of the war?

   A. D-day

   B. Pearl Harbor

   C. Germany's invasion of Poland

   D. The Allies victory in North Africa

3. The **best** caption for the picture above would be

   A. WACs at Work.

   B. Neutrality in Action.

   C. Wartime Rationing.

   D. Rosie the Riveter.

4. Why was Stalin upset by the western allies decision to focus on North Africa?

   A. The Soviets controlled North Africa and did not want the Allies to interfere.

   B. It delayed the Allies from attacking the Nazis in Western Europe.

   C. The Germans were too powerful in North Africa, and Stalin feared defeat.

   D. Japan controlled North Africa, and the Soviets were not yet at war with them.

5. What impact did World War II have on the Great Depression?
   A. It ended the depression by creating jobs and demand for products.
   B. It lengthened the depression by causing high military spending.
   C. It had no effect on the depression because it did not impact the economy.
   D. It temporarily improved the depression for a few years.

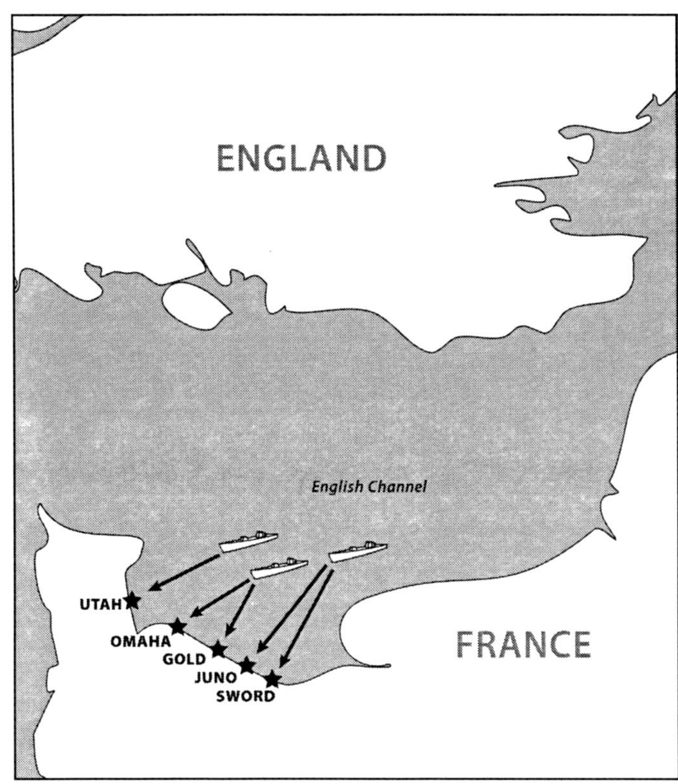

6. The map above depicts which of the following?
   A. Pearl Harbor
   B. V-E Day
   C. D-day
   D. Invasion of Poland

7. What was the Manhattan Project?
   A. Japan's secret plan to bomb Pearl Harbor
   B. The US government's plan to protect New York from invasion
   C. The project that centered around building the atomic bomb
   D. A massive invasion of France by allied forces

8. What tragedy is depicted in the image above?
   - A. Hiroshima
   - B. Nagasaki
   - C. Pearl Harbor
   - D. the Holocaust

9. How were Japanese Americans treated during the war?
   - A. They were honored because of the brave service of the 442nd in Europe.
   - B. They were ignored because citizens were suspicious of German Americans.
   - C. They were suspected of supporting Japan and forced to live in internment camps.
   - D. They were appreciated for their willingness to serve in the US military.

10. Who were the Tuskegee Airmen?
    - A. African Americans who served in the US military
    - B. Native Americans who served in the US military
    - C. Hispanic Americans who served in the US military
    - D. Japanese Americans who served in the US military

Chapter 9
Birth of the Cold War Era

This chapter addresses the following standard(s):

New Indicators	7.4, 7.5, 7.6
Old Indicators	8.5, 9.1, 9.2, 9.4

9.1 The Cold War Begins

Conflict in Europe

Following World War II, tensions were high between the western Allies and the Soviet Union. Neither side trusted the other. The United States and Great Britain felt strongly that the Allies should not occupy the territories they conquered during WWII. The Soviets, on the other hand, had suffered greater losses in terms of life and property than either of them. They were determined not to be invaded again. Stalin decided that he must maintain control over Eastern Europe in order to keep a buffer between the Soviet Union and the nations of the West.

Europe Divided by Iron Curtain

Stalin set up communist regimes answerable to himself in Germany and Poland. The European continent now stood divided between the western democracies and Soviet satellite nations (nations answering to and representing the views of and answering to the USSR). In a speech given by Winston Churchill at Westminster College in Missouri, the former British prime minister said of Europe, "A shadow has fallen... an **iron curtain** has descended across the continent." As a result of his comments, "iron curtain" became the common term used to refer to the dividing line between eastern and western Europe.

US Post-war Policies in Europe

George Marshall

In 1946, a top US diplomat named George Kennan recommended that the US and its allies focus on a strategy of **containment**. Kennan believed that Eastern Europe was firmly in Soviet hands and could not be saved. Therefore, the US and the West should focus on *containing* communism to those countries in which it already existed and not let it spread any further.

Reaffirming Kennan's philosophy, Truman introduced the **Truman Doctrine**. This doctrine stated that the United States would not hesitate to intervene and aid nations overseas to resist communism. It featured a financial plan to build up Europe worked out by former Army Chief of Staff and current Secretary of State, George Marshall. Labeled the **Marshall Plan**, this plan provided nations in war-torn Europe with much needed financial support from the United States. This aid served to spark economic revival and prosperity in these countries, alleviating the suffering of many people. Since communist revolutions often started due to economic hardships, the Marshall Plan went a long way towards preventing Soviet advances into Western Europe and became the crowning achievement of the containment policy. For his efforts, Secretary Marshall received the Nobel Peace Prize in 1953.

A Divided Germany

When World War II ended, the Allies divided Germany among themselves. Part of the country fell under US control, part fell under British control, and part of the nation fell to the Soviets. Out of the portions allotted to the United States and Britain, France received a portion as well. In addition, the German capital of Berlin (although geographically located within the Soviets' territory) was also divided. The western portions of the city went to the western Allies, and the eastern portion fell under the hand of the Soviets.

Berlin Airlift

Great Britain, the United States and France all saw these divisions as temporary. They envisioned Germany eventually being a unified and independent democracy. Stalin, however, had no intention of giving up the Soviet controlled parts of Berlin or Germany. By 1948, it became obvious that Stalin would not relent. Realizing that a unified Germany could not be achieved, the US, Great Britain and France unified their sectors into one nation, the Federal Republic of Germany (**West Germany**), and declared West Berlin to be part of this new nation. The USSR responded by establishing the German Democratic Republic (**East Germany**) under communist rule.

Almost immediately, thousands of people wishing to escape communism fled to West Berlin hoping to make their way to freedom. In an effort to stop this, Stalin decided to force the West to surrender its portion of Berlin. He instituted a blockade of the city, not allowing any needed supplies to reach the people of West Berlin. Wanting to avoid a war, yet deal firmly with Stalin, Truman authorized the **Berlin Airlift**. Over a fifteen-month period, US and British planes delivered needed supplies to West Berlin. The Soviets finally gave up in May of 1949, but the bitterness of the conflict only served to fuel the fires of the **"Cold War."** The term "cold war" was first used by presidential advisor, Bernard Baruch, in 1947; it referred to the tension between the United States and the Soviet Union that dominated both nations' foreign policies and which many feared would lead to actual war.

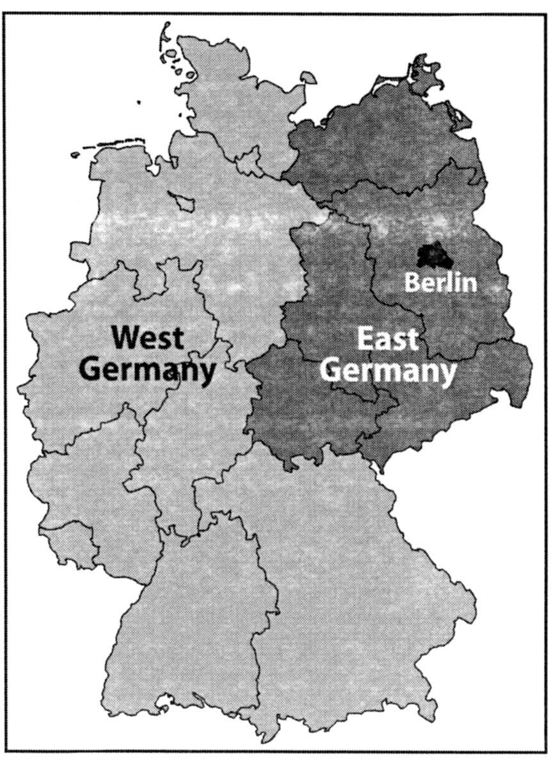

East and West Germany

China and Korea

In 1949, **China** became a communist nation following a revolution. Mao Tse-tung (Zedong) led the revolution and assumed power as the new leader.

Korea was among the countries liberated from the Japanese during World War II. Since both the US and the Soviets played a role in its liberation, the Allies divided the nation along the 38th parallel. The northern half of the country established a communist government while the southern half put in place a pro-US democracy.

Korea

The Korean War

In June 1950, the **Korean War** began when North Korean forces crossed the 38th parallel. The United Nations elected to come to South Korea's aid, and President Truman chose General Douglas MacArthur.

MacArthur's forces pushed their enemy back across the 38th parallel. Continuing to advance north, the UN forces moved ever closer to the Chinese border. Concerned that US-led forces were so close and wanting to maintain a communist regime in North Korea, the Chinese sent troops across the Yalu River to aid the North Koreans. A stalemate soon developed. To make matters more complicated, Truman fired MacArthur after the general criticized the president's handling of the war. After two more long years of fighting, both sides signed a truce in 1953. The agreement left the country divided at almost the same point as before the North Korean invasion.

Chapter 9

THE MIDDLE EAST

THE FOUNDING OF ISRAEL

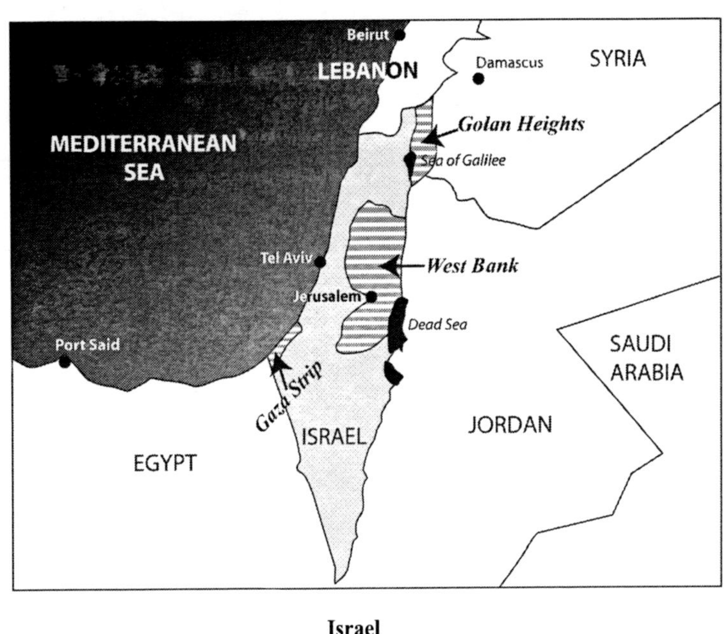

Israel

The discovery of the Holocaust during WWII served to increase support for the founding of a Jewish homeland. Hundreds of thousands of Jewish refugees from Europe wanted to enter Palestine for this purpose. On May 14, 1948, with the support of the newly formed United Nations, the new state of **Israel** officially became an independent Jewish state.

President Truman showed the United States' support for the new nation by immediately recognizing it. Arab nations, however, greatly resented the decision to give part of Palestine to the Jews. They claimed that the entire territory rightfully belonged to Arabs.

Israel's boundary also had an impact on the Cold War. The United States and Israel became staunch allies. The Soviets came to support many of the surrounding Arab states.

THE EISENHOWER DOCTRINE

Elected president of the United States in 1952, **Dwight Eisenhower** (the military hero of WWII) was concerned about the spread of communism and Soviet aggression. Eisenhower believed strongly in the **domino theory**. This theory held that if one nation fell to communism, then its neighboring nations would soon fall as well.

In 1957, President Eisenhower introduced the **Eisenhower Doctrine**. It stated that the United States would not hesitate to aid any country in the Middle East that asked for help resisting communist aggression. A year later, Eisenhower sent troops to Lebanon to help the Lebanese government resist communist backed rebel forces.

The U-2 Incident

Khrushchev

Nikita Khrushchev became the Soviet leader following the death of Joseph Stalin in 1953. In an effort to improve US-Soviet relations, Khrushchev met with President Eisenhower in the United States and invited Eisenhower to also come to Moscow. But in May of 1960, another incident occurred that damaged US-Soviet relations and caused Khrushchev to cancel the invitation. It became known as the **U-2 Incident**. It involved a US U-2 spy plane shot down over the Soviet Union. At first, the US government denied conducting any such spy missions. However, when the Soviets produced evidence, Eisenhower had to acknowledge the Soviet report as accurate. The president accepted responsibility, but refused to apologize for spying on the USSR, thereby infuriating Khrushchev further.

Kennedy, Communism, and Cuba

The Bay of Pigs

Fidel Castro, 1959
(Library of Congress)

In 1959, a young revolutionary named **Fidel Castro** overthrew the Cuban government and assumed control of the nation. He executed more than seven hundred of his opponents and jailed many more. His government also seized control of much of the land and property in the country. Discovering that Castro had ties to communism and that he had seized US property in Cuba, President Eisenhower refused to support the new dictator and broke off diplomatic relations. With US support lacking, Castro allied himself with the Soviet Union.

President John F. Kennedy

When **John F. Kennedy** succeeded Eisenhower as president in 1961, he approved an operation to aid anti-Castro Cubans in an invasion of their homeland. The invasion landed at the Bay of Pigs on April 17, 1961. It turned out to be a terrible failure and a huge embarrassment for the Kennedy administration. It also left many around the world wondering if the young president was up to the task of defending democracy against communism.

The Berlin Wall

Khrushchev was determined to stop the large flow of refugees from East Germany into West Germany through Berlin. The Soviet Union built a wall that separated communist East Berlin from democratic West Berlin. Anyone attempting to cross the wall without permission risked being shot by East German soldiers. For more than a quarter of a century, the **Berlin Wall** stood as a chilling symbol of the Cold War.

Berlin Wall

The Cuban Missile Crisis

Although the Bay of Pigs had been a failure, Castro still feared a future invasion by US forces. Knowing he needed a strong ally, Castro allowed the Soviets to secretly put nuclear missiles in Cuba, just 90 miles off the coast of Florida. When US spy planes spotted these missiles in October 1962, Kennedy responded by authorizing a naval blockade of the island.

For thirteen days, the world watched as the **Cuban Missile Crisis** brought the two superpowers to the brink of nuclear war. Finally, after heated arguments in the UN and much diplomatic maneuvering, Khrushchev agreed to withdraw the missiles in exchange for a US pledge not to invade Cuba. In addition, the US also offered the Soviets a secret assurance that it would eventually remove US missiles stationed in Turkey as well.

International Alliances of the Cold War

The United Nations

UN Building

The Cold War basically divided the world in half between countries that allied with the United States on one side, and those allied with the Soviet Union on the other. In the hopes of avoiding conflict, the international community founded the **United Nations (UN)** after WWII. Much like the former League of Nations, it was intended to provide a place where countries could negotiate rather than go to war.

Within the UN was established a Security Council that consisted of representatives from the United States, the Soviet Union (this seat is now occupied by Russia), Great Britain, France, and China. In addition to these permanent members, other nations could serve two year terms on temporary seats. To this day, the Security Council has the authority to investigate disputes and even authorize military action. Such actions, however, require the approval of all five of the permanent members.

NATO and the Warsaw Pact

Because most nations did not possess nuclear weapons, many relied on alliances to provide collective security. In April 1949, the United States signed a treaty with several European nations. The North Atlantic Treaty allied these nations with one another and stated that each country would come to the defense of any of the others if ever they were attacked. It also formed **NATO** (the North Atlantic Treaty Organization) which would provide a combined military force if such an attack occurred. A few years later, other countries (including West Germany) became part of NATO as well.

The **Warsaw Pact** was the USSR and its allies' answer to NATO. The Pact was formed in 1955 after NATO expanded and admitted new countries. It united the communist countries of eastern Europe in a similar pledge to defend one another and fight collectively if attacked by NATO.

Southeast Asia and Latin America

In an effort to prevent the spread of communism in Southeast Asia, the United States formed the **Southeast Asia Treaty Organization (SEATO)** with Australia, New Zealand, the Philippines, Thailand, Pakistan, France and Great Britain. The United States also led the way in forming the **Organization of American States (OAS)** in 1948. The organization's purpose was to forge cooperation and prevent Latin American nations from becoming communist.

Practice 9.1: The Cold War Begins

1. What did Winston Churchill mean by the term "iron curtain"?

2. The Truman Doctrine and Eisenhower Doctrine were similar in that they were both designed to do which of the following?

   A. support West Berlin during the Soviet blockade

   B. increase Israel's security against Arab states

   C. assist nations abroad to resist communism

   D. pledge to use negotiations rather than military action to solve international disputes

3. Why was the Marshall Plan considered to be so important to the stability of democracy in western Europe after World War II?

4. The term "Cold War" refers to which of the following?

   A. the conflict in Berlin because it occurred during the middle of winter

   B. the conflict in Korea

   C. the tension that arose after the Soviets shot down a US spy plane

   D. the tension and potential for war that existed between the US and Soviet Union

9.2 The Postwar United States

The Rise of the Middle Class

With large numbers of discharged soldiers returning from the war, the nation faced the problem of assimilating these veterans back into US society. To help, Congress passed the "**GI Bill**" (Servicemen's Readjustment Act). The initials "GI" stood for "government issue" and came to be a slang term for US soldiers. This legislation provided military veterans with benefits such as job priority, money for furthering their education, training, and loans for purchasing homes and property.

1950s Suburb

Because of the support the GI Bill provided, the nation witnessed a social revolution. For the first time, large numbers of "common people" could afford to buy their own homes. As a result, developers like William Levitt became rich building entire communities of new houses as a new **middle class** emerged, and people began moving to the suburbs.

Suburbinization (the rapid growth and spread of suburbs) changed US culture. More people purchased houses and cars and commuted to cities for work and leisure. Suburbs also led to more racial division. Most middle-class whites moved out of urban areas to homes in outlying neighborhoods, leaving inner-cities to be occupied mostly by lower-income minorities.

In addition, the nation experienced a population explosion known as the "**Baby Boom**." Baby Boomers are members of the generation born within the first few years after World War II. With the war over, spouses were reunited and couples got married. Many of these people started or expanded their family. What resulted was a "boom" in the number of babies born in the United States during the late 1940s and early 50s.

Education

The GI Bill also had lasting effects on education. Prior to the war, most working class citizens did not go to college. However, with the benefits offered veterans, many returning soldiers enrolled in colleges and universities despite their social class. The US population became more educated and the middle class grew as college degrees translated into better paying jobs.

Such prosperity meant that more parents eventually sent their kids (the "baby boom" generation) to college as well. For the first time in US history, getting a college education became the social norm among middle class citizens. The exception was among African Americans. Because most institutions of higher education remained segregated and because there was limited space in black colleges/universities, most African American veterans did not enroll in colleges or universities after the war. Many of them were also hindered by a lack of formal education prior to entering the armed forces.

The Cold War also impacted education. In 1958, Congress passed the National Defense Education Act. This law provided aid for education and was geared towards boosting the study of science, math, and foreign languages. It was intended to propel the US ahead of the Soviet Union in both the space race and in nuclear technology.

Prosperity and Consumerism

With the end of the war, the US entered a period of great prosperity. The availability of jobs and the boom in economic production during the war meant that people had money. However, due to rationing and other government policies to support the war effort, it wasn't until after the war that citizens spent and purchased what they wanted. The nation once again became a **consumer society**.

People bought sewing machines, washing machines, refrigerators, and a new invention: the **television**. The automobile industry also boomed as more and more people bought cars for their commute from the suburbs to the cities where they worked. Advertisers promoted products trying to make consumers feel they had to have them. Many of their efforts were aimed at housewives. One department store executive commented during the period that, "...we must make women unhappy with what they have... we must make them so unhappy that their husbands can find no happiness or peace in their excessive savings."

More and more, people in the US judged their social status and importance by what kind of car they drove, what clothes they wore, what house they lived in, etc. In order to purchase what they desired, citizens began to rely on credit cards which allowed them to buy products right away and then pay for them over time with interest. As a result, people stopped saving money, and debt increased. Shopping centers popped up across the nation as shopping became a popular pastime.

Women in Society

With the men home from the war, "Rosie the Riveter" was encouraged to put down her tools and return to the kitchen. A woman's place was widely believed to be that of a **housewife**, whose purpose is to raise the kids, clean the house, cook the meals, and be devoted to her husband, all the while remaining pretty and happy.

Housewife

Although some women continued to work after the war, and some even resisted the idea that a woman's greatest purpose was that of a housewife, most (men and women alike) accepted the notion. The image was also reinforced by the wives and mothers portrayed on the nation's most popular television shows.

Chapter 9

A New Red Scare

In addition to fears of nuclear war, a new wave of fear about communism swept the country. During the Great Depression, many citizens had joined the Communist Party or at least voiced agreement with certain communist ideals. Most did this because they felt communism offered the economic relief that they needed. When economic times got better and people learned more about Stalin's brutality in the USSR, most no longer had an interest in being Communists. In the late 40s and into the 50s, the government harassed and arrested many people due to their alleged connections to the Communist Party. This period became known as the second **"Red Scare."**

Government Policies Dealing with Communism and the Threat of Nuclear War

Concerned with the threat of communism, President Truman signed the National Security Act in 1947. This act created the President's National Security Council for the purpose of coordinating national security policies, and the Central Intelligence Agency (CIA). The CIA became the nation's first peacetime intelligence agency and is responsible for covert (secret) operations meant to ensure national security. Originally, the CIA's top mission was to spy on the USSR and its allies.

Congress also relied on the House Un-American Activities Committee (HUAC). First established in 1938, this committee was responsible for rooting out Communists in government and US society.

Since the government suspected many people in the movie-making industry of being Communists, HUAC called a number of Hollywood actors, producers, and writers to testify in 1947. Out of fear that they might be targeted, a number of movie executives developed a Hollywood blacklist. The list consisted of writers, actors, directors, and so forth, that producers refused to work with because of suspected ties to communism.

Joseph McCarthy

One of the most interesting characters to arise as a result of national concern about communism was Wisconsin Senator **Joseph McCarthy**. McCarthy believed Communists had infiltrated high levels of government and the US military. He even accused former Army Chief of Staff and Secretary of State, George Marshall.

Joseph McCarthy

At first, Communist aggression in Korea served to help McCarthy and his ideas gain popularity. Eventually, however, McCarthy had to defend his views in a series of televised hearings. By the time the hearings ended in June 1954, most US citizens viewed McCarthy as paranoid at best and downright crazy at worst. "McCarthyism" (the ideas and fears of communism voiced by McCarthy and his supporters) began to collapse, and the irrational fear that "Communists are everywhere" subsided.

Preparing for Possible War

Interstate System

The Cold War meant that a strong military force needed to be maintained. The Selective Service Act of 1951 allowed the government to draft men between the ages of 18 and 26. Meanwhile, concerns about a nuclear strike against the United States led President Dwight D. Eisenhower to strongly support the National Highway Act of 1956. The act called for the construction of a federal **interstate highway system**. The highway system provided improved mobility for citizens, more and more of whom owned automobiles. Just as importantly, however, the federal highways served a military purpose. The improved roads would allow military troops and personnel to move quicker, and cities could be evacuated much faster, in the event of a nuclear attack.

President Eisenhower

During his farewell address on January 17, 1961, President Eisenhower introduced the term **"military-industrial complex."** The term refers to the important link between the US military, the Congress (which allocates money for military spending), and the civilian industry that produces needed military goods (weapons, uniforms, supplies, etc.). After WWII, mistrust of the Soviets led to the belief that the United States must build up and maintain a strong military force. As a result, the military-industrial complex grew and became an important component of US strategy and policy during the Cold War. This relationship between Congress, the military, and civilian industry continues to remain important today.

Demographic Changes

The changing economy and culture led to **demographic changes**. The western population grew as areas like Orange County, California, became home to the emerging post war defense industry. Meanwhile, other industries created growth in other US regions. As people flocked to new areas to pursue postwar job opportunities, towns grew into bustling cities. In addition, more minorities migrated from southern rural areas to northern urban areas to pursue work. Minority populations in urban areas grew in the years during and after the war. New interstate highways made migration easier and aided population shifts that occurred after the war.

Practice 9.2: The Postwar United States

1. Which of the following people would have benefited from the GI Bill?
   A. a US Marine returning home from the Pacific who wants to buy a home
   B. a sailor who served in the war who has been accused of a crime
   C. a member of the WACs who was wounded in combat
   D. an African-American worker who had moved north during the war

2. The term "baby boomer" refers to which of the following?
   A. soldiers returning home from the war
   B. housewives who gave up their jobs to stay home and have babies
   C. children born in the years immediately following the war
   D. houses built quickly and in large numbers to form suburbs

3. Society in the United States during the late 1940s and 1950s is **best** described by which of the following statements?
   A. It was made up largely of a growing middle class.
   B. Fewer citizens bought appliances and automobiles.
   C. Minorities started attending college in large numbers.
   D. Women's abandoned the role of housewife to go back to work.

4. What are some ways that the second Red Scare and the threat of nuclear war impacted government policies and the lives of US citizens after World War II?

Chapter 9 Review

Key Terms

iron curtain
containment
Truman Doctrine
Marshall Plan
Berlin Airlift
Cold War
China
Korea
Korean War
Israel
Dwight Eisenhower
Eisenhower Doctrine
Nikita Khrushchev
U-2 Incident
Fidel Castro
John F. Kennedy
Berlin Wall
Cuban Missile Crisis
United Nations (UN)
NATO
Warsaw Pact
SEATO
Organization of American States
GI Bill
middle class
suburbanization
Baby Boom
postwar education
consumer society
television
housewife
Red Scare
HUAC
Hollywood blacklist
Joseph McCarthy
interstate highway system
military-industrial complex
demographic changes

Chapter 9 Review Questions

1. To which of the following did the term "Cold War" refer?
   A. The fighting that took place in Europe during World War II.
   B. A war between the US and Soviet Union fought shortly after World War II.
   C. The search for communists within the US government after World War II.
   D. Tensions between the US and USSR that could lead to war after World War II.

2. Following World War II, the United States adopted which of the following policies towards Soviet communism?
   A. containment
   B. aggression
   C. military action
   D. acceptance

3. Which of the following contributed to demographic changes after World War II?
   A. interstate highways
   B. communism in Hollywood
   C. the Truman Doctrine
   D. the Marshall Plan

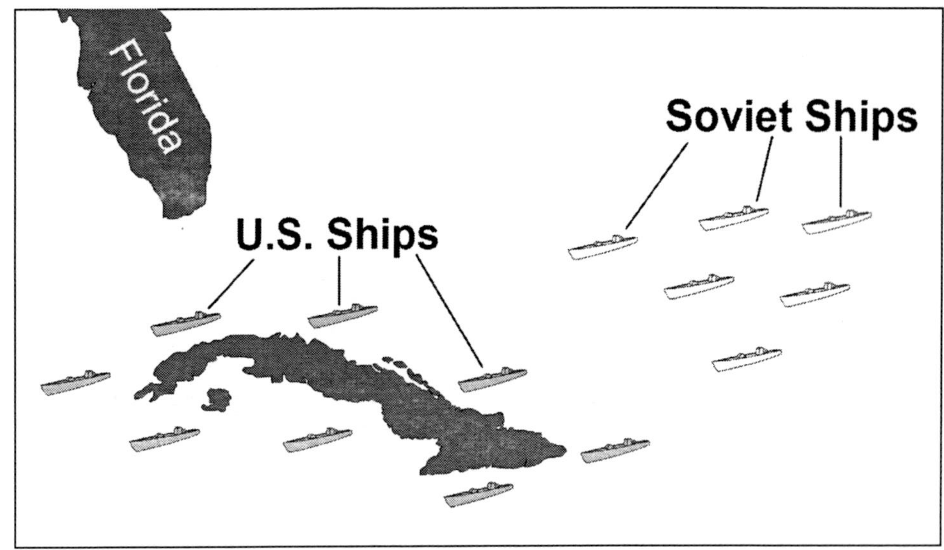

4. Which of the following is depicted by the map above?
   - A. the iron curtain
   - B. containment
   - C. Cuban Missile Crisis
   - D. Berlin Airlift

5. Which of the following was a Cold War conflict that occurred in Eastern Asia?
   - A. Berlin Airlift
   - B. U-2 Incident
   - C. Korean War
   - D. the founding of Israel

6. Which of the following **best** describes the role of women in middle class America after World War II?
   - A. They worked in factories.
   - B. They were housewives.
   - C. Most did not get married.
   - D. Few owned televisions.

7. The image above depicts which of the following?

   A. military-industrial complex
   B. interstates
   C. suburbanization
   D. urban growth

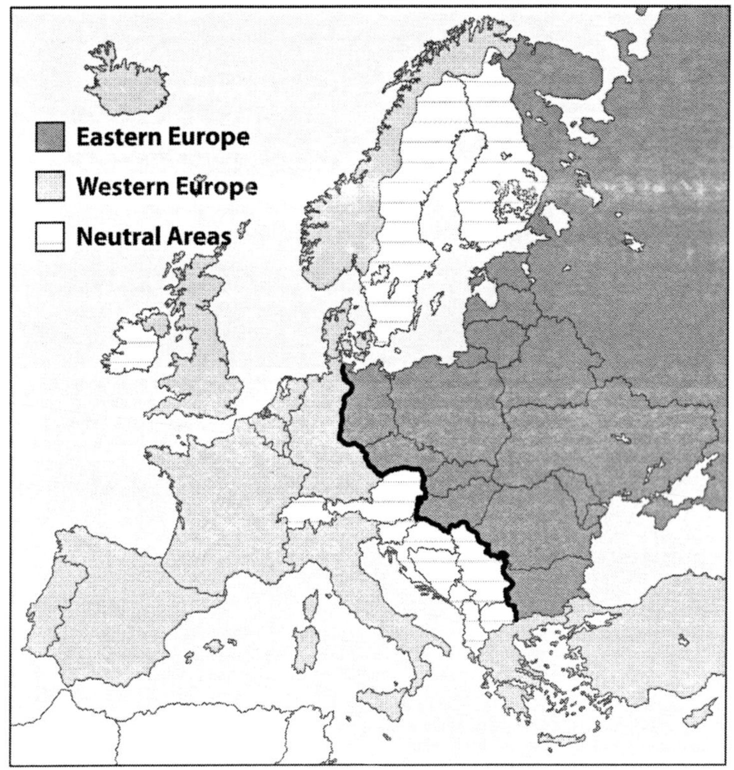

8. The map above depicts the

A. 38th parallel.

B. iron curtain.

C. Berlin Wall.

D. Cuban blockade.

Chapter 10
Transformational Years

This chapter addresses the following standard(s):

New Indicators	8.1, 8.2, 8.3, 8.4
Old Indicators	9.3, 9.4, 9.5

10.1 The Civil Rights Movement

Civil Rights March

Following World War II, African Americans still endured racial discrimination. In the South, state laws continued to sanction segregation (separation by race). In northern states, whites often looked down on and segregated themselves from blacks even where segregation was not endorsed by law.

Most African Americans resented unjust segregation laws. Many expressed outrage that African Americans had fought valiantly for the cause of freedom overseas, only to be treated as second-class citizens once they returned home. This discontent gradually gave birth to a **civil rights movement**. This movement featured African Americans fighting for their constitutional rights. It ultimately changed US society forever.

Civil Rights in Education and Public Accommodations

Brown v. Board of Education

In the early 1950s, the NAACP sued the Board of Education of Topeka, Kansas because it would not let a black girl, Linda Brown, attend an all-white school near her home. In ***Brown vs. Board of Education* (1954)**, the Supreme Court reversed the *Plessy* decision and ruled that racial segregation in public schools is unconstitutional. The Court, led by Chief Justice Earl Warren, found that separate facilities were inherently unequal because they did not present minority students with the same opportunities that were offered in white schools.

Earl Warren

Heart of Atlanta Motel v. United States

Later, in ***Heart of Atlanta Motel, Inc. v. United States (1964)***, the Supreme Court went even further in dealing with segregation. The Court ruled that Congress could use its authority to regulate interstate commerce to outlaw segregation in privately owned businesses. The court said that such policies potentially hinder interstate business transactions. Although many considered the Court's reasoning a stretch, it represented another step towards striking down state sanctioned segregation.

White Resistance

Despite the Court's decision in *Brown*, many southern leaders were determined to maintain segregation as long as possible. In 1957, national attention turned to Arkansas when the governor refused to obey a federal court order to integrate Little Rock Central High School. He called in the Arkansas National Guard to prevent nine black students from entering the school, prompting President Eisenhower to nationalize the Guard and send them home. Eisenhower then mobilized elements of the 101st Airborne to enforce the court's ruling.

Little Rock Students

Resistance also occurred at the college level when the governor of Mississippi defied the Supreme Court and attempted to prevent an African American named James Meredith from enrolling at the University of Mississippi. The university finally admitted Meredith after President Kennedy sent federal authorities to deal with the situation.

George Wallace Defies Integration
(Library of Congress)

Alabama's governor, George Wallace, tried to prevent the integration of the University of Alabama by physically blocking the entrance in protest. The incident ended when federal authorities again intervened and forced Wallace to comply.

Martin Luther King, Jr. and Nonviolent Protests

The Montgomery Bus Boycott

Segregation laws in the city of Montgomery, Alabama required African American passengers to sit in the rear of public buses. Blacks also had to give up their seats to white passengers if the bus was crowded. On December 1, 1955, a bus driver ordered **Rosa Parks**, an African American woman, to give up her seat to a white passenger. When she refused, the bus driver called the police who arrested her and took her to jail.

Rosa parks

Rosa Parks' arrest quickly united the black community of Montgomery in a city-wide protest. NAACP leaders formed the *Montgomery Improvement Association* and selected a young Baptist minister named **Dr. Martin Luther King Jr.** to lead them in a boycott of city buses. Almost overnight, the city's fifty thousand blacks united in walking to work or carpooling rather than riding buses. The boycott cost the city of Montgomery large amounts of money. It lasted over a year until, in November 1956, the Supreme Court ruled that buses in Montgomery must be integrated (desegregated). The **Montgomery Bus Boycott** was a major victory for African-Americans and served to make Martin Luther King Jr. a national figure.

Rev. Martin Luther King, Jr.

Dr. Martin Luther King Jr

Dr. King, was an incredibly intelligent man and a gifted public speaker. He became the recognized leader of the civil rights movement. King was greatly influenced by his religious faith and the philosophy of Gandhi, the leader who had used non-violent protests and **civil disobedience** (non-violent refusal to obey unjust laws) to win India's independence from Great Britain in the 1940s. Dr. King effectively used non-violence to win support for the civil rights movement. Although King was opposed to the use of violence, the same could not be said for many of his enemies. A gunman shot and killed King in April 1968 as he stood on the balcony of the hotel where he was staying in Memphis, Tennessee.

Sit-ins and Freedom Riders

On February 1, 1960, four black college students at North Carolina A&T University protested racial segregation in restaurants by sitting at a "whites only" lunch counter in Greensboro, North Carolina. When the management ordered them to leave, they peacefully refused. Within days, "**sit-ins**" (nonviolent protests in which blacks sat in segregated places until they were served or arrested) spread across North Carolina. Within a few weeks, such protests spread to cities throughout the South. As the movement grew, students gathered in Raleigh, North

Carolina in April 1960, and formed the Student Nonviolent Coordinating Committee (SNCC). These students devoted themselves to the use of non-violent protests to demand civil rights for African Americans.

In 1960, the Supreme Court ruled that segregation was illegal in bus stations open to interstate travel. In 1961, the Congress of Racial Equality or CORE (an organization founded in 1942 and devoted to social change through nonviolent action) organized **Freedom Rides** to test the Court's decision.

That summer, an integrated group of black and white "Freedom Riders" boarded a bus in Washington, DC and traveled south. The trip was mostly peaceful until the bus reached Anniston, Alabama. In Anniston, a white mob attacked the bus and set it on fire. Then they beat the passengers as they fled the burning bus. While the Freedom Rides resulted in the desegregation of some bus stations, perhaps their most important contribution was in drawing national attention to the cause of civil rights.

The March on Washington

King Addresses Crowd in Washington, D.C.

Civil rights protests continued in the South through 1962 and 1963. Wanting to keep pressure on President Kennedy and Congress to pass civil rights legislation, national civil rights leaders planned a march on the nation's capital. On August 28, 1963, Martin Luther King Jr. stood before the Lincoln Memorial at the **March on Washington** and addressed a crowd of more than 200,000 civil rights supporters. In perhaps his most famous speech, King spoke of his dream that the US would become a desegregated society. He challenged his listeners to envision with him a day when white and black people would live peacefully together with equal rights and equal justice.

Malcolm X and the Rise of Black Militant Movements

Malcolm X

Malcolm X was another famous leader. In contrast to the nonviolent approach of other leaders of the civil rights movement, Malcolm X preached that blacks should use "any means necessary" to secure their rights. Malcom Eventually went on a Muslim pilgrimage (a journey for a religious purpose) to the Islamic holy city of Mecca, Saudi Arabia. There he saw black and white Muslims praying and living together peacefully. Following this experience, Malcolm returned to the United States with less militant views. He stopped preaching that all white people are evil and began calling for whites and blacks to work together.

The softening of his views meant that many black militants, now considered Malcolm to be a traitor. On February 21, 1965, three African American men shot and killed Malcolm X while he spoke at a rally in Manhattan.

Inspired by the teachings of Malcolm X, some workers in the SNCC began to reject nonviolent protest as being too slow and ineffective. This militant faction took over leadership of the group when Stokely Carmichael became chairman of the SNCC in May 1966. He called for **Black Power**, a term that included pride in African heritage, separate black economic and political institutions, self-defense against white violence, and sometimes violent revolution. Black Power caused controversy at the 1968 Olympics when several black US medal winners raised black-glove-covered fists as a show of African American pride during the playing of the National Anthem rather than placing a hand over their hearts.

In 1966, **Black Panthers** emerged. This group advocated African Americans leading their own communities and demanded that the federal government take action to rebuild the ghettos of the nation's big cities. While the Panthers did have some violent encounters with police and often preached violent revolution, they also made positive contributions by setting up programs to aid poor, urban blacks.

Legislative Changes Brought About by the Civil Rights Movement

After the March on Washington, President Kennedy proposed new civil rights laws. Following Kennedy's assassination, the new president, **Lyndon B. Johnson**, strongly urged Congress to pass these laws in honor of the late president. Despite fierce opposition from southern members of Congress, Johnson pushed through the **Civil Rights Act of 1964**. The act prohibited segregation in public accommodations and discrimination in education and employment. It also gave the president the power to enforce the new law.

President Lyndon B. Johnson

1964 was also the year that the states ratified the **Twenty-fourth Amendment** to the Constitution. This amendment served to protect blacks' voting rights by making the poll tax illegal.

Congress passed the **Voting Rights Act** in 1965. It authorized the president to suspend literacy tests for voter registration and to send federal officials to register voters in the event that county officials failed to do so. This new law led to a huge increase in African American voter registration, as well as an increase in the number of African American candidates elected to public office. The Voting Rights Act and the Twenty-fourth Amendment were seen as huge victories by civil rights leaders who had always felt that the key to African American's advancement rest in securing the right to vote.

Civil Rights and the Cold War

The **Cold War** impacted the US civil rights movement. Across the globe and particularly in the underdeveloped nations of Africa, Asia, and Latin America, the United States and the USSR tried to out maneuver one another for influence. Each sought to make these nations allies. The Soviets pointed out to the leaders of developing nations the hypocrisy in US ideology. They argued that all the US talk about freedom and democracy was just words. Soviet leaders tried to convince non-white peoples that the United States only offered freedom to people of white European descent and that people of color could not trust the United States.

US presidents like Truman, Eisenhower, Kennedy, and Johnson understood this. They supported new civil rights legislation meant to increase US credibility in places like Africa and diffuse the Soviet's arguments. Martin Luther King Jr. and other civil rights leaders understood this too. King and others used the Cold War to their advantage to put pressure on the federal government to support civil rights.

Civil Rights and the Media

Civil rights leaders also understood the **power of the media**. Beginning in the 1950s and continuing into the 1960s, more and more US citizens owned televisions. Average people saw much of the civil rights movement unfold as they watched in their own living rooms. Rather than simply reading about civil rights demonstrations at which police beat and arrested peaceful demonstrators, TV viewers could see it with their own eyes. Many Americans, including whites, found the violence appalling. The media helped expose the brutality of southern officials in putting down non-violent protests. As a result, many people flocked to support the civil rights movement.

Practice 10.1: The Civil Rights Movement

1. Which of the following actions is illegal based on the Supreme Court's ruling in *Brown v. Board of Education*?

   A. a white principal turning away an African American student because there is a separate school in town for black children

   B. forcing elderly African-American women to have to give up their seats on a public buses

   C. the use of national guardsmen to settle racial disputes

   D. public officials using violence to break-up peaceful protests

2. Which of the following does **not** describe Dr. Martin Luther King Jr.?

   A. He admired the teachings of Gandhi and believed that nonviolence was the best way to bring about change for African Americans.

   B. He was a gifted public speaker and leader.

   C. He eventually abandoned nonviolence to lead the Black Militant movement.

   D. His leadership of the Montgomery Bus Boycott drew national attention to the Civil Rights Movement and made him a well-known figure.

3. What effects did the Voting Rights Act of 1965 and the Twenty-fourth Amendment to the Constitution have on African Americans' ability to vote in the United States?

4. How did leaders like Malcolm X and Stokely Carmichael differ from Martin Luther King Jr. when it came to their philosophies about how African Americans should pursue civil rights?

10.2 Johnson, Nixon, and Vietnam

In 1963, Lyndon Johnson became president following the death of John Kennedy. Johnson sought to transform US society using executive power. He launched the most aggressive domestic program since Roosevelt's New Deal.

Lyndon B. Johnson's "Great Society"

In addition to pushing Kennedy's proposed civil rights legislation through Congress, Johnson also set out to implement what he called the **"Great Society."** In addition to civil rights, it consisted of various proposed social programs and centered greatly around Johnson's declared **"War on Poverty."** Johnson was gifted at political dealings and had success pushing his programs through Congress. The Economic Opportunity Act combatted poverty and set aside money to establish VISTA (Volunteers in Service to America). VISTA mobilized volunteers to work in poorer communities within the United States. The act also established Job Corps for the purpose of educating and training inner-city youth for gainful employment.

Other "Great Society" programs included Medicare and Medicaid to ensure medical care for the elderly and poor, Head Start to help ensure better education for children of low-income families, the National Endowment for the Humanities, which gives grants and funding for the arts and scholarships, and establishment of the Department of Housing and Urban Development (HUD). HUD oversees housing needs, rehabilitates urban communities, and provides rent assistance to those living in low-income housing. It was headed by Robert C. Weaver, the first African-American ever appointed to a presidential cabinet. Johnson also endorsed and signed immigration legislation which lifted certain restrictions on new arrivals to the US and led to a massive increase in immigration, particularly from Latin American and Asian countries.

While the Great Society had noble intentions and some successes, it also required large amounts of funding. Government spending increased, and many in the US middle class came to resent the cost of these programs while at the same time criticizing them for yielding what they viewed as limited returns. As a result, political conservatism began to increase towards the latter half of the 1960s.

Lyndon B. Johnson Speech

Chapter 10

Concerns about Vietnam

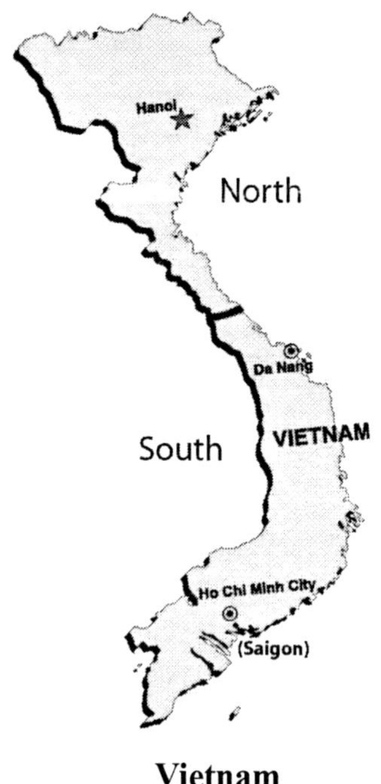

Vietnam

In the 1800s, France established a colony in a small Southeast Asian country called **Vietnam**. Following WWII, fighting erupted as Vietnamese nationalists wanted independence from France. This greatly concerned President Eisenhower because of the nationalists' ties to communism. At a conference in Geneva, Switzerland, countries met to search for a peaceful solution. The **Geneva Accords**, drafted in 1954, called for Vietnam to be divided into two nations.

Ho Chi Minh

The North established a communist-backed government under the rule of Ho Chi Minh. In the South, the United States supported the government of Ngo Kinh Diem. It was not long before war broke out between the two sides.

Even in his own country, Diem faced opposition. He imprisoned people who criticized his government, and he allowed US money sent to help his people end up in the pockets of corrupt politicians. Diem also alienated the mostly Buddhist population by trying to force his own Catholic beliefs on them.

US Involvement Begins

In the early '60s, both Eisenhower and Kennedy feared the spread of Communism. Both sent military advisors to aid South Vietnam against the North and against communist rebels in the South known as the **Viet Cong**. However, Kennedy and his secretary of defense, Robert McNamara, came to realize that Communism could not be defeated in Vietnam so long as Diem's corrupt government controlled the South. In 1963, Kennedy and McNamara contemplated how they might pull US military personnel out of South Vietnam. But an assassin named Lee Harvey Oswald killed Kennedy before any decision was reached. While historians still debate about how Kennedy might have dealt with Vietnam, Johnson's approach was clear. He vowed that he would not lose Vietnam to the Communists.

Gulf of Tonkin Resolution

Johnson won the election of 1964 by portraying his opponent, Barry Goldwater, as a man ready to plunge the US into a nuclear war over Vietnam. Meanwhile, Johnson downplayed his own intentions to escalate US involvement. Once elected, however, Johnson was prepared to increase the US military presence. In August 1964, just 2 months before the election, a key incident occurred in the Gulf of Tonkin. Johnson announced to the nation during his campaign that the North Vietnamese had attacked US ships. Details were sketchy, and some questioned if the event had occurred the way Johnson claimed, but Johnson was able to use the incident to get Congress to pass the **Gulf of Tonkin Resolution**. This resolution gave the president the authority to "take all necessary measures to repel any armed attack against the forces of the United States..." It gave Johnson the power to take military actions in Vietnam without having to get approval from Congress.

THE US WAR EFFORT IN VIETNAM

By 1965, the Viet Cong were continuing to expand as more and more of the poor in South Vietnam were drawn to their cause. Key to the Viet Cong's efforts were the supplies that came from North Vietnam. These supplies made their way south by way of a route through Laos and Cambodia called the Ho Chi Minh Trail. To try and cut off this support — and in response to an attack that killed eight US soldiers — Johnson ordered an intense bombing campaign against North Vietnam. The operation was code named **Operation Rolling Thunder**.

Fighting in Vietnam

During bombing campaigns in Vietnam, the US dropped thousands of tons of explosives (more than in World War II). The bombings destroyed bridges, supply lines, and villages. Sadly, these attacks killed many civilians in the process. Yet Johnson and McNamara refused to bomb certain targets that their military advisors believed were key for fear of starting a war with China and the USSR (both of which were supplying the North Vietnamese and Viet Cong). Between 1965 and 1968, the United States military presence increased dramatically.

THE VIET CONG AND GUERILLA WARFARE

The Viet Cong did not fight a traditional war. Instead they used **guerilla warfare**. This is a strategy in which a weaker army launches surprise attacks against a stronger enemy and then runs away before the stronger enemy can fully retaliate. The Viet Cong used guerilla warfare effectively as they sought to wear down the United States' will to fight.

TET OFFENSIVE

On January 30, 1968, the North Vietnamese and Viet Cong launched a major coordinated attack against the United States and South Vietnamese forces. Known as the **Tet Offensive**, it produced heavy fighting, even in the South Vietnamese capital of Saigon. The Viet Cong and North Vietnamese forces were eventually turned back, but they had won a psychological victory. The Tet Offensive showed that the Communists could launch a coordinated attack. It also led many people in the US to question how the government was handling the war and whether US troops should be there at all.

Attitudes About the War at Home

Few events in US history have divided people in the United States like the Vietnam War. On one hand, many people in the United States believed that it was important to fight communism at every turn. They believed that Vietnam was a noble cause and that it was not wrong to send troops. Such citizens were not upset about fighting the war; instead, they were upset with the government for limiting the military's ability to *win* the war. On the other hand, a growing number of citizens and activists proclaimed that it was wrong for US soldiers to even be in Vietnam. Some even viewed the US actions as "criminal."

Peace Symbol

Such unrest led to a large **anti-war movement**. Especially on college campuses, mass demonstrations against the war took place. Some protestors favored peaceful protest. Others went further and advocated violent revolution to overthrow what they saw as an unjust US government.

President Johnson found himself caught in the middle. His popularity plummeted as he was continuously blamed for failures in Vietnam. So great was the weight of the ordeal that Johnson decided not to run for re-election in 1968.

President Richard Nixon and Vietnam

President Richard Nixon took office in January 1969. He vowed to get the United States out of Vietnam. He advocated a policy of "Vietnamization." He wanted South Vietnamese soldiers to take the place of the US soldiers in Vietnam. However, while Nixon wanted to reduce the numbers of US troops in Southeast Asia (a promise he'd made during the presidential campaign), he was also determined to make sure that South Vietnam did not fall to the Communists. He combined his withdrawal of US troops with renewed bombing raids against North Vietnam and the neighboring countries of Cambodia and Laos. He believed that certain areas of these countries were supporting the Viet Cong.

Richard M. Nixon

In April 1970, Nixon went even further and authorized US troops to invade Cambodia for the purpose of destroying Communist training camps. Nixon did not expect these moves to win the war, but he hoped that they would give him more negotiating power for ending the war on favorable terms for the US.

THE END OF INVOLVEMENT

PARIS PEACE ACCORDS

The United States, South Vietnam, North Vietnam, and leaders of the Viet Cong finally met together in Paris, France in January 1973. There they signed the **Paris Peace Accords**, officially ending US involvement in Vietnam. The Paris agreement called for:

- The withdrawal of US troops from Vietnam within sixty days.
- The release of prisoners of war.
- All parties involved would end military activities in Laos and Cambodia.
- The 17th parallel would continue to divide North and South Vietnam.

FALL OF SAIGON

Following the US withdrawal, however, fighting quickly resumed. In the spring of 1975 (after Nixon had left office), North Vietnamese forces finally surrounded the South Vietnamese capital of **Saigon**. On April 29, the United States carried out a last-minute evacuation of the city. Military helicopters airlifted more than one thousand US personnel and six thousand South Vietnamese citizens to aircraft carriers offshore. The next day, April 30, Saigon fell to the North Vietnamese. Twenty-one years after the signing of the Geneva Accords, Vietnam was firmly in the hands of the Communists.

WAR PROTEST CONTINUE

KENT STATE

By invading Cambodia, Nixon set off a firestorm of protest at home. At **Kent State University**, the protest turned violent. When angry students attacked businesses and burned the army ROTC building on campus, the governor of Ohio sent in National Guard troops. When students started throwing rocks and other objects, the guardsmen retreated to higher ground and opened fire on the protesters. When the shooting ended, guardsmen had killed four people and left nine others seriously injured.

Shooting at Kent State

THE PENTAGON PAPERS

Another factor that caused public support for the war to dwindle occurred in 1971.The New York Times began publishing portions of the **Pentagon Papers**. The Papers were a study ordered by former secretary of defense, Robert McNamara, and documented the history of US involvement in Vietnam. They revealed that the executive branch had lied to Congress concerning the war. Presidents had made secret decisions and undertaken unapproved military actions. Many in the public were shocked and appalled, and support for the war quickly dwindled.

THE MEDIA AND VIETNAM

Much like the civil rights movement, the visual images of Vietnam greatly impacted people's attitudes about the war. Prior to Vietnam, citizens learned about foreign conflicts through newspapers and news reels. (These were news clips that preceded movies and usually portrayed any American war effort in a positive light.) Vietnam was the first conflict in which citizens could witness the death and destruction of war in their own living rooms. Such exposure to the war, coupled with the country's inability to win, led many to doubt or oppose the war.

Practice 10.2: Johnson, Nixon and Vietnam

1. Which of the following points would Presidents Eisenhower, Kennedy, Johnson, and Nixon all have agreed on regarding Vietnam?

   A. Vietnam is such a small country that the United States cannot afford to become involved there.

   B. The United States must escalate the US military presence in Vietnam.

   C. South Vietnam should not become a communist nation.

   D. To bring US troops home, the war must expand to Cambodia and Laos.

2. Congress passed the War Powers Act of 1973 to make sure that the president could no longer deploy military troops without the knowledge and approval of Congress. Which of the following legislative acts was it meant to reverse?

   A. Gulf of Tonkin Resolution

   B. the Geneva Accords

   C. the Paris Peace Accords

   D. the Pentagon Papers

3. What were the Paris Peace Accords and how effective were they in helping the United States achieve its goals for Vietnam?

10.3 SOCIAL REVOLUTION

As the nation entered the mid 1960s, fighting began in Vietnam, and the civil rights movement had raged for roughly a decade. The "baby boom generation" had matured and was now going off to college. The period marked a time of social revolution as the new youth generation questioned social norms and challenged traditional ideas about gender, race, government, and morality.

WOODSTOCK AND POLITICAL ACTIVISM

The Woodstock Music and Art Fair (known better as Woodstock) took place in upstate New York in 1969. Hundreds of thousands of people came to this festival to promote peace, hear the latest bands, use illegal drugs, and engage in behavior that many in the nation found shocking and immoral. The event, and peoples' varying reactions to it, served to illustrate the cultural division that was taking hold in the US during this time period and became a symbol of the **counterculture** forming among many of the nation's youth.

Woodstock

As young soldiers died in Vietnam, many citizens questioned the nation's objectives. At home, the civil rights movement, the women's movement, and protests against Vietnam continued to divide the country as never before. Meanwhile, television brought all of this conflict into the living rooms of US citizens on a daily basis. Out of the new wave of activism that arose on college campuses came the **Students for a Democratic Society (SDS)**. The SDS began with students who had taken part in the Civil Rights Movement and eventually expanded to include other social causes. They launched large protests and called for radical steps to deal with poverty, inequality, and ending the war in Vietnam. Many of its members played key roles in the emergence of what came to be called the "New Left." Individuals in this movement rejected many of the traditional views in society regarding race relations, gender roles, politics, and morality, and called for government action to bring about radical social change.

CAUSES AND SOCIAL MOVEMENTS

Not only did the civil rights movement of the 1950s and 60s serve to improve the social status of blacks in the US, but it also helped inspire and ignite other social movements as well. Other minorities, women, and those promoting political change were all influenced by the civil rights movement.

MIGRANT WORKERS

The United Farm Workers (UFW), founded in 1962 by Cesar Chavez, supported the rights of migrant farm workers, many of which were poor Hispanic immigrants. Chavez went to great lengths to improve the conditions under which migrant workers toiled, including personally conducting hunger strikes. Chavez and the UFW used the same type of non-violent protests that had proved effective by Martin Luther King, Jr. Perhaps the most famous campaign of the UFW was its boycott of California table grapes which led to a 1970 labor agreement.

The Women's Movement

Phyllis Schlafly

The **women's movement** often referred to as "women's liberation" or "women's lib," rejected traditional gender roles and advocated equality between men and women. Advocates of such positions became known as "feminists." Betty Friedan, a feminist author, wrote The Feminine Mystique. On the opposing side was Phyllis Schlafly who campaigned against the Equal Rights Amendment. For her, women can be mothers and later pursue a career in the workplace.

Betty Friedan

The Women's Movement led to a campaign to amend the Constitution to make sexual discrimination illegal. In 1972, the **Equal Rights Amendment** passed Congress and was sent to the states for ratification. The amendment was highly controversial, however, and therefore ran into opposition from women as well as men. It failed to be ratified by enough states and was never added to the US Constitution.

Many of the same people who mourned the death of the Equal Rights Amendment cheered what they saw as a great victory in the case of ***Roe v. Wade***. Prior to 1973, states could outlaw or restrict abortions during a woman's pregnancy if they so wished. Citing an *implied* (not directly stated in the Constitution) right to privacy, the Supreme Court ruled state laws restricting a woman's right to an abortion during the first three months of pregnancy to be unconstitutional. Nearly forty years later, *Roe v. Wade* remains one of the most controversial decisions in US history.

Practice 10.3: Social Revolution

1. Which one of the following people would have been **most** inspired by Woodstock?

   A. a migrant worker excited to know someone is fighting for his welfare

   B. a housewife wanting to feel like it's ok to have a life outside of the home

   C. US citizens holding traditional rallies

   D. a college student who wants to rebel

2. Which statement would a member of the women's movement have **most disagreed** with?

   A. "There is no reason why women should not be allowed to serve in combat as part of the US military."

   B. "Women are fulfilled by being good wives and mothers, but husbands need to show more appreciation for what their wives do."

   C. "If a woman does not want to get married, that's fine. If she does, that's fine too. What's important is that she is not defined by whether or not she's a '*good wife*'."

   D. "The idea that women should refrain from being sexually active before marriage while men run around 'sowing their wild oats' is a ridiculous and outdated way to think."

3. What was SDS and what was its purpose?

10.4 The Nixon Presidency

Detente

Before 1968, US presidents traditionally took a tough, militaristic stance towards the USSR and China. Things began to change with the election of **Richard M. Nixon**. President Nixon believed in **detente**. Under this policy, Nixon sought to ease the tensions that existed between the US and these nations through diplomacy rather than intimidation or force. Nixon became the first president to publicly acknowledge the Communist government of **China** and even visited that nation during his first term. Nixon also met with the leader of the USSR and negotiated a treaty lessening the number of nuclear missiles.

President Nixon and Secretary of State Kissinger

Domestic Policies and Issues

Nixon launched a domestic set of policies he referred to as **"New Federalism."** Nixon wanted to cut government programs and spending and give more power back to the states. He wanted to turn back the aggressive tide of civil rights legislation and advocated a "middle road" between instant integration and "segregation forever" (a cry of many southern politicians of the 1960s).

Despite Nixon's efforts, civil rights continued to advance during his time in office and even won key court victories. In ***Swann v. Charlotte-Mecklenburg Board of Education (1971)***, the Court tackled the issue of **school busing** (the practice of having students attend schools outside the boundaries of what might normally be their district in order to achieve racial integration).

Although Nixon sided with those who opposed the practice, the Supreme Court agreed with a lower court decision that voluntary integration was not working and that public schools could integrate through busing.

The Oil Embargo

Gas Lines

Nixon faced a fuel crisis in 1973. In response to the United States backing Israel during its war with Egypt and Syria, the Arab states comprising OPEC (Organization of Petroleum Exporting Countries), imposed an embargo in which they refused to sell oil to the US. As a result, US citizens sat in long lines waiting to pay high prices for the tiny bit of gas that was available. Fortunately, the embargo ended after only a few months, but it served to cause economic hardship and exposed the nation's heavy dependence on foreign oil.

Environmental Protection

The embargo reminded US citizens that natural resources were not limitless. This contributed to the rise of the **environmental movement**, in which citizens advocated conservation and government policies designed to preserve and protect the environment. Congress passed legislation to maintain clean air and water and the administration established the **EPA** (Environmental Protection Agency) to be responsible for setting and enforcing national pollution-control standards.

Watergate

Despite some of the social conflicts and economic woes facing the nation, most citizens felt far more positive about Nixon than they did the liberal Democratic candidate, George McGovern, in 1972. As a result, Nixon easily won re-election to a second term. War protests and social unrest, however, left President Nixon and those close to him fearing the possibility of political conspiracies (plots to undermine the government). Prior to the 1972 election, officials loyal to the president devised a number of schemes meant to protect him. One such plan involved wiretapping phones at the Democratic National Committee headquarters. The attempt failed, and police arrested five men for breaking into the Watergate office complex (site of the Democratic headquarters). What followed came to be known as the **Watergate scandal**.

Watergate Hearings

Nixon had not known about the plan; but he did participate in the cover-up. Washington Post reporters Bob Woodward and Carl Bernstein pursued the Watergate story and played a major role in revealing how high up the scandal went. In 1973, the US Senate formed a Watergate Committee to investigate the scandal. The hearing revealed a secret taping system in the president's office. Nixon refused to release the tapes, claiming that he was not required to do so by law. The Supreme Court ruled that Nixon had to deliver the tapes, however, and he finally complied. Although the released transcripts had an 18 1/2 minute portion that was suspiciously missing, there was still enough on the tapes to seriously damage the president. Four days later, Richard M. Nixon became the only president in history to resign from office. Had he not done so, he would have been impeached by the House and likely found guilty by the Senate. Watergate seriously damaged many citizens' trust in their government.

Woodward and Bernstein

Practice 10.4: The Nixon Presidency

1. Which of the following statements **best** describes Nixon's "New Federalism?"

   A. It was an aggressive effort to promote civil rights legislation.

   B. It was an attempt to give more authority back to the states.

   C. It represented a new approach to dealing with the USSR.

   D. It was designed to impose sanctions on nations who supported OPEC.

2. What role did Nixon play in the Watergate scandal and why did he choose to resign?

CHAPTER 10 REVIEW

Key terms

civil rights movement
Brown v. Board of Education
Heart of Atlanta Motel, Inc. v. United States
Rosa Parks
Dr. Martin Luther King Jr.
Montgomery Bus Boycott
civil disobedience
sit-ins
Freedom Rides
March on Washington
Malcolm X
Black Power
Lyndon B. Johnson
Civil Rights Act of 1964
Twenty-fourth Amendment
Voting Rights Act
Cold War
power of the media
Great Society
War on Poverty
Vietnam
Gulf of Tonkin Resolution
Operation Rolling Thunder
guerilla warfare
Tet Offensive
anti-war movement
Richard Nixon
Paris Peace Accords
Saigon
Kent State University
Pentagon Papers
counterculture
Students for a Democratic Society (SDS)
United Farm Workers
women's movement
Equal Rights Amendment
Roe v. Wade
détente
New Federalism
Swann v. Charlotte-Mecklenberg Board of Education
school busing
environmental movement
EPA
Watergate scandal

Chapter 10 Review Questions

1. Dr. Martin Luther King Jr.'s philosophy regarding the civil rights movement can **best** be described as what?

   A. civil disobedience meant to win public support to the cause of civil rights

   B. a militant movement that called for African Americans to resist unjust laws by any and all means

   C. merely political because he advocated no action other than to encourage blacks to vote for pro-civil rights candidates

   D. secular and innovative because he rejected religion and ignored any attempts by past leaders to bring about social justice

2. On which of the following points would Malcolm X and Martin Luther King Jr. have **most agreed**?

   A. the need for African Americans to obtain civil rights

   B. the methods that should be used by African Americans to pursue civil rights

   C. the effectiveness of civil disobedience

   D. the willingness to use violence, if necessary, to obtain social justice

3. What impact did the Voting Rights Act of 1965, the Civil Rights Act of 1964, and the Twenty-fourth Amendment to the Constitution all have?

   A. They guaranteed blacks the right to vote by making it illegal to impose a minimum voting age on African Americans.

   B. Together, they protected African Americans' voting rights and struck down segregation in public accommodations.

   C. They removed race restrictions on who could run for office and protected African Americans' freedom of speech.

   D. They granted African Americans the right to vote in the US for the first time since Reconstruction.

4. The Viet Cong can **best** be described as what?

   A. Communist invaders from North Vietnam

   B. pro-US rebels helping US forces during the Vietnam war

   C. South Vietnamese supporting Ho Chi Minh

   D. Cambodian Communists launching raids on US forces in South Vietnam

5. The effects of the Paris Peace Accords are **best** described by which of the following statements?

   A. They marked a new era in US-Chinese relations, in which the US finally acknowledged Mao's communist government.

   B. They continued relations with the Soviets after Ford became president of the United States.

   C. They resulted in a peaceful resolution to the war in Vietnam, with the boundary between north and south returning to what it was before the war.

   D. They served to technically end US involvement in Vietnam but failed to bring about peace, leading to the eventual fall of South Vietnam.

6. Which of the following is **true** regarding President Richard Nixon?

   A. He is the only president in US history to resign after it was discovered that he planned the Watergate break-in.

   B. He was only the second president ever impeached.

   C. He was forced to resign for his participation in a cover-up.

   D. Despite his failures in foreign policy, he was admired as a staunch defender of civil rights prior to resigning from office.

7. US society during the 1960s can **best** be described as what?
   A. calm, reserved, and traditional
   B. full of unrest, divisions, and social transformation
   C. unpatriotic and favoring communism
   D. a time in which political authority was unquestioned

8. What was Johnson's Great Society?
   A. a movement to end communism in Asia.
   B. a piece of civil rights legislation.
   C. a set of programs aimed at ending poverty.
   D. a war resolution giving the president more power.

9. Why did Lyndon Johnson **not** run for re-election in 1968?
   A. He was disappointed that his Great Society had failed.
   B. He found himself unpopular due to the war in Vietnam.
   C. He had already served two terms and could not run.
   D. He did run, but lost the election to Richard Nixon.

10. The image above depicts the
   A. Great Society.
   B. civil rights movement.
   C. Tet Offensive.
   D. Anti-war movement.

Chapter 11
End of the Cold War and Modern America

This chapter addresses the following standard(s):

New Indicators	8.4, 8.5, 8.6
Old Indicators	9.4, 10.1, 10.2

11.1 Conservatism, Reagan, and the End of the Cold War

The Rise of Conservatism

During the 1960s, many US citizens called for political and social transformation. Groups like SDS protested against the Vietnam War and accused the United States of fostering a corrupt political and economic system. Some groups even identified with communist movements in developing countries. Meanwhile, a new youth counterculture challenged traditional views regarding family, religion, and morality.

Barry Goldwater

Many citizens, however, pushed back against such social and political movements. They comprised a new **conservatism** that championed traditional values, opposed extensive government regulations, favored private property rights over newly passed civil rights legislation, and supported a strong military to oppose the Soviet Union and the threat of communism.

The Election of 1964

The nation first took notice of this rising wave of conservatism during the election of 1964. To the surprise of many, conservative candidate, Barry Goldwater, bested his opponents to become the first conservative to win the Republican nomination for president. President Johnson soundly defeated Goldwater in the general election. But Goldwater's candidacy had great impact for three predominant reasons. First, it proved that conservatives' message resonated with many citizens. Second, it showed conservatives' ability to organize well enough to win the nomination of a major political party. Third, Goldwater's argument that civil rights legislation violated constitutional property rights allowed him to become the first Republican candidate to win southern states since the end of Reconstruction, bringing an end to the "Solid South."

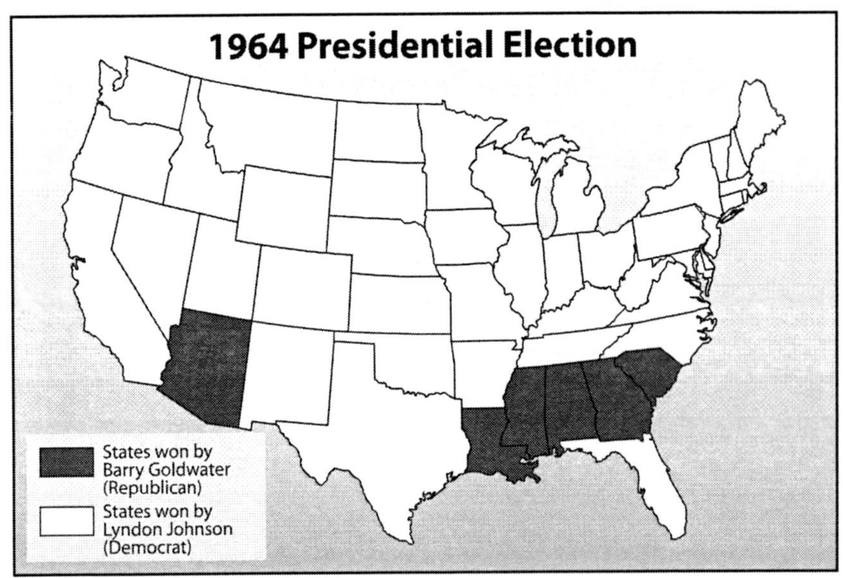

Electorial Map 1964 showing Goldwater Won South

Ronald Reagan

Out of Goldwater's defeat arose a new conservative champion: **Ronald Reagan**. Formerly a Hollywood actor, Reagan was a charismatic communicator who believed in the conservative message. He won political notoriety campaigning for Goldwater in 1964. Then, in 1966, Reagan shocked many experts when he won election as the governor of California. He served two terms before running for president in 1976. He lost the nomination to Republican President Gerald Ford. But Reagan's popularity made him a key political player. He ran again in 1980, this time winning the nomination and defeating the Democratic President Jimmy Carter in the general election.

The Reagan Years

"Reaganomics"

Reagan

When Ronald Reagan entered office in 1981, he introduced a plan that his critics quickly labeled **"Reaganomics."** It was a plan that was based on supply-side economics. Reagan believed that the economy would be stimulated and would recover quickest if the supply of goods increased. He backed policies and supported corporate tax cuts designed to benefit producers (corporations, small business owners, investors, etc.). This reasoning was often referred to as the **"trickle-down theory,"** because it advocated that the benefits felt by business owners would eventually "trickle down" to consumers and the average working class. By cutting taxes imposed on businesses and corporations, Reagan believed that business owners and employers would spend more money to hire workers and increase production.

Initially, Reagan's approach was the object of ridicule as the nation experienced a recession in the early '80s. Eventually, however, the economy did get better during his first term. One of Reagan's most famous quotes as the economy improved was, "You know its working, because they (his critics) aren't calling it 'Reaganomics' anymore."

National Debt

US Military

When Ronald Reagan became president, he believed that two major things needed to happen. First, the size and role of government needed to decrease. Second, the US military had to be strengthened. This meant that at the same time Reagan was spending big bucks on the military, he was cutting taxes and decreasing government regulation in other areas. The massive spending combined with less revenue from taxes contributed to a record **national debt**.

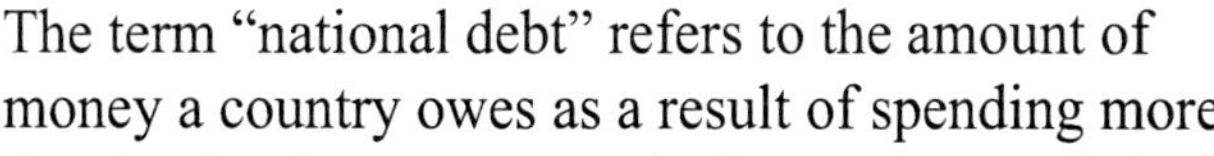

The term "national debt" refers to the amount of money a country owes as a result of spending more than it takes in as revenue. At first, most people in the United States didn't care. As they saw it, Reagan had strengthened the armed forces and his tax cuts were tremendously popular. It would be his successor, George H.W. Bush, who would have to deal with the debt of the Reagan years.

Reagan and the "Evil Empire"

Reagan was convinced that the Soviet Union could not be trusted and that they would stop short of nothing but worldwide domination. Reagan made headlines during his first term when he referred to the USSR as an "evil empire." To make matters more complicated, Soviet leader Brezhnev and his first two successors died during the first few years of Reagan's presidency, giving the president no time to build any kind of diplomatic relationship.

Reagan believed that the Soviet's communist economy could not survive an arms race much longer. He believed that a military buildup by the United States would not only increase the nation's defenses, but that it would bring about the ultimate collapse of communism in the Soviet Union as well. Reagan set about pouring $1.5 trillion into the nations' military.

Reagan and Gorbachev

In 1985, a young and progressive leader by the name of **Mikhail Gorbachev** became the leader of the USSR. Despite Reagan's misgivings about the Soviets, the two struck up an unlikely friendship. In 1987, Reagan and Gorbachev signed a treaty, which reduced the number of US and Soviet missiles in Europe.

Mikhail Gorbachev

The Iron Curtain Comes Down

Gorbachev realized that the hurting Soviet economy could not sustain an escalated arms race with the US. He initiated *glasnost* (political openness) and *perestroika* (a restructuring of the economy to allow limited free enterprise). These changes, along with the economic collapse of communist nations in eastern Europe, paved the way for the fall of communism in the Soviet Union and its satellite nations.

Ronald Reagan and Mikhail Gorbachev

On November 9, 1989, the East German government announced that people could travel freely to West Berlin. Germans flocked to the Berlin Wall and began tearing it down with sledgehammers and anything else they could find. The wall, and the "iron curtain," had fallen. Except for a failed coup (attempt by certain members of the government to overthrow those in power) in the early '90s that was meant to remove Gorbachev and reverse his policies, the Cold War was over. Just a few years after the fall of the Berlin Wall, the Soviet Union itself dissolved. It had survived less than eighty years.

Reagan's Final Years and Legacy

Iran-Contra Hearings

Reagan's presidency was not without its trials. During the early 1980s, Reagan committed US forces to Lebanon as part of a UN peacekeeping mission after Israel invaded to attack Palestinian camps it suspected of launching attacks against northern Israelis. Over two hundred US soldiers died as the result of a suicide bombing while stationed there. The US eventually withdrew its troops without peace being restored to the region.

Later, Reagan's administration also suffered the embarrassment of a scandal known as the **Iran-Contra Affair**. Administration officials secretly negotiated the sale of weapons to Iran in exchange for US hostages being held in the Middle East. They then funneled the money illegally to fund anti-communist rebels in Nicaragua known as the Contras. Although investigators never determined that Reagan knew about the deal, several Reagan officials ended up facing criminal charges.

Still, despite the challenges and a scandal, many US citizens remember Reagan as one of the nation's foremost presidents. The economy did well under his leadership, the US military became stronger, and conservatives credited his foreign policies with pressuring the Soviets in a manner that led to the end of the Cold War. Reagan won re-election easily in 1984 and left office in 1989 immensely popular. He did, however, run up a massive national debt which his critics often point to as one of the greatest fallacies of his presidency.

Practice 11.1: Ronald Reagan and the End of the Cold War

1. Which one of the following policies would Ronald Reagan have **most agreed** with?

   A. cutting taxes on small business owners

   B. cutting military spending

   C. raising taxes on businesses

   D. increasing the size of government

2. The term "Reaganomics" refers to which of the following?

   A. Reagan's approach to the Cold War

   B. Reagan's economic policies

   C. Reagan's desire to strengthen the military

   D. Reagan's desire to raise taxes

3. In what way did Reagan's decision to increase military spending affect the Cold War?

11.2 Events and Issues: 1990–2000

George H.W. Bush

After two terms as president, Reagan left office in January 1989. His vice president, **George H.W. Bush**, succeeded him. Bush was in office when the Berlin Wall came down and when the Soviet Union finally collapsed in the early 90s.

President George H. W. Bush

The Persian Gulf War

Saddam Hussein

Bush acted as commander-in-chief over the nation's military during the Persian Gulf War in 1991. In 1990, Iraq's leader, Saddam Hussein, invaded the neighboring country of Kuwait. Due in part to the reliance on oil from Kuwait and nearby Saudi Arabia, Saddam's actions concerned the United States. President Bush worked through the UN to coordinate an alliance of twenty-eight countries that took military action against Iraq after Saddam refused to withdraw back across the Iraqi border. The war lasted only forty-two days and resulted in the liberation of Kuwait.

Foreign Oil

Events like the OPEC oil embargo of the early '70s and the Persian Gulf War of the early '90s served to shine a spotlight on a growing concern in the United States: the nation's dependence on **foreign oil**. Most US citizens believed that the nation should not rely so heavily on foreign oil supplies, especially from nations that did not maintain good relations with the United States. Some called for more oil drilling and mining to access rich fuel reserves at home. Others feared the damage that such practices could do to the environment. They emphasized the need to pursue alternative sources of fuel.

THE ECONOMY AND THE ELECTION OF 1992

President Bill Clinton

The presidential election of 1992 was one of the most memorable in history. The Republicans put their hopes in President Bush. The Democrats nominated Arkansas's governor **Bill Clinton**. Clinton understood that Democratic candidates had suffered in recent elections because voters perceived them as being "tax and spend liberals" who would raise taxes to fund big government. Clinton successfully portrayed himself as a "New Democrat" who was moderate (in between conservative and liberal) rather than liberal.

H. Ross Perot

What made the '92 election so different was the fact that it featured a formidable third party candidate.Texas billionaire businessman, H. Ross Perot, entered the race for president as an independent candidate. Because of the discontent many felt with the federal government and the traditional two-party system, Perot gained a great deal of national support. At one point, Perot was actually even with Clinton and Bush in the national polls. But Perot dropped out of the race unexpectedly, only to change his mind and re-enter. Perot's indecisive behavior cost him the loyalty of many of his supporters and his campaign never regained its momentum. In the end, Bill Clinton won with less than 50% of the popular vote.

THE CLINTON PRESIDENCY

ECONOMIC AND DOMESTIC AFFAIRS

The economy saw an upswing during the Clinton presidency. Under Clinton, the nation went from having a massive **budget deficit** (spending more money than the government has in a given year) to a **budget surplus** (spending less money than the government has in a given year). The United States also ratified **NAFTA** (The North American Free Trade Agreement). NAFTA promoted free trade (no trade restrictions) between the US, Canada, and Mexico, and caused considerable controversy in the United States. Many labor unions feared that the agreement would encourage US businesses to relocate to Mexico where they'd face fewer restrictions and be able to pay lower wages. Proponents of NAFTA, however, argued that it would create jobs in the United States by increasing foreign markets for US business.

Clinton sought to improve the US **healthcare system**. Disturbed that nearly forty million US citizens still had no medical insurance, Clinton appointed his own wife, Hillary Clinton, to head a task force to analyze health care and propose reforms. Clinton ended up presenting to Congress a plan that called for a government-supervised health insurance program that guaranteed affordable health coverage to every US citizen. The plan was rejected by Congress after roughly a year of debate. Many insurance and business interests had opposed the plan and did an effective job of lobbying and building political support against it. In addition, many conservatives felt that it was too expensive and another example of "tax and spend liberalism" to fund government programs. Critics also argued that government control would ultimately hurt the quality of health care in the US and pointed to examples in other countries to support their claim.

THE "CONTRACT WITH AMERICA" AND THE '94 ELECTION

Newt Gingrich

The Clinton administration experienced a setback in the face in 1994 when the Republicans won control of both the House and the Senate. Georgia Republican representative, Newt Gingrich became a nationally-known politician when he instituted the Contract with America. The "contract" was a pledge by conservatives to scale back the role of government, cut taxes, and balance the budget. It helped propel the Republicans to victory in the 1994 congressional elections and enabled Gingrich to become the Speaker of the House.

A huge showdown between Clinton and Gingrich's Republican-led Congress occurred in 1995 over proposed budget cuts. When the two sides could not compromise, the federal government was forced to temporarily shut down and cease services to millions of people. It was the spring of '96 before the two sides reached an agreement. The **budget battle** turned out to be a plus for Clinton. Prior to the showdown, Clinton's popularity had been fading. Fortunately for the president, however, most people blamed Congress for the government shutdown.

Clinton Signing Welfare Reform

In August of 1996, Clinton signed into law a sweeping **welfare reform**. Declaring it "the end of welfare as we know it," Clinton placed new restrictions on entitlements (special programs and benefits from the government, like welfare) and scaled back social spending. The reforms also placed lifetime limits on the amount of aid families could receive, required most adults to find work within two years of applying for aid, and placed more conditions on qualifying for food stamps (vouchers from the government that can be used by low-income families to purchase food). The policy boosted Clinton's popularity just before the election. He easily defeated Republican Bob Dole and Ross Perot (this time the nominee of the newly-created Reform Party) to win the 1996 presidential election.

SCANDAL AND IMPEACHMENT

Bill Clinton is acknowledged by many to have been a brilliant politician and an effective president. His legacy is forever attached, however, to a series of scandals that dogged his candidacy and his administration.

Clinton and Lewinsky

The final scandal to hit the Clinton White House was by far the biggest. A young woman named Paula Jones accused Clinton of sexual harassment before he had become president. During the investigation, officials asked Clinton about the nature of his relationship with a White House intern named **Monica Lewinsky**. Under oath, before a grand jury, the president denied that he had ever had any sexual relationship with the young lady. As more evidence came to light, however, it became apparent that Clinton had lied.

In August 1998, Clinton went on national television and admitted having a relationship with the Lewinsky that was "inappropriate."

On December 19, 1998, the House voted to **impeach** President Bill Clinton. He was only the second president in history to be impeached; the first being Andrew Johnson (Nixon was never impeached because he resigned before he could be). Clinton's presidency survived because the Senate voted to acquit him.

THE PRESIDENTIAL ELECTION OF 2000

Decided by a mere 537 votes in the swing state of Florida, the **election of 2000** is to date the closest election in US history. It is also one of the few in which the winner in the Electoral College failed to win the popular vote.

Al Gore

The Democratic candidate for president was Vice President Al Gore. The Republicans nominated former Texas governor, **George W. Bush** (the oldest son of President George HW Bush). On election night, the outcome was decided by Florida's vote count. Florida had twenty-five electoral votes. All of them would go to whichever candidate got the most votes, giving the candidate the electoral votes he needed to win the presidency. Early in the evening, the media reported that Al Gore had won in Florida based on exit polls. But these predictions were made before voting in the panhandle (the western part of Florida that sits in the central, rather than the eastern, time zone) had finished. As the evening wore on and the votes were counted, members of the press switched gears and announced that Florida was still up for grabs. A few hours later, news agencies announced that Bush had won Florida, and with it the election.

President George W. Bush

Al Gore called Bush and congratulated him. Then, he climbed into his limousine to make the short drive to address hundreds of his supporters and let them know that he had conceded the election. But on the way, Gore received word that the race in Florida had tightened and that the two candidates were now separated by fewer than one thousand votes. Gore stopped his limo and turned around. He called Bush, who was preparing to make his victory speech, and informed him that he was taking back his earlier concession. Voters sat up late into the night and into the early morning hours, waiting to hear who their next president would be. They went to bed still not knowing.

George W. Bush Inauguration

What followed was a month of debate. Bush had won more votes in Florida, but a number of voting irregularities suggested that some of the votes intended for Gore had accidently been cast for third party conservative candidate, Patrick Buchanan. On December 12, 2000, the United States Supreme Court voted 5 – 4 to stop any future recounts. Gore finally conceded the election, and George W. Bush became the 43rd president of the United States. Many Democrats accused Bush of stealing the election. Meanwhile, some Republicans sarcastically responded that if Democrats in Florida were "too dumb to vote correctly," then they didn't deserve to win anyway.

Practice 11.2: Two Bushes and a "New Democrat"

1. President George H.W. Bush gained great popularity for which of the following?

   A. handling of the nation's economy

   B. victory in the Persian Gulf War

   C. balancing the budget

   D. NAFTA

2. Which president helped lead the nation's government from a budget deficit to a budget surplus?

   A. George H.W. Bush

   B. Bill Clinton

   C. George W. Bush

   D. No president has ever presided over a budget surplus.

3. What was welfare reform and how did it impact the 1996 election?

4. What key roles did the state of Florida and the Supreme Court play in the presidential election of 2000?

11.3 The Middle East and the Rise of Terrorism

Since the founding of Israel in 1948, Arab and Persian Gulf nations which are predominantly Muslim have harbored great hostility towards the predominantly Jewish Israelis. Many Middle East nations refuse to recognize Israel's right to exist because they view Palestine (Israel) as rightfully belonging to the Arab Palestinian people. The conflict has led to a number of wars in the region as well as ongoing violence between Palestinians and Israelis. Because the United States has traditionally shown support for Israel, many in the Middle East have feelings of anger and animosity towards the United States as well. In recent years, this alliance with Israel has been one of the factors making the United States a major target of Islamic **terrorists** (criminals who destroy property and kill innocent civilians in the name of a political or social cause). These terrorists subscribe to a radical form of Islam which advocates violence to overthrow the United States and other western nations.

The most formidable and best known Islamic terrorist group is **Al-Qaeda** (Al-kīda). The group's founding leader was **Osama bin Laden**. Al-Qaeda first gained international attention when it was linked to US embassy bombings in Tanzania and Kenya. Then, in 2000, terrorists attacked the *USS Cole* as it sat anchored in a harbor in Yemen.

Osama bin Laden

The Terrorist Attacks of 9/11

Firemen with Flag

Life in the United States changed forever on **September 11, 2001**. That morning, people across the country watched in shock as terrorists flew hijacked commercial airliners into the World Trade Center in New York City and the Pentagon in Washington, DC. The attack killed thousands as the Twin Towers of the Trade Center came crashing down, and the Pentagon burst into flames. Meanwhile, another hijacked plane crashed in a field in Pennsylvania, killing everyone on board. It went down when the passengers revolted and prevented the airliner from reaching its intended target (believed to be either the Capitol or the White House). In one day, four planes were hijacked, the World Trade Center was destroyed, and the Pentagon had been badly damaged. Far more tragic, however, were the many lives that had been lost. The date remembered as **9/11** brought the reality of terrorism home to the United States and shook people's sense of national security more than any event since the bombing of Pearl Harbor.

The War on Terror

President Bush responded by declaring a **"war on terror."** He created a new government department for the purpose of preparing and protecting the nation against future terrorist attacks — the Department of Homeland Security. Among other things, it greatly increased airline security to prevent future hijackings and instituted a color-coded terrorist alert system to warn the public when there is increased reason to fear a terrorist attack.

Bush also signed into law the US PATRIOT Act. The new law increased the authority of US law enforcement agencies and allowed them greater latitude in what measures they used to obtain information. Although the law came to be criticized by some as infringing too much on civil liberties, it was renewed by Congress and the president in March 2006.

Afghanistan

Having confirmed that Al-Qaeda and bin Laden were responsible for the attacks of 9/11, President Bush set about forming an international coalition of nations to take military and diplomatic action. The government knew that bin Laden was in **Afghanistan**, enjoying the protection of the Taliban government. When the US insisted that the Taliban hand over bin Laden, the Taliban refused. In October of 2001, the US military launched Operation Enduring Freedom. Within weeks, the invasion succeeded in toppling the Taliban and making it impossible for Al-Qaeda to train and plan its operations as it had before. Today, international troops remain in Afghanistan, rebuilding the country, supporting the new government, battling pockets of resistance, and continuing the search for terrorists. In spring 2011, US troops finally tracked Osama bin Laden to a compound in Pakistan, where they shot and killed him.

War in Iraq

As part of his strategy in the war on terror, Bush felt that the US could not simply sit back and defend against future attacks. He believed that the US needed to strike first against terrorists and state-sponsored terrorism (terrorism officially supported by a national government). In 2003, this policy resulted in the **War in Iraq**. Believing Saddam Hussein had weapons of mass destruction that might be used to support terrorism, the United States and several allies invaded Iraq and removed Saddam from power.

Statue of Saddam Hussein Being Torn Down in Baghdad

US Helicopter in Iraq

For all of the excitement over Saddam's fall from power, however, major problems followed in Iraq. Most notable, the US forces never found the alleged "weapons of mass destruction." The Bush administration came under harsh criticism because it was on the basis that such weapons existed and were in Saddam's possession that Congress had supported the war effort. The president's harshest critics accused him of lying. Others defended the president, stating that he simply acted on the information that he had and that Saddam's unwillingness to let the UN inspectors investigate made it necessary to assume that Iraq had weapons it was trying to hide.

Successes in Iraq included the formation of a new democratic government, a new constitution, building projects, and greater opportunities for women. However, terrorist insurgents and religious factions within the country have also served to increase violence. Many US soldiers lost their lives attempting to stabilize the country. In 2011, after more than eight years, Bush's successor, President Barack Obama, announced that he would withdraw the last US troops from Iraq before the beginning of 2012.

US Influence in the Middle East

Historically, the United States has exercised influence in the Middle East, especially since the founding of Israel in 1948. The United States has traditionally been an Israeli ally and has supported Israel during several Arab-Israeli conflicts. In 1978, President Jimmy Carter played a key role in negotiating a successful and long-lasting peace agreement between Israel and Egypt: the **Camp David Accords**.

Today, the United States continues to exercise influence in the region. This often causes conflict. American ties to Israel have made the nation an object of resentment for Arab and Persian countries. In recent years, US leaders have had to deal with the threat of Iran building nuclear weapons. In 2011, a wave of revolutions took place in the Middle East, beginning in Egypt and toppling leaders in several countries. Because of its rich oil supplies, key trading routes, and important geographic location, the Middle East will remain a region of interest for the United States.

Practice 11.3: The Middle East and Terrorism

1. What was significant about September 11, 2001?

2. Which of the following countries was attacked for harboring Al-Qaeda?

   A. Afghanistan

   B. Iraq

   C. Iran

   D. Israel

3. What country was attacked because the United States believed its leader had weapons of mass destruction?

   A. Afghanistan

   B. Iraq

   C. Israel

   D. Egypt

11.4 Key Issues Facing Modern America

Immigration

One of the greatest reasons for racial and cultural diversity in the United States is **immigration**. In recent decades, more and more immigrants have come from Latin America. While there are many people who immigrate to the United States legally each year, a growing number tend to be **illegal immigrants** who enter the United States across its southern border. As a result, the US Hispanic population has grown tremendously in recent decades.

Illegal Immigrant Protesting

One of the effects of this increase has been a controversial acceptance of **bilingualism** (accommodating for the use of more than one language). As the number of people in the US who speak Spanish as a first language grows, more and more states and government institutions are beginning to communicate in Spanish as well as English. In public schools, there is some emphasis on bilingual education. First mandated by Congress in 1968, this is the practice of providing students with access to public education taught in their own language. Some have argued that such practices are destructive because they hinder newcomers to the United States from learning English and serve to divide rather than unite people in the US. Proponents point out that it enables immigrants to learn more easily and maintain their cultural identity. They also argue that, because the United States has no official language, there is no reason why education and public information should not be offered in other languages as well as English.

United States and Mexico Border

Because many immigrants are here illegally, some citizens want existing immigration laws strictly enforced and illegal immigration halted. Advocates of such positions point out that the millions of illegal immigrants who live in the United States cause a drain on the nation's health care system and public services without contributing enough taxes to cover the costs. Critics of this position, however, point out that the vast majority of illegal immigrants are decent, hard working people who just want a better way of life. They also claim that many of these immigrants are necessary to sustain the nation's economy because they do many of the menial tasks and manual labor jobs that US citizens will not do.

Economic Disparity

Economic disparity refers to the differences in income and assets that exist when comparing individuals and/or different populations within a society. It is important to remember that, compared to the rest of the world, just about every US citizen compares favorably on an economic basis. However, within the United States, there is a great deal of disparity. The bulk of the nation's wealth is in the hands of a relatively small percentage of US citizens. On average, white US citizens tend to do better economically than minority citizens. Due to **urban flight** (trend in which middle class citizens leave the cities to live in the suburbs) inner cities tend to be economically worse off than the suburbs.

Upper Class and Lower Class

How to deal with the reality of economic disparity is often an issue of political debate. Conservative politicians tend to advocate less government control. They believe that the government should simply provide equal opportunity for all citizens to pursue success without hindering the process with high taxes or excessive regulation. By contrast, more liberal politicians believe that it is up to the government to get involved. They tend to favor higher taxes for raising revenue that can then be pumped into government programs designed to help those who are economically disadvantaged.

Contemporary America

President Barack Obama

The **election of 2008** proved to be another historic presidential campaign. Having served two terms, President George W. Bush could not run for re-election. Several Republicans tried to win the nomination. The party eventually nominated John McCain, an experienced senator from Arizona. McCain then made history when he became the first Republican to choose a woman to run as his vice-presidential running mate, Alaska's Governor Sarah Palin. (Congresswoman Geraldine Ferraro had run on the Democratic ticket in 1984.)

Barack Obama

The Democrats nominated a young Illinois senator named **Barack Obama**. Most experts thought that the Democrats would nominate former first lady and current New York Senator Hillary Clinton. Obama ran a masterful campaign, however, and defeated Clinton to become the Democratic candidate. Two months later, Obama defeated McCain to become the first African American president in US history.

The Real Estate Crisis

President Obama entered the White House during a challenging economic time. During the 1990s and the first few years of the twenty-first century, banks and other lenders had greatly relaxed lending standards in order to finance homes. The lower standards meant that more people qualified for loans to purchase houses. As more people bought homes, the real estate market boomed. Construction increased. Many US citizens found employment in industries connected to the booming housing market.

Real Estate Crisis
Home For Sale

Unfortunately, many of these loans were ballooning mortgages. People who had little money for down payments and normally could not have afforded a monthly mortgage accepted lending terms that allowed them to pay a low monthly payment for a set number of years with the understanding that the payment would "balloon" to a higher rate when the period expired.

As the economy began to contract, people lost jobs. Unemployment coupled with ballooning mortgage payments meant that many homeowners could no longer make their monthly payments. A record number of people went into **foreclosure** (lost their homes to lenders they could no longer pay back). Foreclosed homes created a surplus of houses on the market. Real estate prices dropped drastically. A **real estate crisis** ensued. Construction halted. Many homeowners found themselves "upside down" in their mortgages (owing their lender more money than their house was worth). Thousands of people whose livelihood depended on real estate found themselves unemployed or their businesses failing.

The Stimulus Plan

Obama's first strategy to deal with the economic crisis involved passing a **stimulus package**. It pumped large sums of federal money into the economy with the goal of creating jobs. The plan also provided billions of dollars to save several key businesses from going bankrupt. It also helped prevent the US auto industry from going under. But more than three years into Obama's tenure, unemployment had continued to rise, the real estate market continued to flounder, businesses still weren't expanding, and it appeared to most citizens that Obama's stimulus had failed.

Taxes

Taxes remained a key area of debate. President Obama and others argued that tax cuts passed under President Bush to aid businesses should be ended. The president felt these tax cuts gave too much advantage to big corporations and the wealthiest Americans. Obama also supported raising the tax rate on wealthier citizens, arguing that "Millionaires and billionaires should pay their fair share."

President Barack Obama

Republicans, however, opposed Obama's policies. They argued that ending the Bush tax cuts would take more money away from business owners at the very time that businesses needed money to expand and create jobs. They also pointed out that the nation's wealthiest citizens already paid the vast majority of taxes and that they were also the people who tended to own businesses and employ workers. Forcing them to pay more in taxes, opponents argued, would only discourage them from hiring people, producing goods, and pumping money into the economy.

Globalization

Due to technology and economic ties, today's world is more connected than ever before. **Globalization** has resulted in a worldwide economy and communications that link the world together. What threatens the security or economic stability of one nation quickly impacts others as well. As a result, nations like the United States have a vested interest, not only in their own security and stability, but in the security and stability of countries around the world.

The **European Union (EU)** is one example of economic globalization. The EU is an economic entity consisting of twenty-seven European nations. The EU unites these nations economically and uses the euro as a common currency. In recent years, the EU has faced problems as several member countries have built up massive national debts. A few of these countries have even come close to going bankrupt. Such instability can have drastic effects not only in Europe, but across the globe.

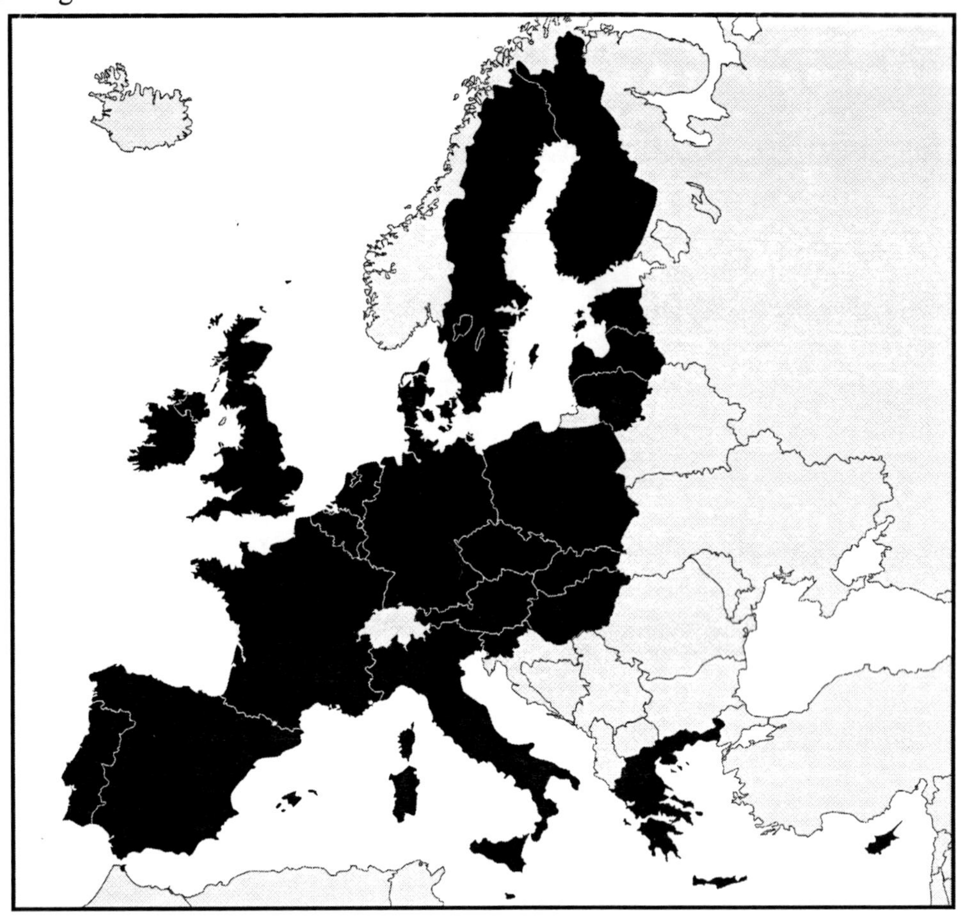

European Union Map

Practice 11.4: Issues Facing the Modern United States

1. Al-Qaeda is **best** described as which of the following?

   A. a group of Muslims

   B. a radical Islamic terrorist group

   C. followers of Islam

   D. rulers of Afghanistan

2. Operation Enduring Freedom was designed to do what?

   A. bring down the Taliban and root out terrorists in Afghanistan

   B. liberate Kuwait

   C. bring down Saddam Hussein and find weapons of mass destruction

   D. maintain peace between Egypt and Israel

3. What were the Bush administration's arguments for going to war with Iraq? What are some of the criticisms of the war?

4. What made Barack Obama's election so historical?

CHAPTER 11 REVIEW

Key Terms

conservatism
Ronald Reagan
Reaganomics
trickle-down theory
national debt
Mikhail Gorbachev
Iran-Contra Affair
George H.W. Bush
Persian Gulf War
foreign oil
Bill Clinton
budget deficit
budget surplus
NAFTA
healthcare system
budget battle
welfare reform
Monica Lewinsky
election of 2000
George W. Bush
terrorist
Al-Qaeda
Osama bin Laden
September 11, 2001
9/11
war on terror
Afghanistan
war in Iraq
Camp David Accords
immigration
illegal immigration
bilingualism
economic disparity
urban flight
election of 2008
Barack Obama
foreclosure
real estate crisis
stimulus plan
taxes
globalization
European Union (EU)

Chapter 11 Review Questions

1. Which US president viewed the USSR as an "evil empire" that could not be trusted and therefore pursued a massive buildup of US military forces?

   A. Barack Obama

   B. Jimmy Carter

   C. Ronald Reagan

   D. George W. Bush

> *"The scene is amazing! All around people are cheering and waving flags. A number of those here have climbed on top and are beating it with sledgehammers, cheering as each piece falls to the ground. Despite the cold, these people seem ready to stay throughout the night to celebrate the fall of what for so long has been a dreaded symbol of communism and the iron curtain."*

2. The above quote is **most** likely from whom?

   A. a western reporter broadcasting from the Berlin Wall

   B. an eastern reporter broadcasting from Afghanistan

   C. an eyewitness to relief efforts following 9/11

   D. a political supporter after Obama's election

3. Critics of Ronald Reagan would **most** likely focus on which of the following facts?

   A. the effects of Reagan's tax cuts on the economy

   B. the end of the Cold War and his relationship with Mikhail Gorbachev

   C. the nation's debt and the Iran-Contra Affair

   D. the state of the nation's military when he left office

4. Which of the following is **true** regarding Bill Clinton?

   A. He gained great national support claiming to be a "tax and spend liberal."

   B. He was only the third president ever impeached, along with Andrew Johnson and Richard Nixon.

   C. He gained popularity that helped him win re-election by signing welfare reform and being perceived as the "good guy" in the battle of the budget with Congress.

   D. He helped negotiate the Camp David Accords between Israel and Egypt.

5. Which of the following contributed to Clinton's victory in the 1996 election?

   A. healthcare reform

   B. welfare reform

   C. Bush's failure to deal with the economy

   D. the Monica Lewinsky incident

> *"I remember we went to bed disappointed. We'd sat up to almost 3 in the morning waiting to see who would be president. We ended up waiting weeks to see who would be our 43rd president. It finally went to Bush once the Supreme Court made them stop counting votes in Florida."*

6. The above quote is referring to what?

   A. the election of 1996

   B. the election of 1988

   C. the election of 2000

   D. the election of 2008

7. Increased immigration creates which of the following problems?

   A. lack of cultural diversity

   B. population decline

   C. neglect of issues like bilingualism and bilingual education

   D. controversy over immigration legislation

8. A conservative politician would be **most** likely to favor which of the following positions in light of the economic disparity that exists in the United States?

   A. raise taxes so that the government can redistribute money to help the underprivileged

   B. lower taxes and reduce government regulations so as to allow people to more freely pursue prosperity

   C. funding government job training programs to help more people get government jobs

   D. increase welfare payments so that people don't need to work to earn income.

9. Barack Obama tried to address the nation's economic crisis by doing which of the following?
   A. cutting taxes
   B. closing government departments
   C. introducing a stimulus package
   D. increasing foreclosures

10. Which of the following is an example of globalization?
    A. an economic crisis in Greece impacts stocks in the United States
    B. US businessmen refuse to expand due to higher taxes
    C. a president introduces a stimulus package
    D. falling home values lead to massive unemployment among US real estate agents

Practice Test 1

1. *Marbury v. Madison* impacted federal power in which of the following ways? 1.7

   A. It increased the powers of the president.

   B. It allowed senators to be elected directly by citizens.

   C. It empowered the government to enforce civil rights laws.

   D. It meant that the courts could strike down laws.

2. What was the purpose of the FDIC established under the Federal Reserve Act in 1933? 6.3

   A. to insure bank deposits

   B. to make it illegal for banks to close

   C. to provide $2000/year in income to every US family

   D. to provide electrical power to parts of the South

3. Alice looks out of the window of the little shack where she lives. She sees her mother and other African Americans working on a plantation. The men pick cotton. The women do other chores. Alice lives every day with the fear that she could be sold away from her mother. Alice lives in which of the following states? 2.4

   A. North Carolina

   B. Ohio

   C. West Virginia

   D. Pennsylvania

4. The Compromise of 1877 resulted in which of the following? 3.4

A. populists farmers supporting bimetallism

B. laws regulating the expansion of slavery

C. removal of federal protection for freedmen

D. Congress assuming control of Reconstruction

5. President Warren G. Harding won the 1920 presidential election advocating a "return to normalcy." To what did Harding appeal? 5.5

A. nationalism

B. isolationism

C. internationalism

D. militarism

2.1

6. The image above depicts which of the following?

A. Native Americans' last stand at Wounded Knee

B. Native Americans being forcibly removed from the Southeast

C. Native Americans searching for buffalo

D. Native Americans migrating to eastern cities

7. Nathan is a freedman living in Louisiana during Reconstruction. He runs for public office and wins a seat in the state legislature. Nathan's accomplishment is a direct result of the 3.3

   A. Emancipation Proclamation

   B. Fifteenth Amendment

   C. Nineteenth Amendment

   D. Voting Rights Act

8. What impact did the transcontinental railroad have on Native Americans? 4.1

   A. They lost land and resources as they moved to reservations.

   B. They benefitted financially by selling land to railroad executives.

   C. They improved their standard of living by working on the railroad.

   D. They gained political power negotiating land rights for railroad construction

9. Citizens enraged by Spanish atrocities in Cuba and calling for the United States to go to war over the territory were often influenced by 5.2

   A. isolationism

   B. abolitionists

   C. yellow journalism

   D. urbanization

10. Which of the following was a demographic effect of the Cold War? 7.6

    A. The US and USSR entered into an arms race.

    B. More citizens migrated west and to suburbs

    C. The United States began a peacetime military buildup.

    D. US leaders feared a domino effect.

U-boat Attack Sinks Lusitania.
Americans Killed!

11. The event depicted in the above news story eventually helped lead to which of the following? 5.4

A. the bombing of Pearl harbor

B. US involvement in World War I

C. the Spanish-American War

D. annexation of the Philippines

12. In 1863, the president issued an executive order stating that all persons previously held as slaves in "states in rebellion against the Union" were henceforth free. What document issued this order? 3.2

A. Declaration of Independence

B. Bill of Rights

C. Fifteenth Amendment

D. Emancipation Proclamation

13. What impact did the New Deal have on the US economy in the 1930s? 6.4

A. It ended the Great Depression.

B. It used government spending to relieve economic suffering.

C. It cut government programs and spending.

D. It caused a stock market crash and created a depression.

14. The US economy boomed during World War II. Yet, the United States did not become a consumer society until the 1950s. To what can this delay in consumerism be attributed? 7.2

   A. citizens conserving for the war effort

   B. citizens still living in an economic depression

   C. too many women working in factories

   D. fears surrounding the Cold War

15. Which of the following was an intended purpose of NAFTA? 8.5

   A. establish free trade between the US, Canada, and Mexico

   B. improve relations between the United States and USSR

   C. establish an alliance against communism in Europe

   D. unite the economic systems of several European nations

- Advocate of Black Higher Education
- Harvard PhD
- Helped Found the NAACP
- Opponent of Segregation

16. The List above is describing which of the following individuals? 3.5

   A. Theodore Roosevelt

   B. W.E.B. DuBois

   C. Alice Paul

   D. Booker T. Washington

17. Which of the following resulted from the Holocaust? 7.4

A. Germany was divided into two nations.

B. Truman initiated the Marshall Plan

C. the UN approved the founding of Israel

D. the Soviet Union built a nuclear weapon

18. Under the Monroe Doctrine, how would the US have viewed a European power attempting to establish colonies in the Americas? 2.2

A. as a friend, so long as it did not set foot on US territory

B. as a military aggressor moving against the interests of the United States

C. with indifferences, because the United States didn't care

D. as an ally to help the US achieve its "Manifest Destiny"

> In 1958, Dr. Martin Luther King Jr. told a reporter:
> "We believe in non-violence and practicing civil
> disobedience to end the evil that is racism and
> the injustices that arise from segregation."

19. To what was Dr. King referring? 8.1

A. The abolitionist movement

B. The anti-war movement

C. The suffragist movement

D. The civil rights movement

20. Which of the following was part of a peace plan drafted by President Woodrow Wilson following World War I? 5.4

A. Missionary diplomacy

B. Espionage Act

C. League of Nations

D. Treaty of Versailles

Policies of President Lyndon B. Johnson

Great Society
War on Poverty
Medicare
Medicaid
____

21. Which of the following would fit in the blank above? 8.2

A. New Federalism

B. Conservatism

C. Trickle-down economics

D. Government housing

22. Which of the following laws was passed in large part due to nativism? 4.5

A. Chinese Exclusion Act

B. Sherman Antitrust Act

C. Civil Rights Act

D. Voting Rights Act

23. When former British prime minister, Winston Churchill, said, "...an iron curtain has descended across the continent..." to what was he referring? 7.5

A. the threat Hitler posed to Europe

B. Hitler's invasion of France

C. the dropping of the atomic bomb

D. the postwar division between Western and Eastern Europe

24. Iron ore, running water, lumber, and oil are all examples of which of the following? 4.2

A. natural resources that helped the US become an industrialized nation

B. natural resources which the US lacked during the age of industrialization

C. natural resources used to produce electricity

D. natural resources used to produce steel

25. Colonial governments could **best** be described as which of the following? 1.1

A. totalitarian

B. appointed by Parliament

C. representative

D. unlimited

In 2011, President Barack Obama stated: "We stand by the people of Egypt as they make the transition from the Mubarak regime to one that we hope will be freely elected."

26. For what was President Obama expressing support? 8.6

A. democratic reform in the Middle East

B. the advancement of democracy in Europe

C. isolationism on the part of the United States

D. international trade agreements with Egypt

27. Virginia's House of Burgesses fulfilled which of the following roles? 1.2

A. It met on board the Mayflower to draft laws for Massachusetts.

B. It helped establish representative government in the southern colonies.

C. It sparked the American Revolution by drafting the Declaration of Independence.

D. It established the first US government under the Articles of Confederation.

28. Japan's need for natural resources and its desire to expand its empire led to which of the following events? 7.1

A. invasion of France

B. Russian Revolution

C. the bombing of Pearl Harbor

D. the Holocaust

29. Which of the following led to the cry, “No taxation without representation!”? 1.3
    - A. the Stamp Act
    - B. the Quartering Act
    - C. the Boston Massacre
    - D. the Declaration of Independence

30. Which of the following presidents based his foreign policy on the idealistic belief that it was the role of the US to promote democracy in the world rather than acquire new territories? 5.3
    - A. William McKinley
    - B. Woodrow Wilson
    - C. William Taft
    - D. Theodore Roosevelt

31. The antebellum Republican party was distinct from the Democrats primarily in what way? 3.1
    - A. Only Southerners supported the Democrats, while Northerners supported Republicans.
    - B. All Republicans wanted to abolish slavery, while all Democrats supported slavery.
    - C. Republicans were united in their support of slavery, while Democrats were divided.
    - D. Republicans opposed extension of slavery to new territories, while Democrats were divided.

32. Ernest is greatly disturbed by the culture he sees around him in the 1920s. He becomes part of a group known as the “Lost Generation.” Ernest is a 6.1
    - A. jazz musician.
    - B. writer.
    - C. politician.
    - D. activist.

33. A reformer in the 1800s who subscribed to the publications of William Lloyd Garrison, was impacted by the writings of Harriet Beecher Stowe, and moved by the speeches of Frederick Douglass would have **most likely** been a member of what reform movement? 2.4

A. the temperance movement

B. the women's rights movement

C. the abolitionist movement

D. the civil rights movement

34. Which of the following is a common criticism of Reagan's presidency? 8.4

A. He was not conservative enough.

B. He ended the Cold War.

C. He left the nation with a massive debt.

D. He led the economy into depression.

35. The relationship between colonial governors and colonial legislatures could **best** be described as what? 1.2

A. always cooperative, because of common goals

B. distant because of geographic separation

C. awkward, because both sides were often concerned about offending the other

D. often tense, because of differing loyalties and goals

36. Ratification of the Fifteenth Amendment meant which of the following? 3.3

A. Blacks had the right to vote.

B. Blacks, immigrants, and women had the right to vote.

C. Blacks were afforded citizenship.

D. Slavery was declared illegal.

37. Which of the following statements was a common criticism of the Articles of Confederation? 1.6

A. "The document is too weak. It gives no power to the people and too much to the government."

B. "This document fails because it once again allows a national government to impose unjust taxes."

C. "The document is not effective because it grants no substantial power to the national government."

D. "The document cannot be accepted because it does not require the British to recognize our independence."

"It was a sight to behold. Why, I don't know how they survived. Whole families sharing small rooms with other families. The smell was horrible, and the Lord only knows what critters were living behind them walls. I guess its good they work sixteen hour days; ain't no room for much except sleeping."

38. The above quote is probably talking about what? 4.5

A. African American sharecroppers

B. immigrants living in a tenement

C. robber barons living in an urban area

D. members of the Populist movement

39. What was the "Manhattan Project"? 7.3

A. It was the code name for an invasion of Europe.

B. It was the code name for construction of the atomic bomb.

C. It was a plan to industrialize New York.

D. It was the political plan introduced by Ronald Reagan.

40. The impact of the Declaration of Independence worldwide can **best** be described as what? 1.3

    A. profound, because its principles have inspired revolutions and political movements worldwide.

    B. oppressive, because it opposes egalitarianism.

    C. moderate, because its effects have been limited outside of the United States.

    D. powerful, because it rejected the idea of "inalienable rights," thereby giving governments more power.

41. Which of the following statements is accurate concerning technology developed during WWII? 7.6

    A. It served a strictly military purpose.

    B. No medical advances of note occurred.

    C. Some technological advances actually occurred by accident.

    D. Computers were not invented until years after the war.

42. Someone who fought for women's suffrage would have been **most** supportive of which of the following? 4.6

    A. poll taxes

    B. laissez-faire capitalism

    C. the Fifteenth Amendment

    D. the Nineteenth Amendment

43. Anti-Federalists insisted that which of the following be adopted to limit the power of the federal government and protect the rights of citizens? 1.5

    A. US Constitution

    B. Declaration of Independence

    C. Bill of Rights

    D. Thirteenth Amendment

44. Someone who wanted to see farmers make more money and supported "greenbacks" would have likely been part of what movement during the late 1800s? 4.4

A. the abolitionist movement

B. the populist movement

C. the progressive movement

D. the labor movement

45. Which of the following lists describes the antebellum South? 2.3

A. factory system, supported tariffs, growing abolitionist movement

B. open to settlement, reservations, large numbers of immigrants

C. supported the Fugitive Slave Law, plantation system, states' rights

D. free states, large number of immigrants, manufacturing

46. Which of the following people would have **most likely** supported the Articles of Confederation? 1.4

A. a Federalist

B. Anti-Federalist

C. John Adams

D. Alexander Hamilton

47. The Harlem Renaissance is **best** described by which of the following statements? 6.1

A. It was a political movement meant to give power to the common man.

B. It was a black militant movement meant to achieve civil rights.

C. It was an artistic movement among the African American community of the 1920's.

D. It was an educational movement among women.

48. Which of the following factors contributed to the South's defeat in the Civil War? 3.2

A. The South had a larger population.

B. The South could not overcome the Union's superior military leadership.

C. The North had too many resources and too much manpower.

D. The South had too many railroads to manage shipments effectively.

49. Which of the following marked the end of any official US involvement in Vietnam? 8.3

A. the Geneva Accords

B. the Paris Peace Accords

C. the Pentagon Papers

D. the fall of Saigon

50. Why did many businessmen in the US who favored imperialism consider the Pacific to be so important? 5.1

A. They feared the Japanese were planning an attack and wanted to strike first.

B. They could not compete in European markets and saw Asian nations as their last hope.

C. They wanted access to the foreign markets of China and Southeast Asia.

D. War with Hawaii meant that the US needed to establish military bases close to the islands.

51. In 1928, Al got rich as a "bootlegger" in Chicago. Al benefitted financially from the effects of 6.2

A. the Sherman Antitrust Act.

B. Prohibition.

C. the Sedition Act.

D. the Nineteenth Amendment.

52. Which of the following describes President Lyndon B. Johnson's domestic programs? 8.4

A. a "Great Society" meant to end poverty

B. a "New Frontier" in which the US will lead the world

C. "Supply-side Economics" in which tax cuts will benefit the average citizen

D. "New Federalism" in which the government will step back from the New Deal

53. Television shows, advertising, and a number of "scientific" books suggested that women should fulfill what roles during the 1950s? 7.6

A. wife and mother

B. wife, mother, and worker

C. wife and career woman

D. single career woman

54. How did mass media, such as radio, movies, and national publications, help transform US society during the 1920s? 6.1

A. The US began to form a national culture.

B. People stopped watching television.

C. Citizens became more isolated.

D. It had little effect.

55. Which of the following **most** affected John D. Rockefeller? 4.3

A. the Supreme Court's ruling in *Plessy v. Ferguson*

B. the Sherman Antitrust Act

C. the Thirteenth Amendment

D. the writings of Upton Sinclair

Practice Test 2

1. The staple crop tobacco was key to the economic survival of which of the following colonies? 1.1

   A. Virginia

   B. New York

   C. Rhode Island

   D. Massachusetts

2. Which of the following arose as a reaction against new civil rights legislation, the Cold War, and social movements and behaviors that challenged traditional ideas? 8.4

   A. the Republican Party

   B. Students for a Democratic Society

   C. a new conservative movement

   D. a youth counter-culture

"I cannot believe the country has elected that abolitionist-lover. Why, he'll no doubt declare war on slavery the moment he's in the Oval Office. We cannot remain part of this Union. To do so is as good as holding the nail while that Republican drives right through the South's heart."

– Southern politician, 1860

3. Who of the following would have agreed with the above statement? 3.1

   A. Andrew Johnson

   B. Abraham Lincoln

   C. Ulysses S. Grant

   D. Jefferson Davis

4. The Founding Fathers expected only members of an aristocratic upper class to hold political office, and they limited suffrage to only white males who owned property. Such facts are evidence of what? 1.5

A. The Founding Father's belief in limited government.

B. The Founding Father's desire to limit civil rights.

C. The Founding Fathers belief in republicanism.

D. The Founding Fathers trust in democracy.

5. Which of the following hurt US relations with the Soviet Union during World War II? 7.3

A. US reluctance to invade Western Europe

B. the Yalta Conference

C. the Lend-Lease Act

D. the D-Day invasion

6. As settlers moved west and US territory expanded in the early 1800s, supporters of democracy called for which of the following? 2.1

A. an end to slavery

B. more federal regulations

C. equal rights for minorities

D. universal suffrage

7. Why did the United States continually break agreements with Native Americans during the 1800s? 4.1

A. The US government feared a Native American invasion.

B. The US government feared Native Americans would claim US territory.

C. Many US landowners wanted to make Native Americans slaves.

D. US settlers continually wanted more land and resources.

8. In 1998, President Bill Clinton became involved in a scandal after he lied to investigators about his relationship with a White House intern. This scandal eventually led to 8.5

A. Clinton losing the next election.

B. Clinton's impeachment.

C. Clinton's resignation.

D. Clinton's indictment.

9. Who of the following individuals has helped to inspire numerous democratic movements by his assertion that human beings have inalienable rights? 1.3

A. George Washington when he led the Continental Army to victory

B. Thomas Jefferson when he wrote the Declaration of Independence

C. James Madison when he drafted the US Constitution

D. Thomas Jefferson when he supported the Bill of Rights

10. Raymond is a member of the United States Senate. He is an isolationist who does not want the country committing itself to alliances that could lead to war. Which one of the following will Raymond most likely support? 5.5

A. ratifying the Treaty of Versailles

B. sending peace-keeping troops to Europe

C. Warren G. Harding's presidential campaign

D. joining the League of Nations

11. The Berlin Airlift was evidence of 7.5

A. post war radar technology.

B. mass production technologies.

C. the Cold War.

D. detente.

12. Latin American revolutions and the desire to protect US interests during the early nineteenth century led to which of the following executive proclamations declaring the United States' opposition to further European colonization in the Western Hemisphere? 2.2

    A. Monroe Doctrine

    B. Truman Doctrine

    C. Emancipation Proclamation

    D. Roosevelt Corollary

13. Which one of the following was a product of the Harlem Renaissance? 6.1

    A. the writings of Ernest Hemingway

    B. the philosophies of Booker T. Washington

    C. the writings of Langston Hughes

    D. the service of the Tuskegee Airmen

14. The outcome of the Civil War helped establish which of the following? 3.2

    A. The authority of the federal government over that of the states

    B. The right of states to rule themselves

    C. The importance of cash crops to the nation's economy

    D. The constitutionality of secession as a form of protest

15. In 2011, US economists and business leaders were most concerned with the stability of which of the following? 8.6

    A. the Soviet Union

    B. the European Union

    C. the Warsaw Pact

    D. US fundamentalism

16. Which of the following was a political impact of capitalism? 4.3

A. The call for democracy increased.

B. Fewer people supported democracy.

C. Small landowners called on government to regulate land.

D. US manufacturers opposed protective tariffs.

Literacy Tests
Poll Taxes
Jim Crow Laws

17. Which of the following would be the best heading for the list above? 3.4

A. Effects of Emancipation on African Americans

B. Attacks on African Americans' Rights after Reconstruction

C. Laws Limiting Southern Whites During Reconstruction

D. Laws Passed by the Government During the Red Scare

18. Industrial leaders and capitalists supported which of the following? 5.1

A. progressive reforms

B. welfare programs

C. market expansion

D. labor unions

19. "Black Tuesday" refers to what event in US history? 6.3

A. the bombing of Pearl Harbor

B. the day John F. Kennedy was assassinated

C. the day the stock market crashed

D. the day the South seceded from the Union

20. Colonial government and later the US government were both built on the idea of limited government. Which document first established this idea? 1.2

A. Bill of Rights

B. Articles of Confederation

C. Magna Carta

D. Mayflower Compact

21. Ethnic ghettoes, political machines, tenements, slums, and cultural diversity were all consequences of which of the following? 4.5

A. democracy

B. abolition

C. emancipation

D. urbanization

22. Which of the following conflicts led to the United States exercising influence over territories in both the Western and Eastern Hemispheres? 5.2

A. World War I

B. American Revolution

C. Spanish-American War

D. Korean War

23. Which of the following helped African Americans after Reconstruction by teaching them a trade? 3.5

A. Tuskegee Institute

B. Niagara Movement

C. NAACP

D. Hull House

He Kept Us
Out of War!
Re-elect
the President!
1916

24. The poster above is expressing support for which presidential candidate? 5.4

A. Theodore Roosevelt

B. Woodrow Wilson

C. Franklin Roosevelt

D. Richard Nixon

25. Quotas, nativism, and the resurgence of the Ku Klux Klan were all negative responses to 6.2

A. industrialism.

B. urbanization.

C. fundamentalism.

D. immigration.

26. The South's dependence on cash crops and the North's development of manufacturing led to which of the following as the nation expanded? 2.3

A. debates over whether or not to build railroads

B. conflicts over the expansion of slavery

C. lasting alliances with Native Americans

D. fewer markets for US products

27. Which of the following was a product of a "Red Scare" that swept the United States after World War II? 7.5

A. the Palmer Raids

B. the Sacco and Vanzetti trial

C. McCarthyism

D. Students for a Democratic Society

28. Which of the following served as evidence of the "Solid South"? 3.3

A. Democrats winning all major political offices after Reconstruction.

B. Southern states seceding and fighting together during the Civil War.

C. All of the southern states relying economically on staple crops.

D. Southern voters tending to support candidates who supported civil rights.

29. What did President Richard Nixon hope to accomplish through his domestic program known as New Federalism? 8.2

A. pass new civil rights legislation

B. give more power to state governments

C. escalate the arms race with the Soviet Union

D. declare a "war on poverty"

30. The role of the central government in economic affairs during the presidency of George Washington was a key difference leading to which of the following? 1.6

A. conflicts over territorial expansion

B. debates over slavery

C. ratification of the US Constitution

D. formation of political parties

real estate crisis
recession
first woman Republican nominee for vice president
first African American elected president

31. The list above consists of factors that are associated with which presidential election? 8.5

A. 1996

B. 2000

C. 2004

D. 2008

32. What was the "Open Door policy?" 5.3

A. US foreign policy stating that only the US would be allowed to trade with nations in Southeast Asia.

B. US immigration policy that allowed people to immigrate to the US freely.

C. US foreign policy that insisted China be kept open to foreign markets rather than controlled by imperial powers.

D. Japan's policy of open trade with western nations.

33. Which of the following statements describes President Franklin Roosevelt's attitude toward World War II prior to Pearl harbor? 7.1

A. He adamantly opposed war because he was an isolationist.

B. He understood isolationism, but believed that the US could not avoid war.

C. He strongly favored war because the US had been attacked by Japan.

D. He opposed war because he trusted Japan and had no idea the US would be attacked.

34. Which of the following statements is an example of sectionalism? 2.4

A. The South relied heavily on slaves, while the North relied on immigrant labor.

B. the South's decision to fire on Fort Sumter

C. Lincoln's decision to be a Republican

D. many African Americans moving west to become cowboys

35. Franklin Roosevelt's domestic program for addressing the Great Depression that featured deficit spending and which was often criticized as either "too little" or "socialism" was called what? 6.4

A. the New Federation

B. the Fair Deal

C. the New Deal

D. the Great Society

36. What effect did the end of Reconstruction have on African Americans? 3.3

A. It presented them with more opportunities.

B. It resulted in greater education.

C. It led to more oppression.

D. It meant more political influence.

37. In general, how would "robber barons" have felt about tariffs and the Sherman Antitrust Act? 4.2

A. They would have favored both.

B. They would have favored tariffs but opposed the Sherman Antitrust Act

C. They would have opposed both

D. They would have opposed tariffs but favored the Sherman Antitrust Act.

38. The image above depicts which of the following? 2.4

    A. the Harlem Renaissance

    B. a 1950s suburb

    C. the antebellum South

    D. A reservation

39. Which one of the following people might have been labeled a "flapper?" 6.2

    A. a finance capitalist of the early 20th century

    B. an immigrant drafted into the Union army

    C. a progressive woman of the 1920s

    D. a politician speaking out against the US' involvement in WWI

40. The trials at Nuremberg were meant to accomplish which of the following? 7.4

A. avenge the bombing of Pearl Harbor

B. provide justice for the Holocaust

C. put Adolf Hitler on trial

D. execute Tojo Hideki

41. Falling farm prices and increased job opportunities in city factories contributed to 4.4

A. the rise of agribusiness.

B. the birth of textiles.

C. US urbanization.

D. a decline in immigration.

42. Which of the following accurately describes colonial governments? 1.1

A. They tended to be independent due to England's policy of salutary neglect.

B. Due to the necessity for unity, colonial governors and legislative bodies rarely allowed tensions to arise between them.

C. The House of Burgesses established representative government in New England.

D. Desiring to start a country of their own, colonists rejected all previous models of English government in order to experiment with totally new ideas.

43. A supporter of the Fourteen Points would have favored 5.4

A. Wilson's plan for peace following WWI.

B. Germany's reasons for fighting WWI.

C. the Allies' demands before accepting Japan's surrender.

D. Lyndon B. Johnson's domestic program.

44. Which of the following was a product of isolationism? 5.5

A. the military-industrial complex

B. Theodore Roosevelt's foreign policies

C. the Truman Doctrine

D. US refusal to ratify the Treaty of Versailles

45. The WACS, Tuskegee Airmen, "code talkers," and members of the 442nd were all examples of what? 7.2

A. units caught by surprise at Pearl Harbor

B. soldiers involved in combat in the Pacific

C. contributions made by women and minorities to the United States military

D. Mexican American soldiers awarded the medal of honor in WWII

46. Which of the following was a subject of intense debate at the Constitutional Convention? 1.4

A. whether or not the Articles of Confederation needed to be changed

B. whether or not to expand slavery to new territories

C. whether or not to count slaves in the nation's population

D. whether or not to have a king

47. How would a member of the English Parliament have **most** likely felt about the phrase "54/40 or fight!"? 2.2

A. excited, because he would have wanted to retake territory lost during the American Revolution

B. irritated, because the British and US had agreed to occupy the Pacific Northwest jointly

C. angry, because the US and Great Britain had agreed to share territory in New Mexico

D. indifferent, because it referred to a land dispute between the US and Mexico

48. What effect did the Supreme Court's decision in *Brown v. Board of Education* have on segregation? 8.1

A. It reinforced segregation by upholding the concept of states' rights.

B. It struck down segregation in public schools.

C. It had little effect on segregation because states neither acknowledged it nor implemented it.

D. It had limited effect because the executive branch refused to enforce the decision.

49. What effect did the "GI Bill" have on higher education? 7.6

A. Fewer people could afford to go to college.

B. The number of African Americans who went to college drastically increased.

C. More people started going to college.

D. Colleges and universities focused less on science and math.

50. Which early 20th century reformer opened Hull House as a settlement house? 4.6

A. Jacob Riis

B. Upton Sinclair

C. Susan B. Anthony

D. Jane Addams

51. What is "judicial review"? 1.7

A. the power of the Supreme Court to declare acts unconstitutional

B. the power of the Supreme Court to review presidential appointments

C. the power of the president to oversee the appointment of judges

D. the power of the Supreme Court to approve executive orders

52. What effect did the Thirteenth Amendment have on the United States? 3.3

A. It granted African Americans the right to vote.

B. It ended the slavery throughout the United States.

C. It freed slaves in Confederate states while maintaining slavery in the Union.

D. It granted slaves citizenship.

53. The philosophy that the US should accept communism where it already existed and focus its efforts on preventing it from spreading was called what? 7.5

A. detente

B. containment

C. appeasement

D. diplomacy

54. Public reaction in the US to the Vietnam War can be described as? 8.3

A. united.

B. divided.

C. supporting the war.

D. opposed to the war.

55. The fact that the president of the United States cannot do whatever he/she wants but is bound by the laws of the Constitution is evidence of what? 1.2

A. executive powers

B. a belief in "natural rights"

C. limited government

D. common law

Practice Test 2

D

E

F

G

H

N

O

P

Q

U

V

W

Y

Z